AN

HISTORICAL INTRODUCTION

TO THE

LAND LAW

BY

SIR WILLIAM HOLDSWORTH

K.C., D.C.L., HON. LL.D., F.B.A., VINERIAN PROFESSOR OF ENGLISH LAW IN
THE UNIVERSITY OF OXFORD
FELLOW OF ALL SOULS COLLEGE, OXFORD; HON. FELLOW OF
ST. JOHN'S COLLEGE, OXFORD
FOREIGN ASSOCIATE OF THE ROYAL BELGIAN ACADEMY
BENCHER OF LINCOLN'S INN

THE LAWBOOK EXCHANGE, LTD.
Clark, New Jersey

ISBN 978-1-58477-262-0

Lawbook Exchange edition 2004, 2013

The quality of this reprint is equivalent to the quality of the original work.

THE LAWBOOK EXCHANGE, LTD.
33 Terminal Avenue
Clark, New Jersey 07066-1321

Please see our website for a selection of our other publications and fine facsimile reprints of classic works of legal history:
www.lawbookexchange.com

Library of Congress Cataloging-in-Publication Data

Holdsworth, William Searle, Sir, 1871-1944.
An historical introduction to the land law / by Sir William Holdsworth.
p. cm.
Originally published: 1st ed. London : Oxford University Press, 1927.
Includes bibliographical references and index.
ISBN 1-58477-262-X (cloth: alk. paper)
1. Real property—Great Britain—History. 2. Land tenure—Law and legislation—Great Britain—History. I. Title.

KD829 .H65 2002
346.4104'3—dc2l 2002025949

Printed in the United States of America on acid-free paper

AN

HISTORICAL INTRODUCTION

TO THE

LAND LAW

BY

SIR WILLIAM HOLDSWORTH

K.C., D.C.L., HON. LL.D., F.B.A., VINERIAN PROFESSOR OF ENGLISH LAW IN THE UNIVERSITY OF OXFORD
FELLOW OF ALL SOULS COLLEGE, OXFORD; HON. FELLOW OF ST. JOHN'S COLLEGE, OXFORD
FOREIGN ASSOCIATE OF THE ROYAL BELGIAN ACADEMY
BENCHER OF LINCOLN'S INN

OXFORD UNIVERSITY PRESS
LONDON : HUMPHREY MILFORD

OXFORD UNIVERSITY
PRESS
LONDON EDINBURGH GLASGOW
COPENHAGEN NEW YORK TORONTO
MELBOURNE CAPETOWN BOMBAY
CALCUTTA MADRAS SHANGHAI
HUMPHREY MILFORD
PUBLISHER TO THE
UNIVERSITY

First edition, 1927

Reprinted 1935 *photographically in Great Britain by*
LOWE & BRYDONE, LONDON

PREFACE

THE Property Acts have created a serious problem for teachers and students of the land law. Whether or not they result in the long run in a simplification of this branch of the law, their immediate result is to increase the burden of both teachers and students. Several reasons make it imperative that, for a very considerable time, the teacher shall teach, and that the students shall learn, both the old law and the new. In the first place, for many years to come no lawyer will be able to advise on many questions of title unless he has both the old learning and the new. In the second place, much of the old learning is, and I think always will be, essential to an intelligent understanding both of the general principles on which the Property Acts are based, and of their actual contents. In the third place, parts of the existing law are not affected by them. In these circumstances it is obvious that the approach to the study of the modern land law must be an historical approach. The student, before tackling the larger books which deal with the modern law, must learn something of that old law of Real Property, which is the basis upon which the framers of the Property Acts have worked. It is the object of this book to give to students, who are beginning their study of the modern land law, this preliminary historical information. It is not the object of this book to expound the provisions of the Property Acts. All that it attempts to do is, first, to give such an historical outline as will be sufficient to explain the leading principles of the old law of Real Property; and, secondly, to give indications of the manner in which these principles have been modified by the new legislation.

I am indebted to Dr. Hazel, the Principal of Jesus College, and All Souls Reader in English Law, for valuable criticism, and for help in the revision of the proof sheets.

In this edition I have made a few corrections and additions, some of which have been suggested by the reviewers of the first edition, and I have inserted references to the latest edition of Dr. Cheshire's book on the modern law.

W. S. H.

ALL SOULS COLLEGE, OXFORD.

December 1934.

CONTENTS

CHAPTER II

THE SIXTEENTH AND EARLY SEVENTEENTH CENTURIES (1485–1660)

CHAPTER III

THE DEVELOPMENT OF THE MODERN LAND LAW (1660–1833)

CHAPTER IV

THE ERA OF REFORM (1833–1925)

LIST OF CASES

LIST OF ABBREVIATIONS

Ab.	Abridgement.
A. C.	Appeal Cases, *see* L. R.
And.	Anderson's Reports.
Ass.	Liber Assisarum.
Atk.	Atkyns's Reports.
B. and Ad.	Barnewall and Adolphus's Reports.
Beav.	Beavan's Reports.
Bing., N. C.	Bingham, New Cases.
Bl. Comm.	Blackstone's Commentaries.
Bligh	Bligh's Reports.
Bro. P. C.	Brown's Parliamentary Cases.
Burr.	Burrow's Reports.
C. B.	Common Bench Reports.
C. B. N. S.	Common Bench Reports, New Series.
C. D.	Chancery Division, *see* L. R.
Ch. Cas.	Cases in Chancery.
Ch. Rep.	Reports in Chancery.
Cheshire	Cheshire's Real Property (1st ed.).
Cl. and Fin.	Clark and Finelly's Reports.
Cmd.	Papers presented by command to the House of Commons.
Co. Litt.	Coke upon Littleton.
Co. Rep.	Coke's Reports.
Cro. Car.	Croke's Reports, Charles I's reign.
Cro. Jac.	Croke's Reports, James I's reign.
Eng. Hist. Rev.	English Historical Review.
H. and C.	Hurlstone and Coltman's Reports.
H. L. C.	House of Lords Cases.
H. and N.	Hurlstone and Norman's Reports.
Hen. Bl.	Henry Blackstone's Reports.
Hil.	Hilary Term.
Holdsworth, H. E. L.	Holdsworth's History of English Law.
Jac. and W.	Jacob and Walker's Reports.
John.	Johnson's Reports.

K. B.	King's Bench Cases, *see* L. R.
L. Q. R.	Law Quarterly Review.
L. R.	The Law Reports.
From 1865 to 1875—	
L. R. Ch. App.	Chancery Appeal Cases.
L. R. C. P.	Common Pleas Cases.
L. R. Eq.	Equity Cases.
L. R. Ex.	Exchequer Cases.
L. R. H. of L.	English and Irish Appeal Cases.
L. R. Q. B.	Queen's Bench Cases.
From 1875 to 1890—	
App. Cas.	Appeal Cases.
C. D.	Chancery Division Cases.
C. P. D.	Common Pleas Division Cases.
Ex. D.	Exchequer Division Cases.
P. D.	Probate Division Cases.
Q. B. D.	Queen's Bench Division Cases.
After 1890—	
Prefixing the date of the year, as:	
[1891] A. C.	Appeal Cases.
[1891] Ch.	Chancery Division Cases.
[1891] Q. B. or K. B.	Queen's or King's Bench Division Cases.
[1891] P.	Probate Division Cases.
Lev.	Levintz's Reports.
Litt.	Littleton's Tenures.
Ld. Raym.	Lord Raymond's Reports.
M. and W.	Meeson and Welsby's Reports.
Macq.	Macqueen's House of Lords Cases (Scotch).
Mich.	Michaelmas Term.
Mod.	Modern Reports.
My. and K.	Mylne and Keen's Reports.
P. and M.	Pollock and Maitland's History of English Law (1st ed.).
P. Wms.	Peere Williams's Reports.
Pasch.	Easter Term.
Ph.	Phillips's Reports.
Pl.	Placitum.
Pollex.	Pollexfen's Reports.
Q. B.	Queen's Bench Reports by Adolphus and Ellis; Queen's Bench Cases, *see* L. R.
Q. B. D.	Queen's Bench Division, *see* L. R.

R. S.	Rolls Series.
Rot. Parl.	Rotuli Parliamentorum.
Russ.	Russell's Reports.
S. C.	Same Case.
S. S.	Selden Society.
Salk.	Salkeld's Reports.
Sim.	Simons's Reports.
Stubbs, C. H.	Stubb's Constitutional History.
Surt. Soc.	Surtees Society.
Swanst.	Swanston's Reports.
T. R.	Term Reports.
Taunt.	Taunton's Reports.
Trin.	Trinity Term.
Vent.	Ventris's Reports.
Vern.	Vernon's Reports.
Ves.	Vesey Junior's Reports.
W. Bl.	William Blackstone's Reports.
Wilm.	Wilmot's Reports.
Wms. Saunders	Saunders's Reports, edited by Williams.
Y. B.	Year Book.

INTRODUCTION

The Property Acts,[1] which came into force on 1st January 1926, have gone a considerable way towards giving to the land law a statutory form; but they have not by any means gone the whole way. They have both changed and restated the law on a scale never before attempted; but there are still considerable parts of law outside their scope, which are dependent upon the law laid down in older statutes, decided cases, and books of authority.

In order to understand the changes made by these Acts, it is necessary to know what the old law was. For instance, it is hardly possible to grasp the meaning of the clauses of the Law of Property Act, 1925, which make large changes in the incidents of an estate tail,[2] without some knowledge of the pre-existing law. Similarly, a knowledge of the old law is no less necessary to understand the clauses of the Acts which restate the old law. In many cases they are codifications of preceding case law, or of the practice of conveyancers; and it is never possible fully to grasp the brief clauses of a codifying Act,

[1] The series of these Acts is as follows: the parts of the Law of Property Act, 1922, which have not been repealed, as amended by the Law of Property (Amendment) Act, 1924; the Law of Property (Amendment) Act, 1924; the Law of Property Act, 1925; the Land Charges Act, 1925; the Settled Land Act, 1925; the Trustee Act, 1925; the Administration of Estates Act, 1925; the Land Registration Act, 1925; the Universities and College Estates Act, 1925.

[2] §§ 130, 133, 176; for the estate tail see below, pp. 55–60.

without recourse to the material on which these clauses are based. Obviously the parts of the land law, which are not touched by the new Acts, cannot be understood without some knowledge of history, because the authorities on which many of its rules are based depend upon old statutes or cases.[1]

Whether we are considering the law which is contained in the Property Acts, or whether we are considering the law which is outside their scope, some knowledge of the history of the land law will always be needed to understand it; and, for at least the next quarter of a century, this historical knowledge will be more especially necessary. In the first place, when cases arise as to the construction of the clauses of the new Acts, arguments based on reasonings and analogies suggested by the old law will often play a considerable part. To understand the reasons for the decisions in these cases a knowledge of the old law will be necessary. In the second place, over the greater part of England a compulsory system of registration of title is not in force. A landowner who has contracted to convey his property cannot prove his title by reference to a register. He can only prove his title by producing documents which show that he is entitled to the interest in the land which he has contracted to convey. The purchaser must carefully examine these documents to see whether the vendor is really entitled to this interest. It is clear that to understand these documents, which may often go back a very long way, a knowledge of the old law is essential.

The fact that a knowledge of the history of the land

[1] For an illustration see below, p. 7, n. 3.

law is necessary to understand its present form is, it is true, a characteristic which is not peculiar to the land law. But this historical knowledge is, and always has been, more especially essential to the understanding of this branch of the law, for two closely connected reasons. First, all through its history, the importance of the land law has caused it to be influenced by all those social, political, and economic ideas which make up the public opinion of any given period; and, secondly and consequently, the rules of law relating to it are derived from many different periods in its history, and have been evolved under the influence of ideas which come from all these different periods. Let us glance rapidly at these two connected phenomena.

(1) The rules which regulate the manner in which land can be owned, and used, and disposed of, must always be of very great importance to the state. The stability of the state and the well-being of its citizens at all times depend, to no small extent, on its land law. This is as true to-day as it was in earlier periods of our history. But I think that it is also true to say that the reasons for, and the nature of, the importance of the land law have varied at different periods of our history, and that its importance increases as we go back to more remote periods.

In the primitive agricultural communities, which made up the Anglo-Saxon kingdoms, the land and the land law are so important, that almost all questions of Anglo-Saxon law and history seem ultimately to depend upon the original condition and gradual evolution of modes of cultivation, land measurement, and land owning.

The growth of feudalism in the tenth, eleventh, and twelfth centuries increased the importance of the land law. 'Feudalism' is a vague term. But I think that, in general terms, it can be described as comprising two things—a system of land tenure and a system of government. Land is held by tenants of lords; the relationship of lord and tenant gives the lord a certain jurisdiction over the tenant, and imposes upon the tenant the duty of attending upon the lord's court; and thus governmental powers and duties are split up among the holders of land. This tendency to split up the powers of government among the landholders of the country is the effect of the absence of efficient central government; and it is a phenomenon which has occurred in many countries, and at many periods, historically unconnected.[1] The effect is to make the land law something very much more than mere property law. Since it is bound up with jurisdictional and governmental rights, it comes to have a close connexion with constitutional law. In England, the strength of the monarchy, after the Norman Conquest, succeeded in reducing to very small dimensions the governmental aspect of feudalism; but the strong central court, which effected this result, made the feudal conception of tenure universal in our land law. The strength of the centralized institutions created by the Norman and Angevin kings made the English government the least, and the English land law the most, feudal of any in Europe. All through the Middle Ages this feudalized land law was the most important and the most highly developed branch of the common law.

[1] See Holdsworth, H. E. L. (3rd ed.), i. 17–18.

It did not lose its importance in the new age of Reformation and Renaissance which opened in the sixteenth century. Except in the cities and boroughs, it was on the great landowners of the country that the burden of local government rested. It was landowners who elected landowners to represent them in the House of Commons. And, since it was upon the land, and upon the efforts of those who cultivated it, that the food supply of the nation depended, the parts of the law which regulated the position of these cultivators of the soil were then, as they must always be, of great importance to the state. By the efforts of the Legislature and the courts these and other branches of the medieval land law were adapted, in the sixteenth and early seventeenth centuries, to the needs of the modern state. As so adapted, the land law was settled and elaborated during the latter part of the seventeenth and eighteenth centuries.

The new era, which opened at the end of the eighteenth century, was necessarily an era of great changes in the land law. It was necessary to adapt a land law, which had been made to suit the needs of a society in which the great landowners were the governing class, to the needs of a society which was becoming more and more democratic ; and to adapt the land law of an agricultural and a mainly rural society to the needs of an industrial and a mainly urban society. It is for this reason that, throughout the nineteenth and twentieth centuries, the Legislature has, in the case both of the land law and of other branches of law, taken an increasingly large share in its development. The series of Property Acts which came into force on 1st January 1926 is the logical culmination of these legislative changes.

(2) It follows from this account of the influences which have, from age to age, shaped the evolution of the land law, that, in the earlier periods of English legal history, the land law was the most important branch of English law. Indeed, it was not till the eighteenth century that commercial law began to be the rival of the land law. And, even when the industrial revolution had given to commercial law a position of importance, equalling, if not rivalling that of the land law, the land law still retained its importance. Now the development of the land law, like the development of the English constitution, has been very continuous. Statutes of all periods in English history, from the reign of Henry II to modern times, have guided its development. From the reign of Henry II onwards, it has been shaped by the legal profession through the agency of books of authority, such as Glanvil, Bracton, Littleton, and Coke ; and through the agency of the decisions of the courts of common law and equity. Both the Legislature and the legal profession have introduced into it principles and rules which, since they come from all periods of its long history, represent ideas drawn from all those periods.

Some of the customs which regulated copyhold tenure,[1] and some of the primitive modes of cultivation, which existed till the nineteenth century,[2] were reminiscent of the Anglo-Saxon agricultural com-

[1] For this tenure see below, pp. 39–48.
[2] For these see below, pp. 39–40.

munity. The feudal conception of tenure dominated the land law till the reforms made by the Property Acts; and, though it is now by no means so important as it was, it will still be an important principle so long as the relation of landlord and tenant exists. The strictness of the rules of the medieval land law had been modified, during the latter part of the medieval period, by the development in the Chancery of uses and trusts.[1] But these uses and trusts had raised many problems, some of which the Legislature had attempted to settle by the famous statutes of Uses (1535), and of Wills (1540).[2] Those statutes gave to landowners a very wide range of powers over their land, and to the law a much needed flexibility; but they made it very complicated. To the old complications of the medieval land law were added the new complications introduced by this legislation. In the course of the seventeenth and eighteenth centuries the courts of common law and equity, assisted by the conveyancers, worked out from this basis the principles of the modern land law. When the era of legislation set in in the nineteenth century, legislative changes were made piecemeal, so that the law consisted of a mass of rules, statutory or otherwise, which came from all periods in the history of English law. It might be necessary to go back to legislation of the thirteenth century to decide a modern case—in 1922, for instance, a case turned upon the correct interpretation of the statute Quia Emptores (1290).[3]

[1] See below, pp. 147–51.

[2] See below, pp. 151–61.

[3] *In re Holliday*, [1922] 2 Ch. 698; for the statute Quia Emptores see below, p. 106.

In the following pages I propose to give a short sketch of the main lines of the development of the land law. I hope that this sketch will help those who are beginning the study of the modern law to understand the reasons for the provisions of the Property Acts in which the modern law is now largely contained, and for the rules of law which still depend either on earlier statutes or on the common law. As it is an historical sketch, I shall deal with the land law mainly on chronological lines. But, in certain cases, it will be necessary, for the sake of clearness, to depart from the strictly chronological order.

From the chronological point of view the land law falls into four main periods: (1) the medieval period (1066–1485). It was then that the main outlines of the law were fixed with respect to such fundamental matters as tenures and their incidents, estates, inheritance, conveyance, seisin and possession. (2) The sixteenth and early seventeenth centuries (1485–1660). It was then that economic changes and the rise of uses and trusts created new problems for the State. The legislation of this period, and more especially the legislation of Henry VIII's reign on the subject of uses and wills, introduced a new era in the land law, and a new starting-point, from which the Legislature and the judges of the courts of law and equity began to develop the modern law. (3) The late seventeenth, the eighteenth, and the early nineteenth centuries (1660–1833). It was then that the modern law was developed, from its medieval and sixteenth-century bases, into the definite and very logical system, which the Legislature in the nineteenth century set out to reform. (4) The nineteenth and twentieth centuries (1833–1925). This was the era of reform, during which the land law was gradually recast by the Legislature, till, from the legislative experiments of a century, the Property Acts have emerged. To each of these four periods I shall give a chapter, and I shall describe the main features of the law of each period in separate sections.

CHAPTER I

THE MEDIEVAL LAND LAW (1066–1485)

I shall relate the history of the medieval land law under the following heads: § 1. Leading Distinctions; § 2. Tenures; § 3. Estates and Interests; § 4. Inheritance, Dower, and Curtesy; § 5. Incorporeal things; § 6. The Power of Alienation; § 7. Conveyancing; § 8. Seisin and Possession; § 9. Special Customs; § 10. General Conclusions.

§ 1. Leading Distinctions.

'So great is the ascendancy of the Law of Actions in the infancy of Courts of Justice, that substantive law has at first the look of being gradually secreted in the interstices of procedure; and the early lawyer can only see the law through the envelope of its technical forms.'[1] It follows that when, as at Rome and in England, a legal system is gradually and continuously developed from its origins in a primitive society, the subject matter of its rules long retains the marks of the period when the law of actions was the substantive part of the law. There is no better illustration of this fact than the English land law. The earliest rules of the land law grew up round the real actions; and, right down to the passing of the Property Acts, the leading distinctions in that law were traceable ultimately to the sphere which those actions occupied in the Middle Ages. I shall therefore, in the first place, say something of the real actions, and then show how they created the leading distinctions in the land law.

[1] Maine, Early Law and Custom, 389.

The Real Actions.[1]

Long before the close of the medieval period a real action had come to mean an action in which the specific thing demanded could be recovered. As, in the great majority of cases, it was only certain interests in or incorporeal rights over land [2] which were so recoverable, real actions could be defined with substantial accuracy by Blackstone as 'actions whereby the plaintiff . . . claims title to have any lands or tenements, rents, commons, or other hereditaments, in fee simple, fee tail, or for term of life.' [3] Any action, even an action of covenant, in which the land itself was recovered, was classed as a real action; [4] while certain actions, such as the action of waste, in which both the land and damages could be recovered, were classed as mixed.[5]

The most important of the real actions were those by which a person could assert his right to a freehold interest in land held by one of the free tenures.[6] They fall into three groups: (i) the writ of right group; (ii) the assize of novel disseisin; and (iii) the writs of entry.

(i) There were two chief varieties of the writ of right: the writ of right patent, and the *praecipe in*

1 For a full account see Holdsworth, H. E. L. (3rd ed.), iii. 3–29; Maitland, Forms of Action, 315–31, 334–40.

2 Many incorporeal things, such as offices or corodies, were, from the point of view of remedies, and in some other respects, treated like land; for these things see below, pp. 89–102.

3 Bl. Comm. iii. 117–18.

4 For this action of covenant real, whereon fines were usually levied, see Maitland, Collected Papers, i. 448; Forms of Action, 358.

5 Bl. Comm. iii. 118.

6 For the difference between freehold and chattel interests in land see below, pp. 19–20; for the free tenures see below, pp. 23–9.

capite.[1] The writ of right patent was directed to the lord of whom the land was held, and ordered him to do right to his tenant. It initiated proceedings in the lord's court, and was applicable when land was held of a lord other than the king. The *praecipe in capite* was directed to the sheriff, and was applicable when the land was held of the king. Henry II had attempted to extend the scope of this writ to cases where the land was held of another lord. It was this extension which was checked by the thirty-fourth clause of Magna Carta, which provided that, for the future, the writ *praecipe* should not issue so as to deprive a lord of his court.[2]

These writs of right decided finally which of the two parties to the action had the better right to the land in dispute. To the end they carried with them many marks of their great antiquity. The method of trial was always battle till 1179, when Henry II gave the defendant the option of having the question tried by a jury of sixteen persons, known as the Grand Assize;[3] and till 1819 the defendant could elect to have the question tried by battle.[4] The defendant must always deny the plaintiff's case in every detail and with minute accuracy. We shall see that the

[1] For a third and less important variety used by tenants in ancient demesne, and called the little writ of right, see below, p. 132.

[2] See Holdsworth, H. E. L. (3rd ed.), i. 58–9; the clause runs as follows: 'Breve quod vocatur *Precipe* de cetero non fiat alicui de aliquo tenemento unde liber homo amittere possit curiam suam.'

[3] Holdsworth, H. E. L. i. 327–9.

[4] Ibid., 309–10. In these real actions the plaintiff was generally called the demandant, and the defendant in possession of the land, the tenant. For the sake of clearness I use the modern terms plaintiff and defendant.

plaintiff, in order to succeed in the action, need not prove an absolutely good right, but only a right better than that of the defendant.[1] This shows that the action goes back to the time when the chief concern of the law was to adjudicate upon a dispute between litigants—to a time when it had not begun to analyse the conceptions of ownership and possession. These antique traits of the writ of right were its ruin. As early as the end of the thirteenth century it was regarded as a risky remedy, to be avoided if possible.[2] Newer remedies were invented which met the needs of litigants; and so, although the writ of right survived till the abolition of the real actions in 1834, it was very rarely used.

(ii) The assize of novel disseisin was not, like the writ of right, an ancient remedy. It was a new royal remedy founded on an ordinance made by Henry II. It was invented, not to decide which of the two litigants had a better right to the property in dispute, but to protect the person who was seised or possessed of property; and not only will the person seised and disseised be restored to his seisin, but the disseisor will be punished.

> 'There can be no doubt that this action was suggested by the canonists' *actio spolii* which itself had its origin in the Roman interdict *unde vi*. But when once adopted, English law very speedily made it her own. It soon became an exceedingly popular action. The plea rolls of Richard's reign and John's are covered with assizes of novel disseisin, many of which are brought by very humble persons and deal with minute parcels of land.' [3]

[1] Below, pp. 124–5.

[2] Holdsworth, H. E. L. (3rd ed.), iii. 8, n. 1.

[3] P. and M. ii. 47.

It was popular because it was both speedy and effective. There need not be any pleading; and the proceedings could go on although the defendant made default in appearance. It protected a *de facto* seisin—whether rightful or wrongful; and it restored a person who was disseised if he took proceedings at once. But, for a variety of reasons, the assize gradually ceased to have the qualities of speediness and effectiveness which had made it so popular a remedy. By the end of the medieval period it had become as dilatory as any of the other real actions.

(iii) The writs of entry, like the variety of the writ of right known as the *praecipe in capite*,[1] began with the words, '*Praecipe quod reddat*'; but they did not leave at large, as between the parties, the question of better right. They went on to suggest that the defendant, or his predecessors in title, 'had no entry into the land claimed' except by some means stated in the writ, which means gave no right to the land. The question to be tried, therefore, was limited to the question, Did or did not the defendant come to the possession of the land in the manner suggested by the plaintiff?

The reason for the invention of these writs is to be found first in the cumbersome character of the writ of right, and secondly in the limitations of the original scope of the novel disseisin. It was felt to be hard to drive a man, who might perhaps have a recent and long-continued seisin on his side, to prove his title by means of a writ of right. He was allowed, therefore, to suggest a particular fault in the tenant's title, and to recover if he could show that the

[1] Above, p. 12.

tenant entered by the faulty title suggested. This being the reason for the invention of these writs, we are not surprised to find that some of the earliest of them are the 'writs of entry sur disseisin'.

At first the scope of these writs was limited. A faulty entry by the defendant at any period, however remote, could not be alleged by the plaintiff; [1] but in 1267 the Statute of Marlborough [2] changed the law, and provided that a plaintiff could allege a flaw in the defendant's title at any time in the past.[3]

Writs of entry became very popular. They superseded both the writ of right and the assize of novel disseisin. New writs formed on this model were invented, which were used to protect the many rights in the land which the law recognized. These rights were many and various; and they were each protected by its appropriate real action. Thus the real actions formed a great network of remedies, which protected the multifarious rights which men might have in the land.[4] But most of them were narrow and particular remedies, and it was easy to fail at the outset by choosing an inappropriate action. We shall see that this was one of the many reasons why they were virtually superseded by the rise, in the

[1] A plaintiff might suggest that the defendant had no entry into the land save *per A*, which *A* had disseised the plaintiff or his ancestors; or that the defendant had no entry save *per A* to whom (*cui*) *B* demised the land, which *B* has disseised the plaintiff or his ancestors. It was only 'within these degrees' that the writ lay.

[2] 52 Henry III, c. 29.

[3] The plaintiff was allowed to suggest that the defendant had no entry save after (*post*) a disseisin that *A* had committed against the plaintiff or one of his ancestors; this writ of entry *in the post* was said to be brought 'out of the degrees'.

[4] See Holdsworth, H. E. L. (3rd ed.), iii. 15–26.

sixteenth century, of the action of ejectment,[1] long before their formal abolition in 1834.[2] But, though they were then virtually superseded, they had, as we shall now see, given rise to two leading distinctions in the land law, which remained till the reforms effected by the Property Acts.

The Leading Distinctions Created by The Real Actions.

The two leading distinctions in the land law, which lasted till the passing of the Property Acts, were, first, the distinction between land held by free tenure and land held by unfree or copyhold tenure; and, secondly, the distinction between interests in land which fell under the category of real property, and interests which ranked as chattels real and fell under the category of personal property. Both these distinctions are traceable ultimately to the limitations, which were laid down in the late twelfth and early thirteenth centuries, upon the scope of the real actions. Both, though they owed their origin to a rule of the law of actions, left such enduring marks upon substantive law that they survived the actions to which they owed their origin.

(1) The Distinction between Free and Unfree or Copyhold Tenure.[3] All tenants holding by a free tenure were protected by the courts of common law and by the real actions. The tenant holding by an unfree tenure was protected by neither. He was dependent on his lord's will, and on the custom of the manor, as administered in the manorial court.[4]

[1] Below, pp. 169–75.
[2] 3, 4 William IV, c. 27, § 36.
[3] Holdsworth, H. E. L. (3rd ed.), iii. 29–34.
[4] See below, pp. 41–2.

We shall see that the free tenures covered a wide range [1]—so wide a range that it is sometimes a little difficult to understand the tests applied by the judges to determine whether a given piece of land was held by a free or by an unfree tenure. In fact these tests were often fluctuating and uncertain. Sometimes the judges took some particular incident of the tenure, and treated it as presumptive evidence of unfreedom of tenure. The incident most usually taken for this purpose was Merchet—a fine paid for leave to give a son or daughter in marriage. But this test was not satisfactory, because some of these incidents were also applicable to land held by a free tenure. A more satisfactory test was that based upon the nature and certainty of the services due. The unfree tenant was, in effect, in the position of a labourer, who earned his right to his plot of land, by his agricultural services upon his lord's demesne lands.[2] He was simply a unit in the agricultural organization of the manor; [3] and his duties were uncertain. They were uncertain, not in the sense that they were not fixed—they were usually elaborately fixed by the manorial extent; [4] but in the sense that the lord could order the tenant to do one of several different things. In fact, this distinction drawn by the judges, based on the nature and certainty of the services due, is somewhat similar to the distinction drawn in modern law between a servant and an independent contractor. The free

[1] Below, pp. 23–9.

[2] Below, pp. 41–2; demesne lands are lands which the lord does not let out on some one of the free tenures, but keeps in his own hands, below, p. 41.

[3] For the manor see below, pp. 40–1.

[4] Below, p. 41.

tenant has, subject to the performance of definite services, the ordering and control of his work: the unfree tenant has not. The free tenant is in the position of a man engaged on a venture of his own: the unfree tenant is one of the hands by which the lord cultivates his demesne.

In the days when the land was cultivated by tenants who gave their labour services for their land, this distinction drawn by the royal judges rested on a basis of social and economic fact. Royal jurisdiction had been stretched very far when the king claimed to take cognizance of all disputes between lords and their free tenants. It may well have seemed to the king and his judges that, to extend this jurisdiction further, would have deprived landowners of the powers needed for the management of their estates. We shall see that when, in the latter part of the fifteenth century, the social and economic reasons at the back of this refusal of the common law courts to protect the unfree tenant ceased to exist; when labour services were commuted for money payments determined by the custom of the manor, and the unfree tenant became the copyhold tenant of our modern law, the common law courts began to protect the copyhold tenant.[1] His interest was not, it is true, protected by the real actions; but, in spite of that fact, its incidents were moulded to such an extent on the model of the freeholder's interests, both by the custom of the manor, and later by the common law courts, that it naturally came to be regarded as real property.[2] But the fact that this

[1] Below, pp. 42–3.

[2] Subject to this modification, it would be generally true to say

protection was given to the unfree tenant some two centuries later than it was given to the free tenant left its mark on copyhold tenure. We shall see that the fact that protection was given to the free tenant at an early date by a common law made for much uniformity in the rules applicable to the free tenures; while the fact that this protection was given later to the unfree tenant, the fact that its incidents had, for that reason, long depended on the custom of each individual manor, made for that great diversity in its incidents which was always the chief characteristic of copyhold tenure.

(2) The Distinction between Interests in Land which fell under the category of Real Property, and those which ranked as Chattels Real and fell under the category of Personal Property. The real actions were denied alike to the unfree tenant and to the man who held for a term of years; and therefore the interest of the lessee for years, like the interest of the unfree tenant, fell apart from the law relating to the free holder. But the ground upon which these remedies were denied to the lessee for years was very different from the ground upon which they were denied to the unfree tenant. The denial of these remedies to the lessee for years was not, in the first instance, founded upon any great social or economic division. It was founded, as Maitland has shown, upon an arbitrary and unfortunate application of Roman doctrine of possession. The Roman doctrine of possession seemed to compel the judges to hold that 'there

that real property included all those interests in land, corporeal or incorporeal, which were protected by the real actions.

are some occupiers who are not possessors'; and by reason of this supposed necessity, they laid it down that the man who held for a term of years had not possession, and could not therefore make use of the possessory assizes and the other real actions. We shall see that in later law he got possession;[1] but this reasoning had a permanent and unfortunate effect upon English law. Its effect was to exclude interests for a term of years from the category of real property —to divide our land law into halves. 'English law for six centuries and more', says Maitland, 'will have to rue this youthful flirtation with Romanism.'[2] The subsequent history of the lease for years has thus been very different from the subsequent history of unfree tenure. We have seen that the latter was gradually absorbed into the law of real property under the name of copyhold tenure:[3] the former became a chattel real and remained personal property.

The Property Acts have effected a great simplification in the land law by getting rid of both these distinctions. The Law of Property Act, 1922 has abolished copyhold tenure,[4] and has provided a scheme for getting rid of the incidents of that tenure at latest by 1936;[5] and it is one of the objects of the series of Property Acts to assimilate the law of chattels real to the law of real property.[6] In fact, these Acts have gone far to create what this country has never had before—a uniform land law. But all this we shall see more clearly when we have examined

[1] Below, pp. 72–3.

[2] P. and M. ii. 114.

[3] Above, p. 18.

[4] § 128.

[5] § 138 (1).

[6] See the title to the Law of Property Act, 1922; cp. Cheshire, Real Property (3rd ed.), 33–4.

the history of tenure, and the history of the different estates and interests in the land which the law formerly recognized. These two topics are the subject of the two following sections.

§ 2. Tenures.

The doctrine of tenure is a doctrine of universal application in the land law. It was applied to the free tenures, to unfree tenure, and to the relation of lessor and lessee for years. We shall see that, as the result of the Property Acts, its application to the relation of lessor and lessee for a term of years is its chief application of practical importance in our modern law.[1]

The doctrine of tenure, as it existed before the Property Acts, is thus stated by Maitland:

> 'Every acre of English soil and every proprietary right therein have been brought within the compass of a single formula which may be expressed thus: *Z tenet terram illam de . . . domino Rege.* The king himself holds land which is in every sense his own; no one else has any proprietary right in it; but if we leave out of account these royal demesnes, then it is true that every acre of land is held of the king.'[2]

The man who holds directly of the king is the tenant *in capite.* He may either keep the land in his own hands—hold it in demesne, or he may grant it to some one else. In the latter case he holds the land in service, and is the mesne lord of his tenant, who holds by a mesne tenure. The fact that this doctrine of tenure was applied universally to the land law is a purely English phenomenon. Other countries

[1] Below, pp. 38, 235. [2] P. and M. i. 210–11.

knew feudal tenure; but the law governing it was applicable only to noble or military tenure. The feudal law was not the ordinary law of the land. But in England the royal courts, while strictly curtailing the governmental aspect of feudalism, generalized its proprietary aspect, so that the feudal conception of tenure was made part of the ordinary law.

The conception of tenure, therefore, was hard-worked by English law. It covered very different sets of relationships. The earl, the knight, the church, the tenant who performed labour services, the tenant who paid rent, all held the land of some lord, and ultimately of the king. Thus one piece of land might be held by very various tenures. *A*, holding by military service of the crown, might enfeoff *B* to hold of him by a money rent (socage), and *B* might enfeoff *C*, a church, to hold on the terms of praying for the souls of *B*'s ancestors (frank-almoin).[1] *A*, *B*, and *C* all had rights in the same piece of land. As between the crown and *A*, as between *A* and *B*, as between *B* and *C*, each tenant owed the service promised; and the service thus due as between grantor and grantee was called *intrinsec*. But all these various services due from *A*, *B*, and *C* were imposed upon the land and, so to speak, ran with it. If *A* made default in his service the king could distrain upon the land in the hands of *C*. The service thus imposed upon and due from the land, irrespective of any bargain made between subsequent holders, was termed *forinsec*. *A*'s military service due to the crown was outside any bargain made

[1] For these tenures see below, pp. 23–9.

between *A* and *B*, or *B* and *C*.[1] If, however, *A* made a default in his service, so that the king distrained, and thus disturbed *C*, *C* might by writ of *mesne*[2] proceed against *B*, and *B* might by the same writ proceed against *A*.

We have seen that the leading distinction between tenures is that between the free tenures and unfree tenure.[3] I shall, therefore, in the first place, describe briefly the free tenures and their incidents; and, in the second place, I shall describe unfree tenure, and the manner in which the modern copyhold tenure was evolved from it.

The Free Tenures and their Incidents.

At the latter part of the thirteenth century the free tenures and their incidents had attained substantially their final form. I shall deal (1) with the free tenures; (2) with their incidents; and (3) with the manner in which the law relating to these tenures and to their incidents has been modified by the Legislature.

(1) The Free Tenures.[4] English law, at the end of the thirteenth century, recognized four kinds of tenure, which originally corresponded to four different types of social relationship. These four kinds of tenure were frank-almoin, knight service, serjeanty, and socage.

1 For the rule that military service is always due to the crown see below, p. 25.

2 For a specimen of this writ see Holdsworth, H. E. L. (3rd ed.), iii. 660.

3 Above, pp. 16–19.

4 For a full account see Holdsworth, H. E. L. (3rd ed.), iii. 34–54.

Frank-almoin, or free alms, was a tenure by which only a church or monastery or man of religion might hold land.[1] Such persons or bodies might hold land by other tenures; but no one else could hold land by this tenure. Its main characteristic was the absence of any obligation to perform secular services. The services due were religious services of a general kind, such as prayers or masses, which were unenforceable by a secular tribunal.[2] The statute of Mortmain (1279), which prevented indiscriminate grants of land to religious houses,[3] tended to stop the growth of this tenure. Moreover, it was made still more uncommon as the result of the statute Quia Emptores (1290).[4] We shall see that this statute provided that, on every alienation for an estate in fee simple, the grantee should hold, not of the grantor, but of the grantor's lord. But, as tenure in frank-almoin could only exist as between the grantor and grantee, no new grants of land to be held by this tenure for an estate in fee simple could be made except by the king, to whom the statute Quia Emptores did not apply.

Knight service was the typical tenure of the feudal system; and, as we have seen,[5] the feudal system was far more than a system of land tenure. In the twelfth century a tenant holding by this tenure often

[1] Litt. § 133.

[2] If a special and definite service of a religious kind was reserved it was called tenure by Divine Service, and the lord could distrain if the service were not performed, Litt. § 137.

[3] 7 Edward I; see below, pp. 109–10, for this and other statutes of Mortmain.

[4] 18 Edward I, c. 1; see below, p. 106, for this statute.

[5] Above, p. 4.

filled a public position of no mean importance. His military service (in theory) protected the state. He was entitled to a voice in the commune concilium. He had or claimed to have jurisdiction over his tenants. But the development of the art of war, the growth of a centralized government, and the successful competition of the royal courts, had gradually diminished the importance of this tenure in public law. The inefficiency of the feudal levy for any prolonged campaign had soon become apparent, and tenure by barony ceased to be a title to a seat in the House of Lords. The tenant by knight service found his remnant of jurisdiction of little avail, and was often glad to avail himself of the superior processes of the courts of common law. The same causes which destroyed the political influence of feudalism necessarily destroyed the old meaning of tenure by knight service.

In the twelfth century those who held by this tenure must produce the stipulated quota of knights to serve the king for a period of forty days in the year. In England the king was strong enough to insist that this service was due only to him.[1] But a force of this kind was useless to a king engaged on a distant expedition. Both for this reason, and because a paid army was more useful in coping with baronial disorder, Henry II encouraged his military tenants to commute their service for a money payment, which came to be known as scutage. But Magna Carta limited the royal right to take

[1] No such rule was known in Normandy, Holdsworth, H. E. L. (3rd ed.), iii. 39 ; baronial rebellions showed that it was not well observed in England.

scutages;[1] and, in the fourteenth century, Parliament claimed to exercise the same control over scutages as it exercised over other forms of direct taxation. We hear little of scutage after the end of the thirteenth century. It was remitted in 1385 by Richard II;[2] and we hear no more of it except its formal abolition in 1660.[3]

Thus, by the end of the thirteenth century, tenure by knight service had ceased to provide either soldiers or their pay. 'If', says Maitland,[4] 'tenure of knight service had been abolished in 1300 the kings of the subsequent ages would have been deprived of the large revenue that they drew from wardships, marriages and so forth; really they would have lost little else.' The elements which once made this tenure important in public law had disappeared; and it became a form of land holding and nothing more.

Serjeanty. Serjeanty means service. The serjeant means primarily one who serves—thus those who follow and serve the law are the serjeants-at-law. Tenure by serjeanty means, therefore, tenure by service. All the tenures imply service of some sort. Indeed, the whole of medieval society is held together by the services of tenants—the church is endowed, the kingdom is defended, the land is cultivated. But that which distinguishes the service of one who holds by serjeanty from the service of one who holds by the other tenures is the fact that the service of the serjeant is a pre-eminently personal service.

[1] § 12 of the Charter of 1215, which made the consent of the commune concilium necessary for a levy of scutage.

[2] Stubbs, C. H. ii. 569.

[3] 12 Charles II, c. 24, § 2.

[4] P. and M. i. 256.

In the twelfth and thirteenth centuries this tenure covered a wide field. The great officials of the kingdom or royal household held the hereditary serjeanties of being the king's marshal, his sword-bearer, his seneschal, or his butler; and, as early as the thirteenth century, they were regarded as conferring dignity rather than as involving onerous services. Then, too, a number of persons held of the king and other lords by the tenure of performing an infinite variety of smaller services connected with sport, domestic duties, and smaller governmental duties.[1] Some of these humbler services were connected with military duties. The military serjeanties supplied the feudal army with light auxiliary troops, with attendants on the knights, with military material, and with transport.[2]

The chief cause for the decay of this tenure was the tendency, which became pronounced in the fourteenth century, to substitute contracts with hired servants for the creation of this tenure. As its result, the only two classes of tenants by serjeanty which were left were the dignified class who held by the duty of performing ceremonial services for the king on solemn occasions, and the less dignified class who held by the duty of performing small services of a military kind. The fact that these services were of a military kind led to the rule that tenure by serjeanty could only be tenure in chief; and the difference between the dignified and the smaller serjeanties led to the distinction between grand and petit serjeanty. The former was subject

[1] Red Book of the Exchequer (R. S.), ii. 451–68; Holdsworth, H. E. L. (3rd ed.), iii. 48.

[2] P. and M. i. 264–5.

to the same incidents of tenure as tenure by knight service: the latter to the same incidents of tenure as tenure by socage. The services due from tenants by grand and petit serjeanty were not affected by the Act of 1660, which abolished tenure by knight service,[1] or by the Property Act.[2] They are the last survivors of a tenure which once covered many diverse relationships—political, social, and economic.

Socage. At the end of the medieval period free socage had become the tenure by which all freehold lands were held if they were not held by frankalmoin, knight service, or serjeanty. This negative characteristic of the tenure is clearly brought out by Littleton.[3] It is clear from his account that we can say much as to the services and incidents which are not due from the socage tenant; but that we can say little about the services which are due. Military service or scutage is not due; and above all there is no wardship and marriage. Generally a money rent is due, and occasionally agricultural services. The rent may be nominal or substantial; it may consist in the gift of something of real value, e.g. a pound of pepper, or of merely nominal value, e.g. a rose. Sometimes no rent at all, but only fealty, is due.

In the days before the royal courts had created the four great types of free tenure, socage tenants were a very various class. In fact, there are socage tenants of all kinds, from the substantial rent-paying tenant to the tenant bound to perform labour services

[1] 12 Charles II, c. 24.
[2] Law of Property Act, 1922, § 136.
[3] § 117; cp. §§ 119, 120, 123–5, 128–9, 130–1, 211.

and perhaps personally unfree.[1] It is for this reason that the great dividing line between free and unfree tenure cuts through this class. The law retained traces of the fact that the line had been drawn through it in the existence of both villein socage and free socage.

So wide a tenure can only be described, as Littleton described it, by negative characteristics; and it is exactly these negative characteristics which caused it to be highly valued, for they gave the tenant exemption from scutage and wardship and marriage. It was the least encumbered of all the tenures with obsolete and oppressive incidents, reminiscent of an older day when land-holding involved public rights and duties as well as private rights of ownership. It was because it fitted in best with the newer ideas, which regarded land-holding simply as a form of property, that it finally superseded all the other free tenures.[2]

(2) The Incidents of the Free Tenures.[3] Blackstone[4] enumerates as the incidents of tenure aids, relief, primer seisin, wardship, marriage, fines for alienation, and escheat. I shall deal later with the subject of alienation.[5] Here I shall deal with the other incidents of tenure enumerated by Blackstone, and also with some of the other consequences of tenure, in the following order: (i) homage and fealty; (ii) relief and primer seisin; (iii) wardship and marriage; (iv) aids; (v) escheat and forfeiture.

[1] Vinogradoff, Villeinage, 196–203. [2] 12 Charles II, c. 24.
[3] For a full account see Holdsworth, H. E. L. (3rd ed.), iii. 54–73. [4] Comm. ii. 63. [5] Below, pp. 102–110.

(i) *Homage and Fealty.* Homage is the ceremony which makes the tenant the man of his lord. The oath of fealty is the oath which the tenant swears to be faithful to his lord.

All free tenants were obliged to take an oath of fealty to their lords. Homage, on the other hand, was originally a ceremony only performed by the tenant by knight service. It gave rise to rights and duties on the part both of lord and tenant,[1] and was in fact the cement of those associations of lords and tenants which, when the state was weak, assumed many governmental functions. It declined in importance as the state grew stronger. When the land law became merely property law its consequences became merely proprietary. It gave rise to an obligation on the part of the lord to warrant the tenant's title,[2] and it was extended to the other free tenures. When this obligation came to depend on express covenants it ceased to have any meaning at all, and was abolished in 1660.[3]

(ii) *Relief and Primer Seisin.* At the outset we must distinguish the relief from the heriot. Before the Norman Conquest the man was expected to give his lord an heriot at death. This heriot—the arms of the thegn, the stock of the peasant, perhaps the gift to the lord that he might recognize the will of his tenant—represents in theory the return to the lord of the capital which he has advanced to his tenant. The relief, on the other hand, represents the sum paid by the heir to the lord that he may succeed

[1] P. and M. i. 280–1, 287.

[2] Litt. §§ 143–5; Holdsworth, H. E. L. (3rd ed.), iii. 56, 160.

[3] 12 Charles II, c. 24.

to the property of his ancestor. In the case of the greater military tenants there could be no question of the advance of arms or stock. The land had been granted in return for public services past or future. Reliefs were at first an incident of tenure by knight service, but were gradually extended to the other free tenures. Their amount was at first uncertain, but those payable by tenants by knight service were fixed by the Charter of 1215,[1] and those payable by other tenants in the course of the thirteenth and fourteenth centuries.[2] This incident of tenure was not abolished in 1660.

The king, unlike other lords, was entitled on the death of his tenant to get first seisin (primer seisin) of the land. When the heir had done homage and paid his relief, he could get his land from the king. This royal right was abolished in 1660.[3]

(iii) *Wardship and Marriage.* Though the interest of the tenant had become hereditary, the obligation to pay a relief still reminded the heir of the lord's rights. It is clear that, when the right of the heir was still struggling for recognition, the lord's claim to take back the land on the death of his tenant would be most strongly felt when the tenant's heir was an infant or a woman. The lord, it would be argued, must be allowed to educate the infant heir, so that he might become a worthy tenant, and he must have some say in the marriage of the woman, lest he be forced to accept as a tenant his personal enemy. New point was given to these rights of the lord by the rigid theory of tenure, by the centralized

[1] § 2. [2] Holdsworth, H. E. L. (3rd ed.), iii. 60.

[3] 12 Charles II, c. 24.

administration of the law, and by the power of the crown. The rights of wardship and marriage became definite rights of great pecuniary value both to the king and to the mesne lords. To modern minds such rights seem to be very fiduciary in their nature. The fact that the modern idea as to the fiduciary nature of these rights was so long unrecognized by English law is due to the fact that they formed an increasingly valuable item in the royal revenue.

They were valuable rights because the guardian, though he must not waste the ward's land or marry him or her to a person of lower social rank,[1] had in other respects a free hand; and, being valuable rights, they were freely bought and sold. But since, as the result of the working of the statute Quia Emptores,[2] mesne tenure gradually became obsolete, they tended to become exclusively royal rights; and the king only was compensated when they were abolished in 1660.[3]

These incidents of tenure were confined to the tenures by knight service and grand serjeanty. Tenants by socage and petit serjeanty were under the guardianship of their nearest relatives who were incapable of inheriting.[4] Socage guardianship was thus able to develop into a form of trusteeship, and so became the model to which all forms of guardianship eventually conformed.

(iv) *Aids.* In the days when the feudal group was a little state, associated for mutual help and pro-

[1] Magna Carta (1215), §§ 4, 5, 6, 37; 3 Edward I, c. 21; 6 Edward I, c. 5.

[2] 18 Edward I, c. 1.

[3] 12 Charles II, c. 24.

[4] Glanvil, VII, c. ii; cp. Litt. §§ 123, 124.

tection, the lord could call upon the tenant to help him in emergencies. At first these emergencies were not defined. But the ordinary occasions on which an aid might be demanded were defined by Magna Carta [1] to be the ransoming of the lord's person, the knighting of his eldest son, and the marriage of his eldest daughter. The amount of the aid in the two last-mentioned cases was fixed in 1275; [2] and in 1352 the amounts thus fixed were made binding on the crown.[3] They were abolished in 1660.[4]

(v) *Escheat and Forfeiture.* All land is held of some lord. That lord, or some one of his predecessors in title, is supposed to have given the land to the tenant, or some one of his predecessors in title. Therefore, if the tenant die without heirs, it is only right that the lord should have back again that which he gave to the tenant. This is escheat *propter defectum sanguinis.* Similarly, if the tenant commits any gross breach of the feudal bond—commits, that is, a 'felony' in the original sense of that term [5]—the lord may take again that which he gave. This is escheat *propter delictum tenentis.* The right of escheat was thus a tenurial right, which was dependent upon the fact that the freehold had no tenant. Therefore it could only arise when a tenant in fee simple [6] died without heirs or committed felony. If the estate was a smaller estate, the person or

[1] (1215) § 12; it was only with the consent of the *commune concilium* that they could be imposed on other occasions.

[2] 3 Edward I, st. 1, c. 36.

[3] 25 Edward III, st. 5, c. 11.

[4] 12 Charles II, c. 24.

[5] Holdsworth, H. E. L. (3rd ed.), ii. 357–8.

[6] For the estate in fee simple see below, pp. 52–5.

persons next entitled got the estate if or when it came to an end.[1]

The history of these two varieties of escheat has been dissimilar.

Escheat *propter defectum sanguinis* was part of the law till the Property Acts came into force.[2] But in practice, owing to the fact that the statute Quia Emptores[3] destroyed mesne tenure or the evidence for its existence, it came to be a right more valuable to the crown than to any one else; and even to the crown it came to be of little value when all free tenants acquired the right to dispose of their lands by will.[4]

The operation of escheat *propter delictum tenentis* was extended when felony came to mean, not merely an offence which involved a gross breach of the feudal bond, but any serious crime. When this newer conception of felony had come to prevail, the commission of a felony was supposed to cause an escheat because the felon's blood was corrupted. He could not own any property himself, nor could any heir born before or after the felony claim through him. The same consequences followed upon an abjuration of the realm,[5] and upon a judgement of outlawry upon an indictment for felony.[6] In all these cases of escheat the lord's right was subject to the right of the crown to 'year, day, and waste', a right the origin of which is obscure.[7] In later law this right was always compounded for by the lord.[8]

[1] See below, pp. 66–7.

[2] Below, p. 38.

[3] 18 Edward I, c. 1.

[4] For the history of the will of lands see below, pp. 295–8.

[5] For abjuration see Holdsworth, H. E. L. (3rd ed.), iii. 303–7.

[6] Ibid., 604–5.

[7] Ibid., 69–70.

[8] Challis, Real Property (3rd ed.), 35.

The right of forfeiture did not depend upon tenure. It was the prerogative right of the king, as king, to all the lands of a person convicted of high treason, of whatsoever lord they were held; so that the exercise of this right deprived the lord of his right to an escheat. It was largely this conflict of interest between king and lord which led to the definition of the scope of high treason in Edward III's reign.[1]

In course of time the services due from the different types of free tenure came to be of comparatively small value. We have seen that, by the end of the thirteenth century, the military service of the tenants by knight service was practically obsolete;[2] and the money rents due from the tenants in socage became negligible with changes in the value of money. But the incidents of tenure, more especially the incidents of wardship and marriage, remained very valuable to the king and other lords, and more especially to the king, since, as the result of the working of the statute Quia Emptores,[3] more and more land came to be held directly of him. In fact, these incidents of tenure have had an important influence on the development of the land law, right down to the abolition of most of them in 1660. Their influence can be briefly summarized as follows: (*a*) It is probable that they had some influence in settling the rule that land descends to the eldest son, or, if there are no sons, to all daughters equally.[4] (*b*) They were one of the causes of the rule that a landowner could not leave his lands by his will.[5] (*c*) It is

[1] Holdsworth, H. E. L. (3rd ed.), ii. 475–6. [2] Above, p. 26.
[3] 18 Edward I, c. 1. [4] Below, pp. 81–2.
[5] Below, pp. 103–4.

probable that their value had something to do with the manner in which the question of freedom of alienation was settled in 1290 by the statute Quia Emptores.[1] (*d*) They were the chief cause for the enactment of the first statute of Mortmain in 1279.[2] (*e*) They were one of the causes which led to the rule of law known as the rule in *Shelley's Case*.[3] (*f*) The desire to evade them was one of the causes of the popularity of uses; [4] and the restoration to the king of this branch of his revenue was a principal cause for the enactment of the statute of Uses.[5] (*g*) The refusal of the court of Chancery for a considerable period to enforce a use upon a use as a trust was mainly due to the fact that the enforcement of these trusts would have frustrated the main purpose of the statute of Uses by again depleting this branch of the king's revenue.[6] It is not till the importance of these incidents of tenure was diminished by the Legislature that they ceased to influence the land law. To the history of this process we must now turn.

(3) The Modification by the Legislature of the Law relating to the Tenures and their Incidents. The first great modification of the law relating to the free tenures and their incidents was made by the statute of Tenures in 1660.[7] By that Act tenure by knight service was converted into tenure by socage; and

[1] Below, p. 106.
[2] 7 Edward I; below, p. 109.
[3] Below, p. 54.
[4] Below, p. 149.
[5] Below, p. 153.
[6] Below, pp. 160–1.
[7] 12 Charles II, c. 24; for some criticisms on the draftsmanship of the Act, and for difficulties thereby caused in its interpretation, see *In re Holliday*, [1922] 2 Ch. at pp. 711–13.

the incidents of wardship, marriage, aids, primer seisin, and fines for alienation, together with scutage and homage, were abolished. The Act did not affect the other free tenures, except in so far as they were subject to the incidents of tenure which were abolished. Copyhold tenure was excluded altogether from its operation—an exclusion which Roger North, writing at the end of the seventeenth century, thought was unfair.[1] The result of this exclusion was that, till the abolition of copyhold tenure by the Property Acts, the incidents and consequences of tenure continued to possess great practical importance in relation to that tenure.[2] But, with respect to land held by a free tenure, the effects of the Act in diminishing the importance of the consequences of tenure were very great.

In the first place, as Hale pointed out in his introduction to Rolle's Abridgement, it got rid of a mass of obsolete law connected with tenure by knight service and its incidents. In the second place, by eliminating many of the consequences of tenure, it took a long step in the direction of assimilating the law of real and personal property. It is true that a long road remained to be travelled before the assimilation effected by the Property Acts could be attained; but I think that it is true to say that the reform effected by the Act of 1660 was a condition precedent to any sort of progress along that road.

The other important legislative modifications of

[1] 'It was somewhat unequal, when Parliament took away the royal tenures *in capite*, that the lesser tenures of the gentry were left exposed to as grievous abuses as the former', Lives of the Norths, i. 31.

[2] Below, pp. 46–8.

the old law were in respect of the incidents of escheat and forfeiture. Escheat *propter delictum tenentis*, the king's right to year day and waste, and forfeiture, were abolished in 1870.[1] Escheat *propter defectum sanguinis* was abolished by the Administration of Estates Act, 1925. That Act provides that, if the owner of a fee simple estate in land dies, without heirs and intestate, the land shall not escheat, but shall, like personal property, lapse to the crown as *bona vacantia.*[2]

The results of these legislative modifications, and of the changes made by the Property Acts, are, first, that practically all tenure is now socage tenure—frank-almoin and the services attached to grand and petit serjeanty are the only two survivors;[3] and, secondly, that, though in the case of land held by a free tenure for an estate in fee simple, it is still true to say that the land is held of the crown, the consequences of tenure have been reduced to a vanishing-point. It is only in the cases where a person holds an interest less than an estate in fee simple that a tenure exists which has any practical consequences. But this aspect of tenure is intimately connected with the history of the doctrine of estates and interests in the land;[4] and, before dealing with it,

[1] 33, 34 Victoria c. 23.

[2] Administration of Estates Act, 1925, §§ 45 (1) (*d*), 46 (1) (vi); for the evolution of the rules as to the application of escheat and forfeiture to equitable estates see Holdsworth, H. E. L. (3rd ed.), iii. 71–2; the result is that the interest of the *cestui-que* trust, who dies without heirs and intestate, now goes to the crown as *bona vacantia* in the same way as a legal interest; but his interest is not affected by the death, without heirs and intestate, of a sole trustee.

[3] Law of Property Act, 1922, § 136.

[4] Below, pp. 48–77.

I must first relate briefly the history of unfree tenure, and the manner in which copyhold tenure was evolved from it.

Unfree and Copyhold Tenure.[1]

In order to understand the nature of unfree tenure, and the manner in which it developed into copyhold tenure, it is necessary to say something, first, of a semi-communal method of cultivating the land, which we can see in operation from the Anglo-Saxon period right down to the nineteenth century ; and secondly of the manor and its organization.

(1) The semi-communal method of cultivating the land which we can see in operation from the Anglo-Saxon period down to the nineteenth century is that known as the common or open field system.[2] The land of the village community was divided up into two or three open fields (*campi*), which were cultivated in a certain rotation. Each of these fields was divided into a number of strips (*seliones*), which averaged about an acre in extent ; and the strips were divided from one another by turf balks. Each landowner possessed a certain number of these strips in different places in the open fields. It is probable that the strips were scattered in this way in order to give each owner a little bit of the good land, a little bit of the indifferent, and a little bit of the bad. To allot to each owner a continuous area, compensating by extent of area for deficiency in quality, was beyond the powers of a primitive community. In addition, each landowner had certain common rights. One

[1] Holdsworth, H. E. L. (3rd ed.), iii. 198–213, vii. 296–312.

[2] Ibid., ii. 56–61.

and sometimes two of the common fields were left fallow each year, and over these fields there was a right of common of pasture for the cattle of the villagers, which was known as common of shack.[1] There were also rights of common over the extensive waste lands which adjoined the village. In spite of numerous private Acts which provided for the enclosure and partition of these open fields, a committee reported in 1844 that this system still prevailed over a large part of England. An Act passed in the following year, and later Acts, which gave facilities for enclosure and partition,[2] have resulted in its gradual disappearance.

(2) This primitive cultivating community is the essence of the manor. It came, after the Conquest, to be dependent on a lord of whom the land was held; and this lord, by virtue of this tenurial relationship, had the right to hold a court or courts for his tenants.[3] Often, too, the lord possessed a franchise—such as the right to hold a court leet [4]—which gave him an additional jurisdiction. Legal theory, in course of time, added other elements to the manor. The lord might have both free and unfree tenants. The lawyers, therefore, laid it down that he had the right to hold two courts—a court baron for his freeholders, and a court customary for the unfree or villein tenants; and that there was no true manor unless there were both free and unfree tenants. The typical manor, therefore, consisted of

[1] For rights of common see below, pp. 94–7.

[2] 8, 9 Victoria, c. 118.

[3] For the manor see Holdsworth, H. E. L. (3rd ed.), i. 23–4, 28–30, 179–85.

[4] For this franchise see ibid., 135–7.

(*a*) lands kept by the lord in his own hands—his demesne, (*b*) lands held of him by tenants holding by a free tenure, (*c*) lands held of him by tenants holding by an unfree tenure, (*d*) certain rights of jurisdiction over these tenants, and (*e*) certain rights of common belonging to the tenants over the fallow fields or waste lands.

The unfree or villein tenant held of his lord a certain quantity of land in return for his services in cultivating the lord's demesne land. At first, no doubt, those services were imposed very much at the arbitrary will of the lord; and in many cases (though by no means invariably) the villein or unfree tenant was personally unfree.[1] But, in the course of the thirteenth century, the tenant's liabilities to his lord, both in respect of labour services and in respect of other payments, such as merchet and heriots,[2] were written down on the manorial extent and the records of the manor court.[3] And though, as we have seen, the unfree tenant was not protected as against his lord by the king's courts,[4] he did get protection in the manor court, which administered the customary law of the manor. Indeed, it is clear

[1] In fact these tenants were of diverse origins, recruited both from the personally unfree, and from free men who had come to be dependent on a lord (Holdsworth, H. E. L. (3rd ed.), iii. 199–201); the lawyers, from the end of the twelfth century onwards, kept quite distinct the ideas of unfreedom of tenure and unfreedom of status, see ibid. (3rd ed.), ii. 202 and n. 6, 264, 577; for the history of unfree or villein status see ibid., iii. 491–510.

[2] For these incidents see above, pp. 17, 30.

[3] For the manorial extent see Holdsworth, H. E. L. (3rd ed.), ii. 370, 379–80, iii. App. II; for the records of the manor court see ibid., ii. 370–1.

[4] Above, pp. 16, 18.

from the records of these courts, that this customary law was being developed on lines which, in many cases, resembled the development by the king's court of the law relating to land held by free tenure.[1] The result was that the rights and duties of both lord and tenant tended to become fixed and certain. In legal theory the unfree tenant held at the will of the lord; but that will was in most cases controlled by the customary law of the manor.

In the course of the fourteenth century we can see the beginnings of a change in this system. In a few places labour services were commuted for money payments. The Black Death (1348–9), which swept off a large part of the labouring population, strengthened this tendency, by breaking up the solidarity of the manorial organization. Neither the statutes of Labourers, which attempted to keep down wages, nor the villein revolt of 1381, had much effect upon this tendency. The practice of leasing lands for terms of years, and of commuting labour services for money rents, spread rapidly at the end of the fourteenth century, because the old system had become impossible. The change is marked by a gradual change in the name of the tenure. It is coming to be called, not, as formerly, tenure in villeinage, but tenure by copy of the court roll.

It is clear that this commutation of labour services for money rents destroyed much of the original reason for the refusal of the royal courts to interfere with this tenure. Protection given by the royal courts to these tenants would no longer mean an interference with, or an inquiry into, the agricultural

[1] Holdsworth, H. E. L. (3rd ed.), ii. 379–81.

economy of the manor ; it would mean only the due enforcement of a bargain, the terms of which could be easily ascertained by looking at the rolls of the manor court. But this change in circumstances would not by itself have led the common law courts to interfere. There were too many precedents which laid it down that these tenants had no interest save at the will of the lord. But the high-handed proceedings of the lords, who took advantage of the uncertainty of the terms of the tenure under the new leases granted to tenants, made some interference necessary in the public interest. What served well enough when the will of the lord was substantially in agreement with the custom of the manor, no longer served when the will of the lord and the custom of the manor pulled different ways.

It was the Chancery and the Council which were the first to interfere to protect the copyholder against his lord ; and, in the latter half of the fifteenth century, the common law courts began to follow suit. Danby, C.J., in 1467, and Brian, C.J., in 1481, both stated that they would give a remedy if a copyholder was unjustifiably ousted by his lord ; and these dicta were incorporated into the text of Littleton's Tenures in 1530. In fact the settlement of the legal position of the copyholder was a very difficult question ; and its difficulty was aggravated by a growing demand for English wool, which was causing the conversion of arable land into pasture, and a consequent depopulation of the country. It was also a question which was vital to the peace of the country, for Coke, in 1584, testified to the fact that ' great part of the land within the realm is in grant by copy '.[1] It was due to the efforts of the Legislature, royal commissions, the courts of common law, the court of Chancery, the court of Requests, and the Star Chamber, that a fair settlement was made in the course of the sixteenth century.

If a tenant could show that he held land which was anciently copyhold, the lord was compelled to comply with the terms of the tenure as laid down by the custom of the manor. On the other hand, it was held that no land could be accounted copyhold unless it could be shown that it was anciently copyhold. Thus the tenants of land anciently copyhold got security of tenure, and the lord was left free to develop as he pleased other parts of his property. In effect the copyhold tenant got a fully-protected interest in the land on the terms upon which his services had been commuted in the fourteenth or fifteenth centuries. He was fortunate in being thus able to hold upon terms settled at so early a date. The general fall in the value of money, which took place towards the end of the sixteenth century, caused these fixed payments to be much less than the real value of the land. And so the copyholder got a substantial interest in the land, which interest is really, as Maitland has said, ' an unearned increment, the product of the American mines '.[2]

Thus tenure by copyhold became merely a form of landownership, without any servile taint. As Coke

[1] *Heydon's Case* (1584), 3 Co. Rep. at f. 8b ; note that Maine, Early Law and Custom, 299 seqq., points out that grievances, analogous to those which were successfully dealt with by the Tudor statesmen were left unremedied in France, and were among the causes of the French Revolution.

[2] Eng. Hist. Rev. ix. 439.

says, 'in the point of service a man can scarce discern any difference between freehold lands and copyhold lands '.[1] The differences had become merely historical. The wise settlement arrived at in the Tudor period affords abundant justification for Coke's eloquent comparison between the present and the past condition of the copyholder. Time had indeed dealt very favourably with copyholders in divers respects.[2]

The courts of common law gradually assimilated the law of copyhold tenure to the law of free tenure, statutory and otherwise, in so far as the law did not conflict with the custom of the manor. The creation of this body of law was no easy task. It involved, first, a nice adjustment of the conflicting claims of custom and the common law ; secondly, much consideration of the problem of the application of the statutes and doctrines of the common law to copyholds ; and, thirdly, the due recognition and protection of the conflicting interests of lords and tenants. This body of law was never wholly satisfactory ; for it suffered from the defects both of obscurity and technicality. The custom of the manor was often

[1] Complete Copyholder, § 7.

[2] § 9, 'But now copyholders stand upon a sure ground, now they weigh not their Lord's displeasure, they shake not at every sudden blast of wind, they eat, drink, and sleep securely ; onely having an especial care of the main chance (viz.) to perform carefully what duties and services soever their Tenure doth exact, and Custome doth require : then let Lord frown, the copyholder cares not, knowing himself safe and not within any danger. For if the Lord's anger grow to expulsion the Law hath provided several weapons of remedy ; for it is at his election either to sue a *Subpoena* or an action of trespass against the Lord. Time hath dealt very favourably with Copyholders in divers respects.'

uncertain; the procedure of the manor court was often both antiquated and technical; and the technicalities of the common law doctrines, which were applied to eke out the defects of the manorial custom, helped to make this branch of the law very complex.

The changed political and economic conditions of the nineteenth century brought into clear relief the anomalous and inconvenient character of this tenure. Its leading defects were admirably summed up by the Real Property Commissioners in 1832, as follows: First, the customs of different manors were very numerous and very various; and this led to frequent litigation 'between lord and tenant, between vendor and purchaser, and between persons claiming adversely the same interest.'[1]

> 'Each manor', said the Commissioners,[2] 'has for itself a system of laws to be sought in oral traditions, or in the court rolls or proceedings of the customary court, kept often by ignorant or negligent stewards. In some manors the customs are reduced into writing in the shape of a Customary on the presentment of the homage, or by an Act of Parliament; but little benefit is generally derived from these rude attempts at codification.'

Secondly, as freeholds and copyholds were often intermixed, it was often difficult to find out whether a given piece of land was freehold or copyhold. In order to give a purchaser security of title it was sometimes necessary to make both a freehold and a copyhold conveyance of the same land. Thirdly, the rules as to minerals and timber, under which neither lord nor tenant could make any use of them

[1] Report 15. [2] Ibid. 14.

except by mutual agreement, 'directly interfered with the profitable enjoyment of the soil, and materially diminished the public wealth'.[1] The arbitrary fines payable on alienation and descent had the same effect. The principles upon which the amount payable was calculated were not in all cases settled; and the rule that two years improved value could be charged amounted in substance to 'a tax on the capital of the tenant laid out in improvement'. Hence improvements were seldom made.[2] Fourthly, the lord's rights in respect to heriots led 'not only to ill-will and strife between neighbours, but to constant fraud and evasion'.[3] Fifthly, the fees payable to the steward on every step taken in the lord's court were a very heavy burthen on all dealings with the land.[4] Sixthly, the copyhold tenant got a little compensation from the fact that the land was not legally liable to his debts in his lifetime or after his death. But this immunity was, the Commissioners justly said, 'a reproach to the law'.[5] Practically the only points in which the law

[1] Ibid.; the commissioners say that, 'in consequence of the law with respect to timber, generally speaking, no young tree is allowed to stand on copyhold land;' and there is a common proverb, that 'the oak scorns to grow except on free land'. It is certain that in Sussex and in other parts of England, the boundaries of copyholds may be traced by the entire absence of trees on one side of a line, and their luxuriant growth on the other.

[2] Report 15.

[3] Ibid. 19.

[4] Ibid. 16; Roger North, Lives of the Norths, i. 31, said, 'In very good earnest it is a miserable thing to observe how sharpers that now are commonly court keepers pinch the poor copyholders in their fees. Small tenements and pieces of land that have been men's inheritances for divers generations, to say nothing of the fines, are devoured by fees.'

[5] Ibid. 16.

as to copyhold showed any superiority over the law as to freehold were the fact that the court rolls provided a register of title, and the fact that the widow's rights to dower formed no impediment to alienation.[1]

The Commissioners found themselves unable to suggest the compulsory abolition of copyhold—too much land was still held by this tenure. But they recommended, among other things, that greater facilities should be given for its enfranchisement, i.e. for its conversion into free tenure. This suggestion was carried out by a series of nineteenth-century statutes. As the result of this legislation the amount of land held by copyhold tenure was so rapidly diminished, that the Property Act (1922) has been able to do what Roger North in the seventeenth century and the Real Property Commissioners in the nineteenth century thought eminently desirable —provide for its compulsory abolition.

§ 3. Estates and Interests.

The different types of tenure mark out the leading characteristics of the different forms of landholding known to the law; but they tell us nothing of the nature or incidents of the various interests which those who hold by these tenures may have in the land. It is this question of the nature and incidents of these interests with which we are now concerned.

In the case of land held by the free tenures, and also (with local modifications) in the case of land held by copyhold tenure, the law as to the nature and incidents of the tenant's interest depends on the doctrine of estates in the land. The case of the tenant

[1] Report 16, 17; for dower see below, pp. 87–8.

for a term of years is somewhat different. We have seen that he was denied the protection of the real actions;[1] and we shall see that, consequently, he was at first regarded as having, not a definite interest in the land, but simply a personal right against his landlord. But we shall see that his remedies were gradually expanded, so that he came to have a fully protected interest in the land, which was analogous to the freeholder's estate.[2] But, as the nature of his interest fell under the category of personal property, it differed very considerably in its incidents from freehold estates in the land which fell under the category of real property.[3] I must, therefore, treat separately the series of estates which a person holding by one of the free tenures might possess, and the interest of the lessee for a term of years. In conclusion I shall state briefly the simplifications effected by the Property Acts in this branch of the law.

The Series of Estates in Land held by a Free Tenure.

English law, before the Property Acts, recognized a very large number of different estates in the land. There was, in the first place, the following series of estates in possession: the estate in fee simple—the largest estate known to the law—which descended to all the heirs lineal or collateral of the tenant; the estate in fee tail, created by the statute De Donis Conditionalibus (1285),[4] which descended only to the lineal heirs of the donee; the estate for life and other lesser estates. In the second place, if a tenant in fee simple gave less than a fee simple, he had not given

[1] Above, p. 20.
[2] Below, pp. 72–3.
[3] Below, pp. 74–6.
[4] 13 Edward I, st. 1, c. 1.

all that he had to give. He might either retain that interest or give it to another. Hence we get the estate in expectancy—called a reversion when the interest was retained by the donor, and a remainder when it was granted to another. In the third place, estates might be given to two or more persons to hold as co-owners. In the fourth place, estates might be created in favour of a donee as a security or gage for a sum of money which the donee had advanced to the donor. In this way the relations of mortgagor and mortgagee were created.

I shall, in the first place, say something of the origin of the conception of an estate in the land; and then I shall describe briefly these four groups of estates.

(1) The origin of the conception of an estate in the land.

The peculiarly English conception of an estate in the land originates from two causes:

(i) An immature system of law has some difficulty in grasping the idea of a legal right apart from the thing over which that right exists. At the present day we know well enough that ownership means simply a bundle of rights. Early law regards it as control over a thing—hardly conceivable apart from that thing. The distinction, in fact, between a right and the subject of a right is a feat of abstraction of which it is quite incapable. Now it is no doubt true that it is only the tenant in possession who has a present right to the land. But it is clear that others have both rights and actions to enforce them. The interests, for instance, of others, who hold in remainder or reversion, are rights to get possession at a future time. Roman lawyers would have called them *res incorporales*. But, as we shall see, English law at this period had no clear idea of the distinct juristic character of *res incorporales*.[1] Remainders and reversions were therefore treated as if they were corporeal things; and thus this defect in the analytic faculty is one reason why English law has come by its doctrine of estates. These future rights to enjoy are treated as if they were actually existing things.[2]

(ii) There were a large number of different interests, recognized and protected by the law, which might coexist in the same piece of land at the same time. There might, as we have seen, be many different tenants holding by different tenures.[3] Likewise there might be many different tenants holding different interests—in possession, reversion, or remainder. The enjoyment of these interests in reversion or remainder might be postponed; but they were protected by appropriate actions, and they were as definite as the interests of the tenant in possession. Some word was needed to express the interests of these various persons, and the word hit upon was 'status' or 'estate'—perhaps for the following reason: We have seen that in the older law the tenure by which the tenant held his land often told us something of his status.[4] The word 'status' was an apt one to express a man's position with regard to land-holding at a time when so many things turned upon land-holding. As the differences between

[1] Below, pp. 92, 129–30.

[2] For a good account of this peculiarity of English law see Markby, Elements of Law (3rd ed.), 163, 164.

[3] Above, p. 22.

[4] Above, p. 23.

the types of free tenure tended to diminish in importance, the term came to be applied to the quantum of the tenant's interest rather than to the quality of the tenant's tenure. Thus the term 'status' or 'estate', borrowed originally from public law and applied upon feudal principles to land tenure, became acclimatized in private law; and as land-holding became more and more simply property law, it took upon itself the new meaning of an interest in land.

Similarly, the term 'freehold' lost its original connexion with tenure, and came to mean all those estates in the land which, being protected by the real actions, were accounted real property. As Lord Mansfield said, 'the idea modern times annex to freehold or freeholder is taken merely from the duration of the estate'.[1]

(2) Estates in possession.

(i) *The estate in fee simple.*[2] By the end of the thirteenth century it was settled that a gift of land to a man and his heirs gave the donee an estate, which would descend to all his heirs lineal or collateral. The words 'and his heirs' were essential till, in 1881, the Conveyancing Act allowed, as an alternative, the words 'in fee simple'.[3] In 1837, however, the Wills Act had enacted that a gift by will to a person simply should pass the fee simple or other the whole estate of the testator, unless a contrary intention appeared in the will;[4] and this rule has been extended to

[1] *Taylor* v. *Horde* (1757) 1 Burr. at p. 108.

[2] Holdsworth, H. E. L. (3rd ed.), iii. 105–7.

[3] 44, 45 Victoria, c. 41, § 51; by the same section the use of the words 'in tail' were made alternative to the use of the words 'heirs of the body'.

[4] § 28.

conveyances *inter vivos* by the Law of Property Act, 1925.[1]

If in a gift to *A* and his heirs the expression ' to *A* and his heirs ' were interpreted literally, it might seem that the land was given to both *A* and his heirs —in other words that the heirs acquired, or in the technical phrase ' purchased ', something by the gift. This may have been so in very early law. But, as early as the first half of the thirteenth century, it was settled that the heirs acquired nothing. The word ' heirs ' was held in technical language to be ' a word of limitation ', i. e. it marked out or defined the estate taken by the donee, and not ' a word of purchase ', i.e. the heirs acquired nothing by such a gift. The reason for this interpretation of the word ' heirs ' was due partly to the favour which, as we shall see, the king's courts showed to freedom of alienation—they refused to allow the donee's heirs to restrict the donee's freedom of alienation ;[2] and partly to the feeling that any other interpretation might hinder the lord's right to a relief—if the heir took as purchaser, and not by inheritance, it is not at all clear that a relief would be payable to the lord.

Probably it was the same two causes which led to the evolution of the rule which came to be known as the rule in *Shelley's Case.*[3] It is called the rule in *Shelley's Case* because the classical statement of the rule is contained in that case, which was decided in 1581.[4] But though the rule is older than that

[1] § 60 (1).

[2] Below, p. 103.

[3] Holdsworth, H. E. L. (3rd ed.), iii. 107–11. The best account of the rule is contained in Lord Macnaghten's judgement in *Foxwell* v. *Van Grutten*, [1897] A. C. at pp. 667–81.

[4] 1 Co. Rep. 93 b.

case—it was in fact established in the fourteenth century—it is advisable to state it in the classical words used in that case: 'When the ancestor by any gift or conveyance takes an estate of freehold, and in the same gift or conveyance an estate is limited either mediately or immediately to his heirs in fee or in tail; that always in such cases "the heirs" are words of limitation of the estate, and not words of purchase.' [1] Thus, if an estate be given to *A* for life, remainder to *B* for life, remainder to the heirs of *A*, *A* will take both an estate for life, and a fee simple expectant on the death of *B*, which he can alienate as he pleases. His heirs will take nothing. The reasons for the establishment of this rule were as follows: (*a*) It made for freedom of alienation. (*b*) Any other interpretation might have deprived the lord of his relief. (*c*) Any other interpretation might have caused the seisin or possession of the land to be left vacant—it might have caused, to use technical language, an abeyance of the seisin. Thus, if land were given to *A* for life, remainder to *B* and the heirs of his body, remainder to the heirs of *A*; and if *B* died in *A*'s lifetime without leaving an heir of his body, in whom could the fee be vested if it had not vested from the first in *A*? It may be well that no one was entitled to succeed as *A*'s heir either at the time of the gift or at *B*'s death; and it is no answer to say that in such a case *A* might take for life with a contingent remainder in favour of his heirs; for, as we shall see, the law did not, in the fourteenth century, admit the validity of contingent remainders.[2]

The rule was a rule of law and not merely a rule

[1] 1 Co. Rep. at f. 104 a.

[2] Below, p. 68.

of construction—that is, it was applied if the appropriate technical words were used by the donor, irrespective of his intentions. It gave rise to a large mass of litigation in the eighteenth and nineteenth centuries; but it is now abolished by the Law of Property Act 1925.[1] At the present day, therefore, the word 'heirs', if contained in a limitation like that given above, is a word of purchase, and the heir or heirs will take an estate in fee simple. But the Act only applies to instruments coming into effect after 1st January 1926, so that, in interpreting old deeds or wills, it will be necessary to know the meaning of this old rule of law.

(ii) *The estate tail.*[2] Before 1285 a gift to a man and the heirs of his body created a fee simple conditional. That is, it was construed as a gift to a man and his heirs (i.e. a fee simple) conditionally upon his having an heir of his body. Thus, if an heir were born alive (whether he survived or not) the condition was fulfilled, and the donee got a fee simple, which he could alienate, which would be forfeited if he committed treason, or would escheat if he committed felony. If, on the other hand, the donee had never had an heir, or if he had had an heir who had predeceased him and he had not alienated the estate, the land reverted to the donor. This interpretation disappointed the intentions of donors, and so the great landowners procured the passing, in 1285, of the statute De Donis Conditionalibus, which created the estate tail.[3] It was so called because it was an estate

1 § 131.
2 Holdsworth, H. E. L. (3rd ed.), iii. 111–24.
3 13 Edward I, st. 1, c. 1.

the descent of which was cut down (*talliatum*) to the heirs of the body of the donee.

The statute provided that, for the future, the land should descend according to the terms of the gift (*secundum formam in carta expressam*), and that donees should have no power to deprive their issue, or persons entitled in reversion or remainder, of the land given to them. The donee in tail could alienate the property, but the estate which he created could not last for a longer period than his own life; for the statute gave to the issue, the reversioners, and the remainder-men writs of formedon (*forma doni*), by means of which they could recover their interests when they fell into possession. It was ultimately held that the words of the statute must be interpreted to mean that, not only the first donee in tail, but also the whole series of his issue, could thus be restrained from alienating the estate for a longer period than their own lives.[1]

The restrictions placed by the statute, as thus interpreted, upon tenants in tail were soon found to be not only irksome, but productive of great injustice. Parliament was petitioned for its repeal, but these petitions were always rejected.

> 'The truth was that the lords and commons, knowing that their estates tail were not to be forfeited for felony or treason; as their estates of inheritance were before the said Act . . . and finding that they were not answerable for the debts or incumbrances of their ancestors, nor did the sales, alienations, or leases of their ancestors bind them for the

[1] For this interpretation, which was not wholly in accordance with the literal words of the statute, see Holdsworth, H. E. L. (3rd ed.), iii. 114–16.

lands which were entailed to their ancestors, they always rejected such bills.' [1]

In default of Parliamentary aid the ingenuity of the legal profession set itself to work to evade the statute.

The expedients which were ultimately adopted to effect this purpose were the fictitious legal proceedings known as recoveries and fines.

A recovery was a fictitious real action, pursued through all its stages to final judgement. But a recovery by itself would not have been efficacious, since these collusive recoveries were voidable.[2] But the machinery of a recovery was made efficacious by combining it with the doctrine of warranty. If *A* had given land to *B* and his heirs, and had bound himself and his heirs to warrant *B*'s title, and *X* claimed the land from *B*, *B* could call on *A* to fulfil his duty of warranting the title—he vouched *A* to warranty. If *A* admitted his duty to warrant the title, *X*'s action went on against *A*. If *X* succeeded in his action, the court gave judgement that *X* do recover the land from *B*, and that *A* convey lands to *B* of equal value. These rules were applied to the estate tail as follows: *X*, a friend of *A* the tenant in tail, brought a writ of right in the court of Common Pleas claiming the land from *A* for an estate in fee simple. *A* vouched to warranty *Y*—a man of straw. *Y* admitted the duty to warrant, asked to be allowed to talk the matter over out of the court with *X*,[3] and then departed in contempt of the court. *X* therefore recovered the land from *A* for an estate in fee

[1] *Mildmay's Case* (1606), 6 Co. Rep. at f. 40 b.

[2] See L. Q. R. vi. 285–6.

[3] In the technical phrase 'he craved leave to imparl'.

simple—which he at once conveyed to *A*; and *A* got judgement against *Y* ordering him to convey to *A* lands of equal value. This judgement *Y* was wholly unable to satisfy; but this fact the courts regarded as quite immaterial—they had done their best. If, however, lands had been conveyed by *Y* to *A* in accordance with the judgement, all the persons interested in the entailed lands would have been compensated. It was for this reason that a recovery barred all those interested in the entailed lands—issue, remainder-men, and reversioners.[1] In later law all this elaborate process was not gone through. The steps in the fictitious action were merely enrolled on the records of the court. The part of *Y* was played by the crier of the court of Common Pleas, who received for his services the sum of 4*d.* for each occasion on which he acted. He was known as the common vouchee, because he was vouched to warranty by all those who suffered a recovery.[2]

A fine was a fictitious personal action which was compromised—hence the name *finalis concordia.* The statute De Donis had enacted that a fine should have no effect on an estate tail. But, by virtue of statutes of the reigns of Henry VII and VIII, a fine was allowed to bar the issue, but not the reversioners or remainder-

[1] Exactly when this expedient for barring an estate tail was introduced is not certain, Holdsworth, H. E. L. (3rd ed.), iii. 118–19; *Taltarum's Case* (1472), Y. B. 12 Ed. IV, Mich. pl. 25 shows that the expedient of a common recovery was then well known.

[2] As Sir F. Pollock has said (The Land Laws, 84) the crier of the court of Common Pleas thus 'passed his life cheerfully and not ungainfully in perpetual contempt of the court of Common Pleas and liability to be fined at the king's discretion'.

men.[1] Thus the person in whose favour the fine was levied got an estate which was like a fee simple in that it descended to his heirs general. But it was unlike a fee simple in that it was cut short if the issue of the tenant in tail failed. This estate was known as a base fee.

It was therefore only a recovery which completely barred the estate tail. But, because a recovery was a real action, it must be begun against the man in possession of the first estate of freehold. Now estates tail were usually created by family settlements, under the limitations of which the father had an estate for life, and his son the first estate tail. Since the action must be begun against the father, the son could not completely bar the estate tail without his father's consent. That consent was not required for a fine, because, being a personal action, it could be begun against the tenant in tail; but, by the levy of a fine, only a base fee could be created; and that was not a marketable commodity. The result of this procedural rule was therefore beneficial. It is for this reason that it has outlived the old processes to which it owed its origin.

Fines and recoveries were abolished in 1833;[2] and the Act, while retaining the substance of the old law, substituted, as Blackstone had suggested,[3] the simple machinery of a deed enrolled, formerly in the court of Chancery, and later in the Central Office of the Supreme Court. A tenant in tail of full age, whose interest was in possession, could in this way completely bar his estate tail, and turn it into an estate in fee simple. But if the tenant in tail's

[1] 4 Henry VII, c. 24; 32 Henry VIII, c. 36.

[2] 3, 4, William IV, c. 74.

[3] Comm. ii. 361.

estate was not in possession, he could not effect a complete bar without the consent of the protector of the settlement, who was usually the man in possession of the first estate of freehold. If he tried to bar the estate tail without the consent of the protector, he could only create a base fee. The Law of Property Act 1925 has retained the substance of the old law as to barring estates tail; but it has modified it in two ways. In the first place, the disentailing deed need not be enrolled. In the second place, an estate tail can be barred by will, if the property entailed, the instrument under which it was acquired, or entailed property generally, is referred to specifically in the will.[1]

With the other important effects of the Property Act 1925 on estates tail I shall deal later.

(iii) *The estate for life and other lesser estates.*[2] From a very early period it was the rule that a gift of land to *A* gave *A* a life estate only; and this rule may show that, at this early period, the law regarded the life estate as the normal estate in the land. In fact, in the days when the claims of lords and heirs limited the rights of the tenant,[3] it may well have seemed that an estate for life, or something like it, was the largest interest which a tenant could have in the land. It was for this reason that the tenant for life had seisin, i.e. a possession which was protected by the real actions. We shall see that the person seised had very great advantages, not only as against third persons, but even as against others entitled to the land. He could, for instance, dispose of the land

1 §§ 133, 176 (1).

2 Holdsworth, H. E. L. (3rd ed.), iii. 120–5.

3 Below, pp. 103, 104–5.

by a 'tortious' feoffment, and thereby deprive the owner in fee simple of his right of entry.[1] Moreover, there were originally no effective provisions against commission of waste. We shall see that other persons who had rights in the land gradually got better protection against wrongful dispositions by the tenant for life.[2] At this point we must consider the statutes which were passed to prevent the commission of waste.

The statute of Gloucester[3] (1278) provided a writ of waste against tenants for life, years, or a woman holding by right of dower.[4] Those convicted of waste were punished by forfeiture of the thing wasted and triple damages. To come within the statute the waste must have been caused by the voluntary act of the tenant—the fact that it had been caused accidentally or by *vis major* was a good defence. How far tenants were liable for merely permissive waste, i.e. for doing nothing, with the result that the premises decayed, was not settled till a later period. I shall therefore deal with this and other questions relative to waste in a later chapter.[5] In this period, however, it was settled that a grantor could allow a tenant to commit waste. The tenant was then said to be a tenant 'without impeachment of waste'.

A tenant for life was entitled to take reasonable 'botes' and 'estovers' without committing waste.

[1] Below, p. 125.
[2] Below, p. 127.
[3] 6 Edward I, c. 5; an earlier statute of 1267 (the Statute of Marlborough) had contained provisions against waste; later statutes were 13 Edward I st. 1, c. 14, 20 Edward I st. 2, 11, Henry VI, c. 5.
[4] For dower see below, pp. 87–8.
[5] Below, pp. 241–3.

That is, he could cut wood for firing, or timber trees for the repair of the house. To cut timber for any other purpose was waste.

If a tenant for life alienated his estate he created an estate *pur autre vie.* After considerable hesitation, it was decided that such a tenant had the freehold. Since the estate was an estate of freehold, it could not be devised; and what was to happen if the tenant *pur autre vie* died in the life of the *cestui que vie* the lawyers of the fourteenth and fifteenth centuries could not satisfactorily decide. The difficulty was a logical difficulty which specially appealed to the lawyers of this period. If *A*, tenant for life, grants his life estate to *B* for his (*A*'s) life, and if *B* dies in the life of *A*, who will take the land? Not *A*, because he has disposed of his whole interest; not *B*'s heirs, both because they have not been named and because the estate is not an estate of inheritance; not *B*'s personal representatives, because the estate, being an estate of freehold, is real property. The only conclusion we can come to is the conclusion of the reporter in a Year Book of Henry VI's reign, that the estate 'occupanti conceditur'.[1] The estate goes to the first taker—the 'general occupant'. It was perhaps by analogy to this doctrine of general occupancy that the title 'special occupant' was, at the end of the sixteenth century,[2] applied to the case where, the grant being to *A* and his heirs *pur autre vie*, *A*'s heir succeeds on his death.

[1] Y. B. 38 Hy. VI, Pasch. pl. 9.

[2] See L. Q. R. xxxii. 399, where it is pointed out that though the special occupant was known to Coke, he was not known to Littleton (1481) or Perkins (1530).

A's heir takes, not as heir, because the estate is not an estate of inheritance, but as occupant.[1] Statutes[2] passed to abolish the doctrine of general occupancy, by vesting the estate in the personal representatives of the tenant *pur autre vie*, gave to this estate its double character in modern law. If it vested in them under these statutes it was administered as personalty: if it vested in the heir as special occupant it was administered as realty. The Property Acts have made these differences obsolete, by providing a uniform method for the administration of real and personal property.[3]

In conclusion, mention must be made of three varieties of tenancies which do not give a freehold estate in the land. The first is the interest of the tenant at will, the second is the interest of the tenant from year to year, and the third is the interest of the tenant at sufferance.

A tenancy at will is an estate which can be determined at any time by the will of the lessor or the lessee.[4] It is in connexion with this species of tenancy that the law as to emblements grew up. Littleton says:[5]

> 'If the lessee soweth the land, and the lessor after it is sown, and before the corn is ripe, put him out, yet the lessee shall have the corn, and shall have free entry, egress, and regress to cut and carry away the corn, because he

[1] Co. Litt. 41b; Challis, Real Property, 327–8.

[2] 29 Charles II, c. 3, § 12; 14 George II, c. 20, § 9; 1 Victoria, c. 26, § 2 (the Wills Act).

[3] The Administration of Estates Act, 1925.

[4] Littleton's definition implies that it is at the will of the lessor only: but it is clear from Co. Litt. 55a that it can be determined by the will of either party.

[5] § 68.

knew not at what time the lessor would enter upon him. Otherwise it is if tenant for years, which knoweth the end of his term, doth sow the land.'

The principle of this rule was applied, as Coke said, to 'every particular tenant that hath an estate uncertain '.[1] The statutes relating to waste did not apply to the tenant at will, but the landlord could bring an action of trespass if voluntary waste were committed.[2]

It was not till the sixteenth century that the interest of the tenant from year to year arose; and its appearance was due to the inconvenience of a tenancy at will. The tenant at will had no certain interest; and his right to emblements made the land of very little value to the landlord, who was practically deprived of the rent of the land while the right to emblements lasted. It was expedient, both from the point of view of the tenant and of the landlord, that the tenant should have a better defined interest. From the point of view of the tenant, because he had a more assured position; and from the point of view of the landlord, because he got a right to rent to the end of the term. These causes led landowners to create tenancies from year to year rather than tenancies at will. Both for these reasons, and also, perhaps, because it was in accordance with the agricultural policy of the state to encourage agriculture by keeping tenants on the land,[3] the courts began to favour these tenancies; and, for these reasons, to presume that a tenancy from year to year was intended, and not a tenancy at will, whenever a tenant, entering upon or remaining in

[1] Co. Litt. 55b.

[2] Litt. § 71; Co. Litt. 57a.

[3] Above, p. 43; below, p. 73.

possession of premises, paid rent therefor. Thus tenancies from year to year arose not only by express creation, but also by presumption of law.

A tenancy at sufferance is not an interest in the land. It arises when a tenant wrongfully holds on after the expiry of his estate. In these circumstances the tenant was neither a disseisor nor a trespasser, because his original entry on the land was lawful. Having no interest in the land, he has no right to emblements, nor can he take a release from his lessor.[1]

(3) Estates in expectancy—Reversions and Remainders.[2]

Reversions and remainders were the two species of estates in expectancy known to the medieval common law.

The term ' revert ' has been used from the earliest times to signify what will happen when an estate for life expires. The land *revertit* or *redit* to the grantor. The natural contrast to *revertit* or *redit* is *remanet*. The land, instead of returning, remains away from the grantor.[3] In later days the derivation of the terms ' reversion ' and ' remainder ' became obscured. It came to be thought that these interests in land were so called because they were estates left over after a smaller estate had been carved out of a greater estate. ' A reversion is where the residue of the estate always doth continue in him that made

[1] Holdsworth, H. E. L. vii. 243. [2] Ibid. (3rd ed.), iii. 132–7.

[3] P. and M. ii. 21 ; it is there pointed out that the term *revertit* is thus used in an Anglo-Saxon land book ; that we find the term *remanet* used in this sense on the Continent ; and that the two terms are contrasted in this way in a passage of Ulpian's Fragments.

the particular estate.'[1] A remainder is a 'remnant of an estate in lands or tenements expectant upon a particular estate created together with the same at one time'.[2] But, as Maitland points out,[3]

> 'if we look at the documents of the thirteenth century, we soon see that the word *remanere* did not express any such notion of deduction or subtraction. The regular phrase is that, after the death of *A* or if *A* shall die without an heir of his body, then the said land . . . shall remain to *B*, that is, shall await, shall abide for, shall stand over for, shall continue for *B*.'

The later erroneous derivation of these terms was perhaps a natural consequence of regarding these future interests as present existing estates in the land. The common law theory of estates gave a reality—a corporeal character—to that abstract thing, the interest of the tenant in fee simple, and therefore to the various smaller interests, whether in possession or expectancy, which he could create out of his larger interest.[4]

Reversions. It was not till after the statute Quia Emptores (1290) that a clear distinction was drawn between the right of a donor who had given an estate less than a fee simple to a reversion, and the right of a donor who had given an estate in fee simple to an escheat on the failure of the heirs of his donee. That statute emphasized the difference between a reversion and an escheat.[5] We shall see that it provides that, on a grant in fee simple, the grantee shall hold, not of the grantor, but of the

[1] Co. Litt. 22b.
[2] Co. Litt. 143a.
[3] L.Q.R. vi. 25.
[4] Above, pp. 50–2.
[5] Holdsworth, H. E. L. (3rd ed.), iii. 68.

grantor's lord.[1] If, therefore, a tenant in fee simple dies without heirs, his land escheats to the lord of whom it is held; and that lord is not the grantor unless the tenant has taken the land by grant from the crown. If, on the other hand, the interest of a tenant for a smaller estate expires, the land reverts to the grantor who gave the estate, and of whom the estate is held. The statute therefore differentiated the reversion from the right of the lord to take by escheat, and brought the former clearly into view as a distinct estate. The right to escheat depends upon tenure, and upon tenure alone—the land goes back to the lord of whom it is held. This right is not an estate—it is a mere possibility that an estate may arise. The reversion depends also on tenure—the smaller estate is held of the grantor; but it is more intimately related to the quantum of estate taken by the tenant, and it is itself an estate in the land. When the tenant's estate expires, the grantor's estate in expectancy becomes an estate in possession.

Remainders. In modern law remainders are either vested or contingent. The distinction between them is clearly pointed out in Fearne's definition.[2]

> 'It is not the uncertainty of ever taking effect in possession that makes a remainder contingent; for to that every remainder for life or in tail is and must be liable; as the remainder-man may die, or die without issue, before the death of the tenant for life. The present capacity of taking effect in possession, if the possession were to become vacant, and not the certainty that the possession will become vacant before the estate limited in remainder determines, universally distinguishes a vested remainder from one that is contingent.'

[1] Below, p. 106. [2] Contingent Remainders (9th ed.), 216.

Till nearly the end of the medieval period, the law recognized only vested remainders. Littleton states that a remainder must be vested in the remainderman at the same time as the smaller estate, on which the remainder depends, is vested in the donee; [1] and obviously this is impossible if the remainderman has no present capacity to take. The reason for this rule is to be found in the principle that the seisin cannot be in abeyance, i.e. there must be a definite person in existence in whom the seisin is vested. It followed also from this principle that a remainder could not be limited to take effect upon the expiration of an interval of time after the expiry of the particular estate.

But, in the middle of the fifteenth century, one exception was made to the rule that the law would recognize only a vested remainder. It was settled in 1453 [2] that if land were given to *A* for life, remainder to the heirs of *B* a living person, and *B* died leaving an heir before *A*'s death, *B*'s heir could take. This remainder to the heirs of *B* was, when it was created, a contingent remainder, because *B* was then alive, and, till he died, his heir was not ascertained. It was, however, only in this one case that a contingent remainder was allowed at this period. It was not till the sixteenth century that the validity of remainders, which depended upon other contingencies, was admitted, and that the rules which governed them were definitely ascertained. [3]

[1] § 721.

[2] Fitzherbert Ab. *Feffementes*, pl. 99.

[3] Below, pp. 189–97.

(4) Co-ownership.[1]

The law of the fifteenth century knew four kinds of estate held in co-ownership—joint tenancy, coparcenary, tenancy by entireties, and tenancy in common.[2] Each had its peculiar features. Till Henry VIII's reign [3] the estate of the joint tenant could not be partitioned, unless all the joint tenants consented. They were seised 'per my et per tout', i.e. each was seised of the whole property, so that if one joint tenant wished to convey his share to the other or others, he must do so by release. The estate was distinguished by four unities—the joint tenants must get their estate by the same title, they must begin to enjoy it at the same time, they must take the same interest, they had the same possession. If one died the other or others took by survivorship—*jus accrescendi praefertur oneribus*. Coparcenary occurred when several took as co-heirs.[4] Coparceners could compel partition by a writ of partition. They conveyed to one another either by feoffment with livery of seisin, or by release. There was no right of survivorship. Each coparcener's share descended to her heirs. Tenancy by entireties could only exist where an estate was given to husband and wife. During their marriage husband and wife are one person in law; and an estate so given must come to the wife (unless it had been conveyed away by fine) notwithstanding any alienation or forfeiture in-

[1] Holdsworth, H. E. L. (3rd ed.), iii. 126–8. [2] Litt. §§ 277–324.

[3] 31 Henry VIII, c. 1; 32 Henry VIII, c. 32.

[4] Daughters took together as co-heirs, below, pp. 81–2; this was the usual case, but there might be male coparceners in land subject to the custom of gavelkind, below, pp. 133–4.

curred by the husband. Tenancy in common was distinguished by unity of possession only.

> 'A tenancy in common, though it is an ownership only of an undivided share, is, for all practical purposes, a sole and several tenancy or ownership; and each tenant in common stands, towards his own undivided share, in the same relation that, if he were sole owner of the whole, he would bear towards the whole. And accordingly one tenant in common must convey his share to another, by some assurance which is proper to convey an undivided hereditament; and he cannot so convey by release.'[1]

(5) Estates created to secure money lent.[2]

The giving of land as the security for a debt was well known in early law—we can see instances of it in Domesday Book. But the machinery by which this purpose was effected has varied. At the end of the twelfth century, when Glanvil wrote, the estate of the mortagee was an estate which had special features of its own. But, by the end of the thirteenth century, this species of estate had become obsolete, and a mortgage was effected by giving to the mortgagee one of the recognized estates or interests in the land—a fee simple, a life estate, or a term of years.

From the thirteenth to the fifteenth century we can distinguish three different methods of effecting a mortgage. (1) The debtor might give the creditor a lease at a nominal rent. The rents and profits of the land paid off the debt and provided interest for the creditor without giving rise to the suspicion

[1] Challis, Real Property (3rd ed.), 368–9.

[2] Holdsworth, H. E. L. (3rd ed.), iii. 128–30; for the interest of the tenant who takes land in execution by writ of *elegit*, and for the interests of those who hold by statutes merchant and staple, see ibid. 131–2.

that the creditor was committing the sin of usury. (2) The debtor might convey the land to the creditor for a term of years, with a proviso that, if the debt be not paid at the end of the term, the creditor shall keep the land in fee. (3) The debtor might convey the land to the creditor in fee, with a condition that, if the debt was paid by a fixed date, the mortgagor could re-enter;[1] and this condition was strictly construed. Britton distinctly denies that there can be any equity of redemption.[2] It is this third form which ultimately prevailed.[3] The mortgagee took an estate in fee, defeasible upon the condition that the money was paid by the fixed date. It was recognized that his estate was merely a security for money lent. But the strictness with which the condition of payment on the day fixed was construed by the courts of common law obscured this fact; and it was not fully recognized till the court of Chancery began to relieve mortgagors whose property had been forfeited at law for the non-fulfilment of this condition. The elaborate rules evolved by the court of Chancery, on the basis of the narrow rules of the common law, constitute the main part of the rules of the modern law of mortgage.[4]

The Interest of the Lessee for Years.[5]

We have seen that in the twelfth century the lawyers were led, by an unfortunate application of

[1] Turner, Equity of Redemption, xxxviii–ix. [2] Bk. ii. 128.

[3] For a considerable time a variant on this form—the demise of a term to the creditor, with a condition that it should be void when the money was paid off—was more frequently used, see below, p. 323, n. 4. [4] Below, pp. 256–61.

[5] Holdsworth, H. E. L. (3rd ed.), iii. 213–17.

the Roman law of possession, to deny any seisin to the lessee for years.[1] The lessee might, it is true, repel force by force; he might, that is, resist the would-be ejector if he could; but all the legal remedy he had was a personal action against his lessor on the covenant, by which he could recover damages or, if the term had not expired, possession of the land leased. As against third persons he had probably no remedy at all. An ejectment by a third person was a wrong to the freeholder, and it was the freeholder, therefore, and the freeholder alone, who could bring the assize of novel disseisin. The lessee's right was a *jus in personam*, and not a *jus in rem*.

The inconvenience of the rule that the lessee had only a personal right made some change in the law imperative. The writ of *quare ejecit infra terminum* (1235) protected him if he was ejected by one to whom his lessor had sold the property; and, as against ejectors in general, he was protected, from Edward II's reign onwards, by a variety of the writ of trespass known as the action of ejectment (*ejectio firmae*). But the weak part of the latter action was that he could only recover damages for the ejectment and not the land itself.

Towards the end of the fifteenth century, however, it was beginning to be thought that a lessee could recover the land itself by this action; and in 1499 it was decided that this was the law. The reasons why this change was made were mainly economic. We have seen that the decay of the labour-service system was the cause of a great extension in the practice of letting land to lessees for years for longer

[1] Above, pp. 19–20.

or shorter terms.[1] It is quite clear that such lessees, if ejected, would not have been compensated adequately if they had only been given damages. We have seen, too, that the government desired to stop the depopulation of the country caused by the conversion of arable land into pasture for sheep.[2] It is obvious that to continue to enforce the rule that the ejected lessee could not recover the land would have facilitated the operations of landlords who were pursuing this undesirable policy.

But though the lessee for years thus got a fully protected interest in the land, the action by which it was protected was a personal action. His interest therefore continued to be personal property, and so differed considerably from the interests protected by the real actions, which ranked as real property. But of these differences, and of the reciprocal influences which the interest of the lessee for years and the estates of the freeholder have exercised over one another, I shall speak more at length under the following head.

The Effects of the Property Acts.

The effects of the Property Acts upon this branch of the law are very extensive.

In the first place, the Law of Property Act, 1925, diminishes the number of legal estates or interests in the land to two—a fee simple absolute in possession and a term of years absolute.[3] The estate of the tenant from year to year is included in the term of years absolute;[4] and the interests of a

[1] Above, p. 42.
[2] Above, p. 43.
[3] § 1 (1).
[4] § 205 (1) (xxvii).

tenant at will and at sufferance are still recognized.[1] All the other estates exist, but as equitable interests and not as legal estates;[2] but since they exist as equitable interests it is necessary to know the old law relating to them; for, as equity follows the law, their incidents as equitable interests will be the same as their incidents as legal estates.

In the second place, legal tenancy in common is abolished,[3] and the changes made in the law of intestate succession have rendered obsolete the estate in coparcenery.[4] Tenancy by entireties had been rendered obsolete by the Married Women's Property Act (1882); [5] so that, of all the different forms of co-ownership, only joint tenancy exists as a legal estate, and tenancy in common as an equitable interest.

In the third place, the Acts complete the process, which had long been in progress, of assimilating estates of freehold and interests for terms of years. But of this I must speak more at length.

Though, as we have seen, the lessee for years was fully protected at the end of the fifteenth century,[6] his interest was personal property, and differed in many important respects from real property. It is true that, in some respects, rules relating to estates

[1] § 54 (1); Cheshire, Real Property (3rd ed.), 88.

[2] §§ 1 (8); 4 (1); for equitable interests see below, pp. 200–3.

[3] Law of Property Act, 1925, §§ 1 (6); 34; for the reasons for this see below, p. 314; Cheshire, Real Property (3rd ed.), 89.

[4] Administration of Estates Act, 1925, Part IV.

[5] Cheshire, op. cit. (3rd ed.), 554; but, till the Law of Property Act, 1925, § 37, if land were given to *A* and *B*, husband and wife, and *C*, *A* and *B* took half and *C* took half; *A* and *B*, though separate as between themselves for proprietary purposes, were still one person *qua* the outside world; now in such a case *A*, *B*, and *C* will each take a third.

[6] Above, p. 72.

of freehold were applied to leasehold interests. Thus, it was recognized that the lessee held his land of the lessor, just as the tenant for life or in tail held his estate of his grantor; and, similarly, a lessee could lease to a sublessee who would hold of the lessee as his lessor. By the Wills Act of 1540 [1] and the statute of Tenures of 1660 [2] the power, which lessees had always had, of leaving their property by will, was extended to freeholders.[3] But, in many respects, the interest of the lessee for years differed fundamentally from the interest of the freeholder till the changes effected by the Property Acts. A glance at the way in which the main points of difference have been dealt with by these Acts will show the great changes effected by them.

(1) Successive legal estates to take effect by way of remainder or reversion, or under the operation of the statute of Uses,[4] could be carved out of freehold estates. Successive legal interests could not be thus carved out of interests for a term of years, except by will. Out of these interests it was only possible to create successive equitable interests through the medium of a trust. Under the Property Acts it is only through the medium of a trust that successive estates can be created in land, whether held for a freehold estate or for a term of years.[5] (2) Estates tail could be created out of freeholds but not out of

[1] 32 Henry VIII, c. 1.

[2] 12 Charles II, c. 24.

[3] See below, pp. 234–5, 325–6, for other instances of the ways in which the rules as to real property and chattels real have influenced one another.

[4] For uses and the statute of Uses see below, pp. 140 seqq., 151 seqq.

[5] §§ 1 (3); 4 (1).

leaseholds. The Property Acts have abolished legal estates tail, and have permitted equitable estates tail to be created in any kind of property.[1] (3) Till 1897 the rules which regulated the mode in which leaseholds and freeholds were transmitted at death differed. Leaseholds went in the first instance to the executor or administrator: freeholds to the heir or devisee. The Land Transfer Act of 1897 provided that freeholds (with the exception of legal estates in copyhold) should go, in the first instance, to the executor or administrator. But the rules as to the persons beneficially entitled to freeholds and leaseholds on an intestacy still differed. The Property Acts have provided a uniform system of succession on intestacy for all kinds of property.[2] (4) For a long period freeholds were only liable to certain of the debts of their deceased owner: leaseholds were always liable to all the debts of a deceased person which survived his death. Even when freeholds were made liable to all these debts, they were made liable by a different process and in different order from leaseholds. Now a uniform method for the administration of the property of deceased persons is provided.[3]

Thus it will be seen that, in the new scheme of interests in land which has replaced the old, there are present ideas derived both from the law as to freeholds and from the law as to leases for years. Of the extent to which the modern law is in debt to these two separate bodies of doctrine I cannot speak fully till later developments in the law have been considered.[4] In the meantime we must turn to the

[1] § 130 (1). [2] Administration of Estates Act, 1925, Part IV.
[3] Ibid., Part III. [4] Below, pp. 234–5, 325–6.

consideration of the rules which regulated the transmission on death of those freehold estates which were estates of inheritance.

§ 4. Inheritance, Dower, and Curtesy.

The law of inheritance determined the manner in which, on the death intestate of a tenant in fee simple or fee tail, his estate descended to his blood relations. Since estates for years were personal property, the rules as to the persons entitled to succeed to them were governed, not by the law of inheritance, but by the statutes of Distribution.[1] The law as to dower and curtesy regulated the rights of the wife and the husband to succeed to one another's real property. The Property Acts have superseded all these rules by a new scheme of intestate succession.[2] But, as in other branches of the land law, a knowledge of the law on these topics will be necessary for a considerable period to all who are called on to advise upon questions of title; and, in the case of the law of inheritance, we shall see that other reasons make it necessary to continue to have some knowledge of the old law.

Inheritance.[3]

At common law seven rules regulated the descent of estates in fee simple in lands held by free tenure.[4]

[1] For the history of these rules see Holdsworth, H. E. L. (3rd ed.), iii. 550–63; for a short statement of the resulting law see Cheshire, Real Property (3rd ed.), 781–2.

[2] Administration of Estates Act, 1925, Part IV.

[3] Holdsworth, H. E. L. (3rd ed.), 171–85.

[4] Bl. Comm. ii. 208 sqq.; these rules were applied to estates tail to settle the order in which the issue of the original donee in tail succeeded; but, in the case of estates tail, the original donee was the stock of descent.

(1) Inheritances lineally descended to the issue of the person last seised *in infinitum*, but never lineally ascended. (2) Male issue were admitted before female. (3) When there were two or more males in equal degree the eldest only inherited, but the females inherited together. (4) The lineal descendants *in infinitum* of any person deceased represented their ancestor. (5) On failure of lineal descendants of the person last seised the inheritance descended to his collateral relatives being of the blood of the first purchaser, subject to rules (2), (3), and (4). (6) The collateral heir of the person last seised must have been his next collateral kinsman of the whole blood. (7) In collateral inheritances the male stocks were preferred to the female, unless the lands had in fact descended from a female.

These common law rules were modified by the Inheritance Act of 1833,[1] and by Lord St. Leonards' Act of 1859.[2] I shall give a brief account of the common law rules, explaining to what extent they were modified by these two Acts.

(1) Inheritances lineally descended to the issue of the person last seised in infinitum, but never lineally ascended. On this rule the following points may be noted: (i) As to the rule that land, in the first instance, descends, Maitland says that it is the 'natural' rule, i.e. 'we find it in every system that is comparable with our own.'[3] (ii) The rule that the person last seised was the stock of descent was the natural consequence of the importance of seisin in

[1] 3, 4, William IV, c. 106.
[2] 22, 23 Victoria, c. 35, §§ 19 and 20.
[3] P. and M. ii. 258.

the medieval common law—of this I shall speak later.[1] This common law rule, which made the person last seised the stock of descent, was changed by § 1 of the Inheritance Act. By that Act the last purchaser was made the stock of descent; and he was defined to be the person who last acquired the land otherwise than by descent, or in certain other ways,[2] the effect of which was to make the land descendible as land acquired by descent. Thus if *X* inherited land from his father *A*, *A* was the stock of descent; but if his father *A* had devised[3] the land to *X* by his will, or *X* had bought it, *X* would be the stock of descent. To this rule that the last purchaser was the stock of descent the Act of 1859 made one exception. It provided that if there was a total failure of the heirs of the purchaser, the person last entitled should be the stock of descent. This rule might entitle many persons to succeed who would otherwise have had no claim. Thus:

P (the Purchaser) = *A* (*P*'s wife)
|
C

If *C* dies without issue, and all *P*'s ancestors and their issue fail, *A* could not have inherited, because

1 Below, pp. 125–6. The seisin must be a seisin in deed, i.e. possession must actually have been got; this is contrasted with a seisin in law, i.e. a right to get seisin—e.g. the heir had a seisin in law after his ancestor's death and till he entered: when he entered he got a seisin in deed.

2 Escheat, partition, or enclosure; for escheat see above, pp. 33–4; for partition see above, p. 69; enclosure took place when lands held in scattered strips in the open fields were converted into single holdings, see above, p. 39.

3 At common law if land were devised to the heir he took by descent; this was altered by § 3 of the Inheritance Act.

she is not a blood relation to *P*. But she is a blood relation of her son *C*. Now if *C* survived *P* he was the person last entitled to the land. By virtue of the Act of 1859 he will be the stock of descent, and so the land can descend to *A* and her heirs. (iii) At common law the land could not lineally ascend. A father, e.g. could not inherit from his son—though, as we shall see, the descendants from the father, i.e. brothers and sisters, could do so.[1] It is not quite certain what was the origin of this rule. Maitland thinks that it is connected with the principle laid down by Glanvil that a man could not be both lord and heir. If *A* had enfeoffed his son *B* of land, and *B* had done homage to *A*, *A* was entitled to the services due from the land, and *B* was entitled to the land. It was thought that *A*, having the services, could not inherit the land. He, therefore, would be passed over, and the land would go to the next heir. It was only if all *B*'s heirs failed that *A* could get the land—not as heir but as an escheat.[2] This rule was changed by § 6 of the Inheritance Act. On failure of descendants the land went to the nearest lineal male ancestor. We shall see later that the mother and her ancestors were not entitled, till the line of male ancestors and their descendants had been exhausted.[3]

(2) Male issue were admitted before female. 'This preference', Maitland says,[4] 'is far older than feudalism, but the feudal influence made for its retention or resuscitation.' It held good not only in the descending but also in the ascending line; and it

[1] Below, p. 82.
[2] P. and M. ii. 286–93.
[3] Below, p. 85.
[4] P. and M. ii. 259.

was applied to ascertain the order in which the remotest collateral was entitled to inherit.[1]

(3) When there were two or more males in equal degree the eldest only inherited, but the females inherited together. These rules of primogeniture in the case of males, and coparcenery in the case of females, both owe their origin to feudal ideas, but to different stages in the history of those ideas. The rule of primogeniture was first applied to land held by knight service. When land held by this tenure really supplied soldiers it was to the interest of the lord that the inheritance should descend as an undivided whole—that it should be, as Blackstone expressed it,[2] impartible. The eldest son was selected because he would generally be the most capable of performing those services for the sake of which the inheritance had been made impartible. At first he may not have been regarded as absolute owner. He and his younger brothers are sometimes said to hold the land 'in parage'—as equals (*pares*). But he was held responsible for the services to the lord. Being thus held responsible, he was able to assert a claim to absolute ownership, with the result that the claims of the younger brothers became merely moral, and disappeared. The advantages of impartibility were never so strong when a man died leaving daughters only. And, when the incidents of military tenure came to be more valuable than the services,[3] lords found that it paid them best to take the homage of all the daughters, and thus to secure the incidents of tenure from each daughter's share of the land.

[1] Below, pp. 85–6. [2] Comm. ii. 215. [3] Above, p. 35.

Thus the claims of all the daughters were definitely recognized by law, and continued to exist. These rules had spread from tenure by knight service to the other free tenures by the end of the thirteenth century. But at that period the rule of primogeniture could no longer be explained by the needs of the feudal army; and so a better explanation was invented. In Edward I's reign it was justified (not altogether unreasonably) by saying that it was needed to maintain a race of wealthy landowners, who could see that the land was cultivated, and that the cultivators were protected.

(4) The lineal descendants in infinitum of any person deceased represented their ancestor. This principle was fully recognized from the reign of Edward I. It is by virtue of this rule that the children (male or female) of an elder son inherit before a younger son.

(5) On failure of lineal descendants of the person last seised the inheritance descended to his collateral relatives being of the blood of the first purchaser, subject to rules (2), (3), *and* (4). One person is of the blood of another if either (i) he is descended from him, or (ii) if he is descended from common ancestors. A son is of the blood of his father and mother. Brothers and sisters of the whole blood are of the blood of each other. But a husband is not, as a rule, of the blood of his wife; and half brothers and sisters are not of the blood of each other. The Inheritance Act and the Act of 1859 have necessarily affected this rule. Now descent is traced from, and the heir must be of the blood of the *last* purchaser, or the person last entitled, as the case may be.

(6) The collateral heir of the person last seised must have been his next collateral kinsman of the whole blood. At common law kinsmen by the half blood could not inherit from one another. This followed from the rules that the heir must be the heir of the person last seised, and of the blood of the first purchaser. When it was settled that descent must be traced from the person last seised it became clear that, if the common father was the person last seised, a half-brother could succeed to him on the death of the half-brother. There can, of course, be no question of the half blood as between ancestor and descendant. It was for this reason that half blood could always succeed to half blood in the case of an estate tail, because, in the case of these estates, descent was always traced from the purchasing ancestor. But if the person last seised was the son, his brother by the half blood could not succeed to him, because he was a collateral and not necessarily of the blood of the first purchaser. Thus the sister of the whole blood succeeded to the brother of the whole blood—*possessio fratris facit sororem esse heredem.* Half blood could not succeed to half blood; the land would sooner escheat. The rule was productive of hardship, nor was it wholly logical, since there is a chance that a kinsman by the half blood is of the blood of the first purchaser. For this reason Blackstone recommended its alteration.[1] No action was then taken by the Legislature. But all justification for the exclusion of the half blood was lost when the Inheritance Act made the stock of descent the last purchaser, and made it necessary that the heir

[1] Comm. ii. 233.

should be of his blood. Therefore § 9 of the Inheritance Act changed the law. That section provided that a kinsman to the purchaser by the half blood should inherit next after a kinsman of the same degree of the whole blood and his issue when the common ancestor was a male, and next after the common ancestor when such ancestor was a female; so that the brother of the half blood on the part of the father inherited next after the sisters of the whole blood on the part of the father and their issue, and the brother of the half blood on the part of the mother next after the mother. An illustration will show how this rule worked.

```
C = A = B
    |   |
    X   P
```

A is the common father. *P* is the purchaser. He has died without issue. The land would therefore ascend to his paternal ancestors and their issue. Let us suppose that *A* is dead. But for this section the land could not have devolved on *X*, since he was not of the blood of *P*. This section made *X* capable of inheriting from *P*.

We shall appreciate the reason for the apparent difference in the treatment of the half blood when the common ancestor is a female when we have considered the next rule.

(7) In collateral inheritances the male stocks were preferred to the female, unless the lands had in fact descended from a female. When all a given couple's descendants are exhausted, and it is necessary to have recourse to the ascending line, the question

arises, Are we to ascend in the maternal or in the paternal line ? Early law answered this question by the application of the maxim '*paterna paternis, materna maternis*'. If the land has descended from the father we ascend in his line ; if from the mother we ascend in her line. But, having decided whether the estate is to go to collaterals *ex parte paterna* or *ex parte materna*, another difficulty awaits us. How are we to decide between the descendants from the different ancestors of the father and the mother ? Granted that the estate goes to collaterals on the father's side, how are we to decide between the collaterals which descend from that father's two parents ?

The rules relating to this matter were not satisfactorily settled till the Inheritance Act. Sections 7 and 8 of that Act settled the law on the logical lines advocated by Blackstone,[1] though that settlement was not quite in accordance with the rules laid down in the older cases. The provisions of these sections are substantially as follows : The father and all male paternal ancestors of the purchaser, and their descendants, were admitted before any of the female paternal ancestors or their heirs ; all the female paternal ancestors and their heirs before the mother or any of the maternal ancestors or her or their descendants ; and the mother and all male maternal ancestors and her and their descendants before any of the female maternal ancestors or their heirs.[2]

[1] Comm. ii. 238–9.

[2] 3 and 4 William IV, c. 106, § 7, and the definition of descendants given in § 1 ; see Williams, Real Property (22nd ed.), 236 n. (*x*).

The following rule is a corollary from the last. When the descent could no longer be traced along the male paternal line, the mother of a more remote male paternal ancestor and her heirs were preferred to the mother of a less remote male paternal ancestor and her heirs. When the tracing of the descent had entered upon the female line, the same rule applied so often as it became necessary to change from a male to a female ancestor.[1] This rule, for which Blackstone contended, was enacted by the Inheritance Act, so that the preference of male to female was logically carried out throughout the law of inheritance.

It was the preference of male to female which put the half blood next to the sisters of the whole blood, when the common ancestor was a male; and next after the common ancestor when such ancestor was a female. The following table will make this clear:

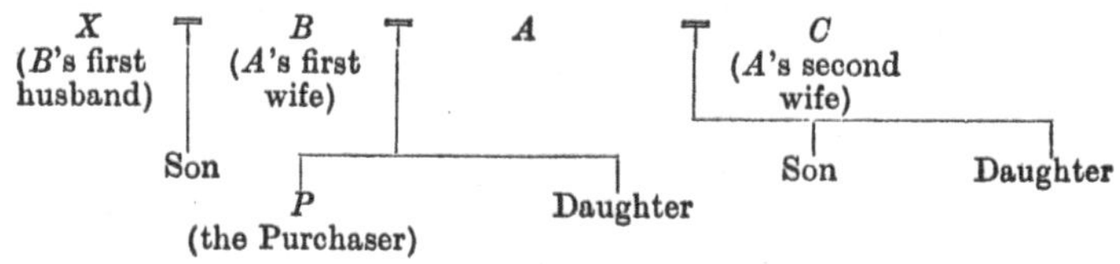

Suppose that *P* has died without issue, and that *A* is dead, *A* and *B*'s daughter will succeed. If she dies without issue, *A* and *C*'s son will succeed, and then *A* and *C*'s daughter. For, by the Act, 'the brother of the half blood on the part of the father will inherit next after the sister of the whole blood on the part of the father and their issue'. Suppose they die without issue, then all the ancestors of *A* and their descendants must be called to the inheritance. If

[1] 3, 4 William IV, c. 106, § 8.

none of them or their descendants exist, then the mother *B* and her heirs will take. Thus if *B* be dead her son by *X* will take ; so that 'the brother of the half blood on the part of the mother will inherit next after the mother'. If *C* had married again and had had a son, that son would be no relation at all to the purchaser.

All these rules are now swept away by the Administration of Estates Act, 1925. But it is necessary to know them, not only in order to be able to advise on old titles, but also for two other reasons. First, the rules for the ascertainment of the persons entitled to succeed to an equitable estate tail are still governed by the law of inheritance. As Blackstone said,[1] 'A gift in tail is a limitation that cannot be perfectly understood without a previous knowledge of the law of descents in fee simple'. Secondly, the abolition of the rule in *Shelley's Case*[2] makes the word 'heirs' or 'heirs of the body' words of purchase, i.e. the gift is to the persons who come under these descriptions. The Law of Property Act, 1925, provides that the question what persons come under these descriptions is to be ascertained by the old law.[3]

Dower and Curtesy.[4]

Dower. At common law the wife had, after the death of her husband, the right to dower. This dower consisted of a life interest in a third of the land of which her husband had ever been solely seised[5] during the marriage for an estate of inheritance, which

[1] Comm. ii. 201. [2] Above, pp. 53–5. [3] §§ 131, 132.

[4] Holdsworth, H. E. L. (3rd ed.), iii. 185–97.

[5] A seisin in law (above, p. 79, n. 1) was sufficient.

issue of the marriage by the husband might inherit. There were several species of dower under the old law; but it was this form of dower, thus fixed by law, which superseded the others.

The widow's right to dower attached to all the lands of which the husband had ever been solely seised. It therefore restricted his right to alienate his property freely. The purchaser could only take the land subject to the chance that the wife might survive and assert her claim to a third of the land for her life. This was in fact the one restriction on the power of free alienation, in the interests of the family, which the common law retained. It was largely for this reason that equity (contrary to its rule of following the law) refused to admit a right to dower out of equitable estates; that in one case the Legislature provided a means for barring dower;[1] and that, in other cases, the lawyers invented ingenious devices for the same purpose. These expedients were rendered unnecessary in 1833. The Dower Act[2] of that year put the widow's rights at the mercy of the husband, and thus destroyed this solitary yet long-lived survival from an age when family rights of many kinds fettered alienation.[3] Till 1926 the widow was entitled to dower, and, by virtue of the Dower Act, out of equitable as well as legal estates; but only out of those estates to which the husband was entitled beneficially at his death, and only if he had not exercised by deed or will his power of taking away her right.

Curtesy. The husband, after the death of his wife, was entitled to an estate by the curtesy out of all

[1] The statute of Uses, 27 Henry VIII, c. 10, §§ 4 and 5.

[2] 3, 4 William IV, c. 105.

[3] Below, p. 103.

his wife's estates of inheritance, provided that, (1) the wife was seised in deed of such an estate of inheritance as the issue, which the husband had by her, might have inherited ; and (2) that a child was born alive during a valid marriage. The right to curtesy was extended to equitable estates. Therefore the husband was entitled to curtesy out of the separate estate of his wife who died intestate, whether that separate estate arose by express limitation or under the Married Women's Property Acts.

The Administration of Estates Act, 1925, has abolished dower and almost abolished curtesy.[1] It is possible that curtesy may still exist in respect of an entailed interest.[2] Unlike the law of inheritance, which the provisions of the Property Acts have kept very much alive,[3] it is only necessary to know the rules as to dower for the purpose of advising on titles ; and, subject to the possibility that curtesy may arise out of an entailed estate, this is also true as to curtesy.

§ 5. Incorporeal Things.

Blackstone tells us that 'incorporeal hereditaments are principally of ten sorts—advowsons, tithes, commons, ways, offices, dignities, franchises, corodies or pensions, annuities, and rents.'[4] This is a heterogeneous list of very different things ; and its composition can only be explained by the light of history. Two main causes have contributed to it.

[1] § 45 (1) (*b*), (*c*).

[2] Law of Property Act, 1925, § 130 (4) ; this section does not mention dower. It is difficult to see why it does not ; for though dower did not at common law attach to equitable estates (which all estates tail now are) it was made to attach to equitable estates by the Dower Act.

[3] Above, p. 87.

[4] Comm. ii. 21.

First, we have seen that feudal ideas tended to annex governmental rights to the tenure of land.[1] The result was to give to many of these governmental rights some of the characteristics of property—they were treated like estates in the land. It was these feudal ideas which gave rise to such incorporeal things as offices, dignities, and franchises. Secondly, all through the medieval period the land law was the most highly developed branch of the law, while the law of contract was comparatively rudimentary. Hence many transactions took the form of the grant of an incorporeal thing which we should now effect by a contract. 'The man of the thirteenth century does not say, I agree that you may have so many trees out of my copse in every year; he says, I give and grant you so much wood. The main needs of the agricultural economy of the age can be met in this manner without the creation of any personal obligations.' [2] This cause accounts for such incorporeal things as rents, annuities, and corodies.

It is impossible to deal fully with this mass of incorporeal things. I shall give a short account of (1) advowsons; (2) rights of common; (3) rents, annuities, and corodies; and (4) easements. These are the classes of incorporeal things which are mainly important in the land law.

(1) Advowsons.[3]

'An advowson is the right to present a clerk to the bishop for institution as parson of some vacant church; the bishop is bound to institute this presented clerk

[1] Above, p. 4. [2] P. and M. ii. 145.

[3] Holdsworth, H. E. L. (3rd ed.), iii. 138–43.

unless he can show one of some few good causes for refusing to do so.'[1] The law as to advowsons is part of the *jus patronatus* of the canon law; and the general idea of an advowson is therefore derived from that law. But, in England, as abroad, it is intimately related to the land law. On that account the title to and possessory rights in an advowson were matters which fell within the jurisdiction of the royal courts, and they were protected by appropriate real actions. For many different reasons, disputes as to the title to and the possession of advowsons, and as to many other matters relating to them, gave rise in the Middle Ages to an enormous mass of litigation. The chief service which this large amount of litigation did for English law was the elucidation of the nature of an incorporeal thing; and that it was able to perform this service was largely due to the fact that English law, like the law of the other countries of Western Europe, had accepted the main conclusions of the canon law as to the nature of the right of patronage.

This right of patronage, which had come to be recognized by the canon law of the twelfth century, was the product of an historical development. During the dark ages which followed on the overthrow of the Roman Empire, landowners of all kinds, lay and ecclesiastical, had put forward claims to be the owners of churches. In fact these churches had come to be regarded as things attached to the land, which could be disposed of by the landowner, just as he disposed of other rights connected with the land. All that the church could do was to take precautions that fitting clerks should be presented, and that they should be

[1] P. and M. ii. 135.

given a sufficient income. It was not till the pontificate of Alexander III (1159–81) that it was recognized that the landowner was not the owner, but the patron of the church—that what he owned was not the church but the incorporeal right of patronage.

The native development of English law, and the cessation of the influence of the civil and canon law at the end of the thirteenth century, made for the survival of the older idea that the advowson is a piece of property, analogous to an estate in the land. But the fact that Bracton had grasped the idea that the advowson was an incorporeal right, quite distinct from the ownership of a corporeal church, and the fact that, in connexion with these advowsons, he had analysed the nature of incorporeal things, helped English lawyers to grasp the nature of these things. Similarly, it was in the law relating to advowsons that we can see the beginnings of the classification of incorporeal things into rights appendant, appurtenant, and in gross. Normally and regularly an advowson was appendant to a manor. An advowson thus appendant passed with the manor without special mention. 'But advowsons are often severed from the manors to which, in legal theory, they had some time or other belonged. The lord gives the manor but retains the advowson, or else he gives the advowson but retains the manor. The latter transaction is common; numerous advowsons are detached from their manors by being given to religious houses. An advowson thus detached becomes, to use a phrase which is current in the last years of the thirteenth century, "a gross", that is, a thing by itself, a thing which has an independent existence.' [1] Thus we get the modern idea of an incorporeal thing in gross as contrasted with one which is appendant. Further, it would seem that if an advowson was annexed, not to a manor, but to a messuage or some other specified piece of land, it was sometimes spoken of as appurtenant. In this we may possibly see the germ of the distinction between rights appendant, i. e. annexed immemorially and of common right to land, and rights which are appurtenant, i. e. annexed by special act of the parties to the land.

In modern times the advowson has ceased to possess the importance which it had at earlier periods in the history of the law. The view that the right to present to a benefice is a species of property has long been out of harmony with the modern view that it is a duty of a fiduciary kind, involving an obligation to appoint a fit person. This was to some extent recognized by the legislation as to offence of simony, i. e. the corrupt presentation to a benefice in return for money.[2] But, till the Benefices Act of 1898,[3] no restrictions were placed on the purchase and sales of advowsons, provided that the transactions were genuine sales, and that they were not tainted by simony. That Act imposed certain restrictions ; and still further restrictions were imposed in 1924 by a Measure of the Church Assembly which will have the effect of making the sale of advowsons, other than those appendant to a manor, impossible.[4]

But, historically, the advowson is perhaps the

[1] P. and M. ii. 135.

[2] For this see Cheshire, Real Property (3rd ed.), 110–11.

[3] 61, 62 Victoria, c. 48.

[4] Cheshire, op. cit. (3rd ed.), 112.

most important of all the long list of incorporeal things which English law once recognized. Blackstone showed an appreciation of this fact when he took the advowson as the type and model of an incorporeal hereditament.[1] The canonists had developed from the old crude idea of the ownership of a church the idea of the incorporeal right of patronage. The common law courts took over this idea when they asserted an exclusive right to jurisdiction over advowsons; and, as we shall now see, it helped them to build up the law as to other kinds of incorporeal things.

(2) Rights of Common.[2]

Rights of common were a necessary part of that common or open field system upon which most of the land of England was cultivated for many centuries.[3] Thus we find common of turbary, or the right to cut turf for fuel; common of estovers, or the right to cut timber, underwood, furze, &c., for fuel or litter; common of piscary, or the right to fish in another's water; and, by far the most important of all, the right of common of pasture. Rights of common of pasture may be divided according to their legal qualities into different classes—common appendant, common appurtenant, common in gross, common *pur cause de vicinage*, and common of shack.

Common appendant is a right of common given by law to the freehold tenants of the manor, to depasture on the waste of the manor their commonable cattle

[1] Comm. ii. 21–2.

[2] Holdsworth, H. E. L. (3rd ed.), iii. 143–51.

[3] Above, pp. 39–40.

levant and couchant[1] on their tenement, provided that the tenement was part of the ancient arable land of the manor. Being thus given by law it is said to be 'of common right'. Common appurtenant is not 'of common right'. It depends on express grant or on prescription.[2] It may be enjoyed by a person not a tenant of the manor; it may exist in respect of cattle other than commonable cattle; and it may be enjoyed in respect of land which is not part of the ancient arable land of the manor. These two rights of common, however, resembled one another in that they were both annexed to the ownership of a dominant tenement. They were both praedial servitudes, and, for that reason, the extent of the right of common was in both cases limited by the needs of the dominant tenement. Common in gross, on the other hand, is not annexed to the holding of any land. It is a personal as opposed to a praedial right. Common *pur cause de vicinage* exists where there are adjoining wastes belonging to two different manors, and the tenants of each manor are allowed to put their beasts on the wastes of the other. Common of shack existed, as we have seen,[3] in some parts of the country, over the lands of the manor after harvest and before the land was sown; or over those parts of the manor which, according to the course of cultivation there pursued, were for the time being lying fallow. During these periods the cattle of the village were pastured promiscuously over the open fields. These rights of common might be, and usually were, enjoyed not

[1] Literally 'getting up or lying down', i.e. the cattle kept by the tenant on his land.

[2] For prescription see below, pp. 279–86.

[3] Above, p. 40.

only by the freehold but also by the villein, or later copyhold, tenants of the manor.

In the course of the thirteenth century the question whether the lord could approve, i.e. bring under cultivation, the waste lands of the manor, arose. It is clear that to allow him an unlimited right to approve might deprive the tenants of the manor of their rights of common. This question was dealt with by the statutes of Merton (1235–6),[1] and Westminster II (1285).[2] These statutes applied to common appendant and common *pur cause de vicinage*; and they were construed to apply to common appurtenant—a construction which is probably due to a mistranslation of the Statute of Westminster II.[3] They did not apply to a right of common in gross. They allowed approvement provided that a sufficiency of common was left to the commoners. Further, the series of Acts which provided for the enclosure of the common fields,[4] provided also for the partition and enclosure of land over which rights of common existed. But these Acts have now done their work; and recent legislation has made enclosure difficult, because it is more concerned to preserve for the general public those rights of common which still exist.[5]

Of the various rights of common which were known in the Middle Ages, common appurtenant was destined to increase at the expense of the others. One effect of the statute of Quia Emptores [6] was to diminish the number of cases in which common appendant

[1] 20 Henry III, c. 4. [2] 13 Edward I, st. 1, c. 46.
[3] See Holdsworth, H. E. L. (3rd ed.), iii. 147–9.
[4] Above, p. 40. [5] Cheshire, Real Property (3rd ed.), 307–9.
[6] 18 Edward I, c. 1; below, p. 106.

could be claimed by a freeholder as incident to his tenure of land of the lord of the manor, because, after the passing of that statute, on a conveyance in fee, the tenant did not hold of the lord of the manor. With the disuse of the common field system of agriculture common of shack went out of use ; and the improvement of the country rendered infrequent common *pur cause de vicinage.* The abolition of copyhold tenure [1] has rendered obsolete the rights of common enjoyed by these tenants. The result is that the two most usual rights of common at the present day are rights of common appurtenant and rights of common in gross. They are not affected by the Property Acts; but, as in the case of corporeal things, there can be no legal estates created in them except in fee simple absolute in possession, or for a term of years absolute.[2]

(3) *Rents, Annuities, and Corodies.*[3]

A rent was one of the services in return for which land might be granted. It issued out of the land. It could be distrained for by the lord in whosesoever's hands the land was. It was treated as a thing—a tenement—just like the land. Such rent service ceased to be rent service if the lord granted it to another. It became rent seck. The grantee, not being the lord, could not distrain ; but, for all that, the rent was still regarded as a thing. The grantee to complete his title must get seisin ; [4] and if he had got seisin he was protected by the real actions. The effect of the statute Quia Emptores [5] was to make a reserva-

[1] Above, p. 48. [2] Law of Property Act, 1925, § 1 (2) (*a*).
[3] Holdsworth, H. E. L. (3rd ed.), iii. 151–3.
[4] Below, pp. 129–30. [5] 18 Edward I, c. 1.

tion of a rent service on a grant in fee simple impossible. Instead, the grantee charged his lands with the payment of rent to the grantor, and gave him expressly a power of distress. Hence we get the rent charge, the grantee of which was, so far as remedies by action went, in the same position as the grantee of a rent seck. We can see these different kinds of rent from an early period. They had attained their modern form by the time of Littleton.[1]

Thus, in the Middle Ages, rent was regarded as a thing issuing from the land, and recoverable by the real actions. It was treated, both from the point of view of procedure, and from the point of view of the rights of the persons entitled, very much like an estate in the land; and this primitive conception of the nature of rent is the source of many of the rules of our modern law on this subject. But, in modern law, rent is not conceived of as a thing, but rather as a payment which a tenant is bound by his contract to make to his landlord for the use of the land. This idea that rent is a payment due by virtue of a contract began to make its way into the law in the cases of rents reserved on leases for years. Rents reserved on such freehold interests as leases for life were governed longer by the medieval idea; and the medieval idea continued to influence the rules applied to rents reserved on leases for years. But, as the conception of contract became more powerful, and as the capacity of contract for effecting the intention of the parties came to be more distinctly realized, ideas derived from this source came to be more extensively used to supplement the deficiencies in the rules as to rent, caused by the pre-

[1] Tenures, §§ 213–40.

valence of the medieval conception; and, in some cases, rules derived from these ideas have, in effect, superseded the older rules, or rendered them comparatively unimportant.

The abolition of the real actions in 1833 [1] gave impetus to the idea that rent is not so much an incorporeal thing as a payment due by virtue of a contract. But the fact that the landlord still has a power to distrain illustrates the close connexion of rent with the land and the chattels thereon. 'Into the land the rent owner enters; he takes the chattels that are found there. In such a case it is easy for us to picture the rent "issuing out of" the land, and incumbering the land.' [2]

Since the modern law has thus been developed under the influence of these two very different conceptions, it is not surprising that it is neither wholly rational nor wholly intelligible. Many of its rules are based ultimately on the medieval conception, while others are based on the more modern ideas; and, as is the case with many other branches of the land law, the mixture of medieval and modern has produced a complex body of very technical law.[3]

The Law of Property Act, 1925, allows a rent charge in possession to exist as a legal estate, provided that it is either perpetual or for a term of years absolute.[4]

A rent is thus a sum of money which issues from or is charged upon land. If a person promised to pay an annual sum of money for services rendered, and no

[1] 3, 4 William IV, c. 27, § 36. [2] P. and M. ii. 129.

[3] Holdsworth, H. E. L. vii. 262–75, 318–19; below, pp. 238–41.

[4] § 1 (2) (*b*).

land was charged with its payment, it was not a rent, and the person entitled could not use the real actions to enforce his claim. But towards the end of Henry III's reign he was given the protection of a writ of annuity. This writ has some affinities with the real actions, and gave rise to the idea that an annuity was an incorporeal thing. Somewhere between the rent which issued out of the land granted and an annuity is the corody. A corody is a grant, usually by a religious house, to some person, of clothing, board, and lodging for a fixed period. It might represent a reward for service done or to be done, or a bargain and sale by one who wished to provide for old age, or an obligation which a religious house owed to its founder or to the crown. The crown often used corodies to reward its servants or officials. A corody issued out of a certain place—it was more real than an annuity. It was not charged on any specific land—it was less real than the rent. However, in 1285 [1] those entitled to corodies were allowed to bring the assize of novel disseisin. If an efficient remedy was wanted the legislator was then obliged to go to the real actions; and this emphasized the reality of what we should now consider to be a merely personal obligation.

It was not till the law of contract developed that the practice of granting annuities and corodies was superseded by the practice of creating contractual obligations. In theory they remained a class of incorporeal things till the abolition of the real actions in 1833, though, by that date, they had long been obsolete.

[1] 13 Edward I, st. 1, c. 25.

(4) Easements.[1]

In modern law an easement is the right either of using the land or streams of another for certain defined purposes, such as walking or driving or turning a mill; or the right of restraining the owner from using his land in certain defined ways, such as building on it so as to obstruct the access of light, or digging in it so as to let down a house. In both cases the duty of the servient owner is to permit; but in the first case the right of the owner of the dominant tenement is to do positive acts: in the second case the right of the dominant owner is merely to prevent acts being done which would interfere with the enjoyment of his property. In the first case, therefore, the easement is called positive; in the second case it is called negative.

From an easement must be distinguished a natural right incident to ownership. A natural right incident to ownership is annexed by law to the ownership of property. On the other hand, an easement is a right additional to these natural rights, specially granted to the owner of the dominant property by the owner of the servient property. It is not till this distinction is firmly grasped that the essential quality of an easement can emerge.

Bracton has something to say about easements; and, in dealing with them, he borrowed the language and some of the rules of Roman law; and, through Bracton, Roman law has had a good deal of influence upon our modern law of easements. In modern times it is well settled that, to use Roman terms, an easement is a praedial servitude. There can be no

[1] Holdsworth, H. E. L. (3rd ed.), iii. 153–7.

such thing as an easement in gross; and herein an easement differs from a profit *à prendre*. But neither when Bracton nor when Littleton wrote was the list of possible easements defined, nor had the lawyers as yet begun to speculate much upon the characteristics of the easement. That there were certain definite rights of this character which one man could give another over his land was clear. That these rights could be acquired by grant or prescription [1] was also clear. But we do not find much positive doctrine as to the nature of these rights. It was not clear, for instance, that there could not be an easement in gross. Such learning as we do find upon the subject is generally connected with proceedings for nuisance —in this period the assize of nuisance, and later the action on the case for nuisance. The fact that this remedy was used to protect both the natural rights incident to ownership and easements, tended to prevent the lawyers from grasping the distinction between these natural rights and easements, and, consequently from grasping the juridical character of an easement. Hence, as we shall see in a later chapter, it is not till very much later that the law of easements was settled in its modern form.[2]

§ 6. The Power of Alienation.

I have now described the tenures by which land could be held, the estates and interests which tenants could have in the land, the rules regulating the devolution of these estates and interests on the death of the tenant, and certain incorporeal rights annexed to landholding. I must now say something of the most im-

[1] For prescription see below, pp. 279–86. [2] Below, pp. 265–76.

portant right of the tenant of land—his power of alienation. In this section I shall deal with the extent of that power, and in the following section I shall deal with the modes in which he was allowed by law to exercise it.

During the twelfth and thirteenth centuries the power to alienate land freely was affected by three sets of causes. In the first place, there were certain restrictions imposed in the interest of expectant heirs. In the second place, there were certain feudal restrictions imposed in the interest of the maintenance of the rights and duties involved in the relation of lord and tenant. In the third place, there were certain restrictions imposed on alienation to corporations—that is, on alienation in mortmain.

Restrictions Imposed in the Interest of Expectant Heirs.[1]

Old rules prevented landowners from completely disinheriting their heirs. Glanvil, writing at the end of the twelfth century, mentions them ; but they had disappeared early in the thirteenth century. When Bracton wrote, the word ' heirs ' was a word of limitation—it marked out or limited the estate given to the ancestor. It was not a word of purchase—the heir acquired nothing.[2] The heir was, to some extent, compensated by the rule which prohibited devises, i.e. gifts by will, of land. The question whether or not devises should be allowed was not settled till the end of the thirteenth century. But at the end of the century it was settled that they were not permissible. Probably the decision not to permit them was caused chiefly by the fact that to permit them would lower

[1] Holdsworth, H. E. L. (3rd ed.), iii. 73–6. [2] Above, p. 53.

the value of the incidents of tenure, and enormously diminish the lord's chance of an escheat. Partly, perhaps, it may have been felt that something was due to the heir; partly that to allow land to pass by will would have created a large exception to the rule that land cannot pass without a genuine livery of seisin.[1] Thus the ancestor could alienate as he pleased in his lifetime; but he could not prevent his heir from inheriting what he had left after his death. It was not till the rise of uses that landowners acquired a power to devise their estates of inheritance.[2]

Feudal Restrictions.[3]

The history of the free tenures has shown us that, to a greater or a less degree, landowning in the eleventh and twelfth centuries was a matter of public law. We at the present day would consider it anomalous if we were told that offices which involved the performance of public duties were freely alienable. Probably something of the modern feeling against the alienability of public offices was, in the twelfth and thirteenth centuries, directed against the free alienation of land; and probably that feeling was stronger in the higher ranks of the feudal hierarchy than in the lower. Such dignified persons as earls, barons, or tenants by grand serjeanty, were expected to fill very public positions and to perform very onerous duties. It is therefore not surprising to find that restrictions upon the power of free alienation lasted longer in the case

[1] For this rule see below, p. 112–13.

[2] Below, p. 149. Estates for years being personal property could be left by will.

[3] Holdsworth, H. E. L. (3rd ed.), iii. 76–86.

of the tenants in chief than in the case of other tenants. We must for this reason distinguish the case of the mesne tenant and his mesne lord from the case of the tenant in chief and the king.

(i) *The mesne tenant and his mesne lord.* How far could the mesne tenant alienate his land without the consent of his lord?

In answering this question we must begin by noting that alienation might take the form either of subinfeudation or of substitution. If *B* is *A*'s tenant, *B* may either enfeoff *C* of part of his land so that he, *B*, is *C*'s lord and remains *A*'s tenant; or he may put *C* in his, *B*'s place, so that *C* is now *A*'s tenant, and he, *B*, drops out entirely. The first is a case of subinfeudation, the second a case of substitution. In the first case Bracton argued strongly that no legal wrong (*injuria*) was done to the lord, though in fact the lord was damaged. *B* was still his tenant. *A* could still distrain for *B*'s services on the whole of the fee which he had granted to *B*. *A*'s incidents of tenure might be diminished in value, but of this the law would take no account. Incidents of tenure were only incidents. If *A* got his services he must be content. The second is a much weaker case for the tenant. Here *B* drops out, and it would seem that the lord might rightly object to having *C*, a poor man perhaps, or his personal enemy, imposed upon him as his tenant instead of *B*.[1] Nevertheless Bracton argued that even in this

[1] There were also difficulties in allowing a lord to alienate his seignory without consulting his tenant, see P. and M. i. 328; Holdsworth, H. E. L. (3rd ed.), 81–3; it was settled that the tenant must attorn to the new lord, i.e. recognize him as his lord; in the thirteenth century a writ called *per quae servitia* was in-

case *B* had full power to substitute without consulting *A*.

The question was finally settled by the statute Quia Emptores (1290).[1] As we have seen, the incidents of tenure were at that date more important to the lords than the services reserved.[2] The tenant wanted the power of free alienation. The lord did not want to lose his incidents. A compromise was made by this statute; and it was a compromise which it was the more easy to make seeing that lords and tenants did not form two exclusive classes. Many, perhaps most, free tenants were both lords and tenants in respect of different parts of their possessions. The statute enacted that 'from henceforth it shall be lawful to every freeman to sell at his own pleasure his lands or tenements or part of them, so that the feoffee shall hold the same lands or tenements of the chief lord of the same fee, by such service and customs as his feoffor held before'. If part of the land were conveyed the services were to be apportioned. The statute was to apply only to conveyances in fee simple. It was settled in Edward II's reign that the lord could not evade the statute by charging fines upon alienation. The result was to give to the tenant in fee simple full power of alienation by way of substitution, but to stop all subinfeudation when a grant was made in fee simple. If a mesne lord has at the present day a tenant in fee simple of lands of free tenure, that tenure must have been in existence before the year 1290.

vented by which the tenant could be compelled to attorn if the conveyance was made by fine.

[1] 18 Edward I, c. 1.

[2] Above, p. 35.

There is an important feature of the settlement made by this statute to which it is necessary to call attention. Because the statute stopped all subinfeudation when a grant was made in fee simple, it set in motion a process by which, in course of time, the importance of merely tenurial principles has been immensely decreased.

> 'It is', says Challis,[1] 'the general effect of the statute of Quia Emptores, so often as a mesne tenure for a fee simple is extinguished by union of the land and the lordship in the same hands, to prevent the mesne tenure from being ever again revived by any act of the parties. Thus, by the gradual extinction of the mesne tenures, the seignory of all freehold lands held for a fee simple tends to become concentrated in the crown.'

This made for the simplification of the rules of the land law which were dependent upon tenure; and, consequently, the removal of a great obstacle to the conception of the land law merely as property law. This is illustrated by the history of the law as to land which is held by copyhold tenure. We have seen that to the end the consequences of tenure formed a real hindrance to its profitable user.[2]

(ii) *The tenant in chief and the king.* In 1256 the king issued an ordinance which forbade all tenants in chief to alienate without his licence. The reason assigned for the ordinance was that, by reason of such alienations, the king lost his incidents of tenure, and that his tenants were so impoverished that they could not perform their services. The statute of Quia Emptores was not binding upon the king, so that he was able to prevent his tenants in chief from freely

[1] Real Property (3rd ed.), 22.

[2] Above, pp. 46–8.

alienating their lands. But he was unable to maintain this restriction. In 1327 tenants in chief acquired the right to alienate freely on payment of a fine for alienation [1]—a payment which was abolished with the other feudal incidents in 1660.[2]

This was the end of feudal restrictions on the freedom of alienation. As the result of these developments the common law came to regard the principle of freedom of alienation as a fundamental principle, based upon public policy. We can find statements of this principle in Bracton in the thirteenth century, in Littleton in the fifteenth century, and in Coke in the sixteenth century. No doubt the grounds which these three authorities assigned for this principle differed. Bracton would have said that they were contrary to the conception of *dominium*, and would also have emphasized the importance of breaking up the solidarity of the feudal group. Littleton would have emphasized the importance of maintaining the principle of freedom of alienation because it was a principle of the common law. Coke would have had in view the attempt of the landowners to create perpetuities;[3] and he emphasized the commercial advantage of a free circulation of property. Though the reasons assigned by these three lawyers would have been different, all had in their minds the impolicy of a general restriction on the power of the tenant in fee simple to alienate. We shall now see that it was this principle which was partly the cause for the legislation against alienation to religious houses, and that it is the reason why

[1] 1 Edward III, st. 1, cc. 12 and 13.

[2] 12 Charles II, c. 24.

[3] For the rules against perpetuities see below, pp. 217 seqq.

this legislation has given rise to the modern prohibition against alienation in mortmain.

Alienation in Mortmain.[1]

If a man gave land to a religious corporation the lord got a tenant who never died, who was never under age, who could never marry, who could never commit felony. It suffered none of those incidents in the life of the natural man which were profitable to the feudal lord. Moreover, land held by religious corporations could not be so freely alienated as land held by individuals. For that reason it was said to have come into a dead hand (*mortmain*). These gifts in mortmain, therefore, were detrimental to the interests of the lords, and were opposed to the leaning of the common lawyers in favour of free alienation. For these two reasons the statute De Viris Religiosis—the first statute of mortmain—was passed in 1279.[2] This statute prevented all alienation in favour of religious houses without the licence of the lord of whom the land was held, and of the king. This prohibition was extended to all corporate bodies in Richard II's reign.[3] Though modern statutes have created some exceptions to the general law,[4] the prohibition has been maintained from the thirteenth century to the present day. It is true that the first and perhaps the chief reason for Edward I's statute no longer exists; for the incidents of tenure are things of the past. But the second reason still holds good. The law is maintained, because to give land to a corporation is to render it

[1] Holdsworth, H. E. L. (3rd ed.), iii. 86–7.

[2] 7 Edward I.

[3] 15 Richard II, c. 5.

[4] 51, 52 Victoria, c. 42; Cheshire, Real Property (3rd ed.), 830–1.

wholly, or almost wholly, inalienable. Though a restriction on the freedom of alienation, it is a restriction in name only ; for, like the modern rule against perpetuities, it is maintained in order to promote the freedom of alienation. And, it should be noted, that this restriction was extended in 1735 by prohibiting a devise of lands to a charity, though that charity is not a corporation [1]—an extension which is due to the fact that, since land held for charitable purposes can only be dealt with for the purpose of giving effect to those purposes, it is not so freely alienable as land held by an individual.

§ 7. Conveyancing.

I must now give some account of the modes by which landowners could give effect to their powers to alienate their property. There are many medieval conveyances, in monastic cartularies and elsewhere, which show us how these powers were used. These conveyances illustrate the actual working of the principles of the land law. They show us how these principles were settled by the endeavours of the conveyancers to satisfy the wishes of the landowners. In fact the principles of the land law were worked out in detail by conveyancers, acting under the criticism and sometimes under the control of the courts. These conveyancers made common forms ; and the common forms, whether of writs or of pleadings or of conveyances, have a habit of acquiring a customary meaning from which the courts will not readily depart, and of thus becoming a part of the law itself.

[1] 9 George II, c. 36 ; for the modern statutes see Cheshire, op. cit. (3rd ed.), 835–7.

With the growth of the complexity of the rules of the land law, and therefore of the forms which were devised to give effect to them, there has grown up a respect for the opinion of those who have constructed these forms, which more nearly approaches to the respect paid in the days of the Roman Republic to the Responsa Prudentum than anything else in English law. In this period, it is true, we are only at the beginning of the process which will make the opinion of the conveyancers almost a source of law. There were many learned amateurs in the monasteries who drew conveyances according to the pattern approved of by the monastery. We can, however, see the beginnings of the process which will eventually lead to this result. Any collection of precedents will show us a growth of uniformity and complexity which points to the rise of a class of professional conveyancers.

We have seen that the leading distinctions in the land law are the distinctions between land held by free and land held by copyhold tenure; and between freehold estates and interests held for a term of years.[1] These distinctions are necessarily reflected in the forms of conveyances. But the rules as to freehold interests held by a free tenure are by far the most important, both because of the great variety of rights included in this category, and because these rules have been the model which conveyances falling within the other two categories have tended to follow.

Freehold Interests in Lands held by Free Tenure.[2]

These conveyances fall into two classes: (1) Those which take effect by the act of the parties, and (2)

[1] Above, pp. 16–20. [2] Holdsworth, H.E.L. (3rd ed.), iii. 220–46.

those which depend for their efficacy on the machinery of the court.

(1) Conveyances which take effect by the act of the parties. The normal and regular mode of creating or transferring a freehold interest in land of free tenure is by a feoffment. 'Feoffment is a species of the genus gift.' [1] It is a gift of a freehold interest in land. But it is not perfected till seisin has been delivered.[2] The essential part of the feoffment is the livery of seisin made with the intention of giving the whole or some part of the donor's interest. Till the passing of the statute of Frauds in 1677 it was unnecessary to evidence the feoffment by any writing, if it was intended to transfer an estate in possession; and, as we shall see, at first writing was equally unnecessary, while something equivalent to livery of seisin was equally necessary, in the case of incorporeal things.[3]

The livery of seisin was given by putting the donee into possession of the land; and, in addition to delivering possession, the donor must quit the land. There could be no livery of seisin unless the land was thus relinquished. Abroad there was a tendency to confuse the actual livery of seisin with symbolical observances (such as handing over a sod, a stick, a ring, or a knife), which were intended to evidence it; and, under the influence of Roman law, there was a tendency to allow the delivery of a document, stating that seisin had been delivered, to operate as an actual livery of seisin. But these developments did not

[1] P. and M. ii. 82.

[2] Bl. Comm. ii. 310–11; P. and M. ii. 82–4.

[3] Below, pp. 129–30.

take place in England. In England an actual livery of vacant seisin was required. The origin of this rigid rule we must ascribe mainly to the importance of the publicity of an actual livery in a system which worked with the jury. Perhaps also it was partly due to the early date at which Roman law ceased to exercise an appreciable influence on English law, and partly to the incapacity of the primitive mind to conceive of a transfer of things without actual *traditio*. Its long continuance in the law we must ascribe partly to the fact that it helped to promote publicity of conveyance and thus to prevent the frauds which secrecy of conveyance renders possible; and partly to the fact that the procedure in the real actions necessitated the presence of a tenant who was seised. As a result of this rule the principle that no freehold can be limited *in futuro* comes to be perhaps the most fundamental rule for the limitation of estates in English law; and the principle was applied not only to estates in possession, but also to estates in remainder and reversion. With some of the important consequences which, in later law, flowed from this principle, I shall deal later.[1]

The livery of seisin is thus the essential part of the conveyance. But gradually the use of writing to show the intent with which seisin had been delivered became more common; and Bracton pointed out that it was convenient for the purpose of perpetuating testimony.[2] As it became more common it became possible to indicate precisely the varying kinds of intent with which seisin was delivered; and, if we look at the large powers which landowners had of making what dispositions they pleased of their pro-

[1] Below, pp. 191, 221; cp. above, p. 68. [2] At f. 33 b.

perty, we shall see that these written charters, which evidenced the livery of seisin, were in practice absolutely necessary, both to show the intent with which seisin was delivered, and to prove that intent in case of litigation. With the history of the forms which they take we began the history of the art of conveyancing.

By the end of the medieval period the form of the charters or deeds, drawn up to show the intent with which seisin was delivered, had become fixed. We get the modern division of deeds into deeds poll and indentures. The deed poll is a deed to which there is only one party. The indenture is a deed to which two or more persons are parties. The names are derived from the old precautions taken against fraud. If several persons were parties to a deed, as many copies of it as there were parties were made on one sheet of parchment, and the parchment was then cut into parts in an indented fashion across some word such as 'Chirograph'. It was thus very difficult to substitute a forged deed for the real one without risk of detection. Such precautions were not considered necessary in the case of a deed to which there was only one party; it therefore had a 'polled' or smooth top. Similarly, we get the various parts of the deed in substantially their modern form—the recitals, showing the occasion for the gift; the habendum, showing the estate taken; the tenendum, showing of whom the land is to be held and by what tenure; the reddendum, showing the services to be rendered; various covenants; clauses of warranty binding the grantor to warrant the title; and the attestation, the sealing, and the delivery of the deed.

Deeds in this form were used to evidence or effect

many different kinds of conveyance. The following are some of the chief varieties: *The release.* This conveyance was used when the tenant was in occupation of the land, and the lord wished to convey to him his rights. It was sometimes used, in conjunction with a lease and entry thereunder, as an alternative method of conveyance to a feoffment with livery of seisin.[1] The converse case to the release was *the surrender*—a tenant of a smaller estate gave up his estate to the reversioner. *The exchange*—no livery of seisin was needed, but the conveyance was not perfect till both parties had entered on the land. *Partitions* were generally made by deed, and a deed was necessary in the case of joint tenants and tenants in common. It was made necessary in all cases by the statute of Frauds. *Deeds of grant* had come, at the end of this period, to be the usual mode of conveying incorporeal things—though, as we shall see,[2] the rule that the grantee was not in all cases fully protected, unless he could prove an actual user of his right, shows that, even in the case of these things, the law required something equivalent to livery of seisin.

It is not always easy to keep apart such distinct things as the transaction itself and the evidence for that transaction. Though the livery of seisin was the essential part of the feoffment, though in the case of certain of these other conveyances some other similar ceremony, such as actual user of the right, actual entry on the land, or the attornment of the

[1] This differs from a bargain and sale and release, below, pp. 293–5, since, by virtue of the statute of Uses, no entry was needed.

[2] Below, p. 130.

tenant,[1] was sometimes necessary ; it was inevitable that the deed, which contained the expression of the parties intent, and preserved it as a perpetual memorial of their title, should assume greater and greater importance. That importance was increased in the following period by the rise of uses, and the consequent development of new and complex forms of conveyance, by means of which the land could be conveyed without the need for livery of seisin.[2] Written documents came to be capable of conveying property. Under these circumstances it is not surprising to find that the ceremonies analogous to livery of seisin, and ultimately even the need for livery of seisin itself, should be abolished by the Legislature. From this point of view the enactment in 1845 [3] that corporeal as well as incorporeal things should lie in grant as well as in livery is the result of a long historical development.

(2) Conveyances which depend for their efficacy on the machinery of the court. These two forms of conveyances are fines and recoveries. Both forms were much used till their abolition in 1833.[4]

Fines. A fine, or to give it its full title, a ' Finalis Concordia ', was an action compromised in court, and by the leave of the court, upon certain terms approved by the court. I have already said something of the fine when dealing with the estate tail.[5] But we have seen that its use in barring an estate tail was a comparatively late development.[6] It had become a very

[1] Above, p. 105, n. 1 ; below, pp. 129–30. [2] Below, p. 290.
[3] 8, 9 Victoria, c. 106, § 2. [4] 3 and 4 William IV, c. 74.
[5] Above, pp. 58–9. [6] Ibid.

important conveyance at an early period, and it retained its importance all through the Middle Ages and later. There were several varieties of fines, and much technical law accumulated round them.

The reasons why so much use was made of fines as conveyances were as follows: (1) A fine 'sets a short preclusive term running against the whole world, parties, privies, and strangers'.[1] This term was fixed as a year and a day. A fine operated therefore to quiet titles, and put an end to litigation. But a statute of 1360[2] deprived it of much of its efficacy, by enacting that it was not to affect the rights of strangers. The results of this statute, in so litigious an age, were very bad; and the old law was restored with some modifications by statutes of Richard III and Henry VII's reigns.[3] (2) The fact that the fine was enrolled gave a guarantee against forgery. (3) It was a conveyance by which a married woman could effectually convey her property. The judges examined her to see if she had freely consented to the conveyance. If they were satisfied, and passed the fine, she could not upset the conveyance after her husband's death. The original reason why the fine had this effect was the fact that it was so solemn in its nature, that, once it has been levied, it stood. But in later law it was considered that it was not so much the sanctity of the fine, as the fact that the married woman had been separately examined, that made the conveyance binding upon her. (4) During this period the fact that the court had passed a fine gave the parties some guarantee of the validity of

[1] P. and M. ii. 100.
[2] 34 Edward III, c. 16.
[3] 1 Richard III, c. 7; 4 Henry VII, c. 24.

the dispositions of the property made by it.[1] That was not the case in later law when the approval of the fine by the court became merely formal.

Recoveries. We have seen that a recovery was a fictitious real action which went through all its stages to final judgement.[2] During the greater part of the medieval period it was not, like the fine, regarded as a regular mode of conveyance. It was regarded rather as a collusive proceeding designed to evade the law. That this was its character in early law is quite clear. It had been used to oust termors of their land,[3] to enable husbands to convey their wives' land,[4] to evade their wives' claims to dower,[5] to defeat the laws of mortmain.[6] In all these cases it had been necessary to pass statutes to nullify the effects of a recovery. Finally, we have seen, it was used, in conjunction with the law as to warranty, to bar an estate tail.[7] It was because this use of a recovery coincided with the policy of the law that it was allowed to operate as a conveyance, and thus at length to attain to the dignity of a common assurance.

Copyholds.[8]

It was during this period that the regular mode of copyhold conveyance, by way of surrender in court and admittance by the lord or his steward, was evolved. The form of this conveyance was one of

[1] Holdsworth, H. E. L. (3rd ed.), iii. 252–3.

[2] Above, p. 57.

[3] 6 Edward I, c. 11.

[4] 13 Edward I, st. 1, c. 3.

[5] Ibid., c. 4.

[6] Ibid., c. 32.

[7] Above, pp. 57–8.

[8] Holdsworth, H. E. L. (3rd ed.), iii. 246–8.

the earliest results of the practice of keeping court rolls, which became general in the thirteenth century. It is the form of the conveyance which has given to the copyholder his name, and has supplied in later law the chief test between free and copyhold tenure.

It is clear that this mode of conveyance emphasized the lord's rights. He was able to charge fines upon admittance and sometimes for enrolment; and therefore, from an early date, the rule was established that the use of any other mode of conveyance was a cause of forfeiture. The lord must not be defrauded of his dues; and, in early days, he was entitled to exercise some discretion as to the admission of persons who proposed to become tenants of his manor. As we have seen, the manor was a little community; and the conveyance which conferred the duties and privileges of membership could not be regarded as merely the affair of the transferor and the transferee. Both the lord and his court were interested in knowing something about it.

In later days, when copyhold custom became stereotyped, and enforceable as against the lord; when copyhold tenure came to denote simply property of a peculiar type; the discretionary powers of lord and court disappeared. By the time of Coke the lord had become simply 'custom's instrument'.[1] He had become merely an agent to carry out the wishes of the tenant in accordance with the custom. The form of the conveyance tells us of a time when his position was very different—but it is a bare form, out of which the reality has departed.

[1] Coke, Copyholder, § 41.

Leases for Years.[1]

The ordinary forms of creating or conveying these interests illustrate very clearly the technicality of the rule which put leases for life and leases for years in different categories. There is often very little difference between the two.

Up till the time of the passing of the Statute of Frauds writing was not required for a lease for years. But, indirectly, the parties were practically compelled to make such leases by deed. It was only if the lease was by deed that the lessee could bring an action of covenant against his landlord—his only remedy until the rise of the newer remedies for the protection of his possession,[2] or that lessor or lessee could enforce the mutual covenants which they had entered into. But the mere making of the lease by deed or otherwise did not suffice to give the lessee any interest in the land. Till entry he had merely an *interesse termini*, a right to enter. It was not till he had entered that he was possessed of his term, so that till then he could take no release, nor was he entitled to use the new remedies for the protection of his possession with which the law had provided him.[3] In this, as in other branches of the common law, writing by itself did not suffice to transfer possession. The need for entry was not got rid of till the Law of Property Act, 1925.[4]

[1] Holdsworth, H. E. L. (3rd ed.), iii. 248–9.

[2] Above, p. 72.

[3] Above, p. 72.

[4] § 149 (1) (2); this rule did not apply to leases which took effect under the statute of Uses, as the lessee got possession by virtue of the statute, below, pp. 156, 294.

§ 8. Seisin and Possession.

We have seen that feudalism had two aspects. It was a branch of public law in so far as it placed governmental rights and duties on the owners of land. It was a branch of private law in so far as it defined the forms and modes of landowning.[1] Our feudalized land law, therefore, had these two aspects. The theory of tenure, and the elaboration of its different forms, with which I have already dealt,[2] were intimately related to the public aspect of the land law. They supplied this aspect of the land law with its background of principle. On the other hand, the theory of seisin and possession supplied the background of principle to the land law regarded as a branch of the private law of property; and, as the public aspect of the land law diminished, and its aspect as a branch of the law of property increased in importance, as the learning which centred round estates and interests in or over the land became more important than the learning which centred round the forms of tenure and their incidents, the theory of seisin and possession naturally began to be of much greater importance than the theory of tenure. In fact it still supplies the background of principle to many parts of the modern land law.

Let us begin by defining our terms. Seisin means possession. It is derived from the same root as the Roman *possessio* and the German *besitz*. 'The man who is seised is the man who is sitting on the land; when he was put in seisin he was set there and made to sit there.'[3] During the medieval period the terms

[1] Above, p. 4. [2] Above, pp. 21–9. [3] P. and M. ii. 29–30.

seisin and possession were used convertibly. One could talk of the seisin of chattels, or the possession of freehold interests in land.[1] But, in the latter part of the fifteenth century, when Littleton was writing his book on Tenures, the term seisin came to be appropriated to describe the possession of freehold estates in the land, while the term possession was appropriated to chattels real and personal.[2] It became definitely wrong to use the term possession in connexion with freehold interests, and the term seisin in connexion with chattels. This change in terminology is due to the fact that the incidents of the seisin protected by the real actions, particularly the conditions under which it could be recovered by these actions, came to differ from the incidents of the possession protected by personal actions. It is true that, fundamentally, the main principles applicable to the seisin of freehold estates were then and always have been the same as those applicable to the possession of chattels.[3] But, for all that, differences had arisen, owing to the development of these two allied conceptions in the sphere of different classes of actions, which could be aptly represented by this differentiation in terminology.

So much for terminology. Let us now endeavour to describe the theory of seisin which the medieval common lawyers worked out. It is necessary to grasp it, because, with some modifications with which I shall deal in a subsequent chapter,[4] it dominates

[1] Maitland, Collected Papers, i. 329.

[2] Holdsworth, H. E. L. (3rd ed.), ii. 581 and n. 2.

[3] Holdsworth, H. E. L. (3rd ed.), iii. 351–4.

[4] Below, pp. 177–83.

our modern land law. But this description will be more readily understood if, by way of preface, we recall the point of view from which modern systems of law regard the allied conceptions of ownership and possession.

Modern systems of law regard ownership as the relation of a person to a thing, which gives to the person indefinite rights enforceable at law to or over the thing. When considering a question of ownership we attend not so much to the physical relation between the person and the thing, as to the question whether the relation between them has been so constituted that the law will annex to it these indefinite rights; for ownership is pre-eminently a right. Possession, on the other hand, expresses the physical relation of control exercised by a person over a thing. The possessor may or may not be owner, according to whether or not this physical relation of control has been constituted under conditions to which the law annexes the rights of ownership. If in all cases where such physical control exists the law annexed the right of ownership, the law relating to possession would merge in the law relating to ownership. But this is not the case. For many causes arising both *ex contractu* and *ex delicto*, the owner of property is not the possessor. Persons lend or let or deposit their things; and dishonest persons steal or otherwise convert them to their own use. The relationships between persons and things grow more complex with the growing complexity of social relations; and the law must define the many kinds of subordinate control exercised by persons over things, which coexist together with or in opposition to the principal control which it calls ownership. Thus we get a law of possession which, both in Roman and in English law, covers many species of subordinate control, and exists side by side with a law of ownership.

This general theory is, of course, a generalization from the rules of mature systems of law. Primitive systems of law have not yet attained these abstract conceptions of ownership and possession. They are concerned rather with the invention and maintenance of rules for the settlement of disputes. Since this is their point of view, they naturally regard the man in possession of land as the owner. If his possession is disputed the plaintiff must prove his case. Till he has proved his case he has no right at all to the land. This was the point of view of the common law in the twelfth and thirteenth centuries. In the writ of right the plaintiff must show that he or his ancestors had a better right than the defendant to the land of which the defendant was seised. This he could do by showing that he or his ancestors had been in possession, or that he or they had done such acts—e. g. collected the rents—as only a possessor could do, and that he or they had been wrongfully deprived of possession by the defendant or his ancestors. The defendant must deny the plaintiff's claim and prove any facts which he has alleged to show that he has the better right to possession. But he could not say to the plaintiff, 'You have not proved your case because *X*, a third person, through whom neither of us claims, has a better right than either of us, and this I am prepared to prove.' Seeing that the plaintiff need only prove a better right to possession, and not an absolute *dominium*, the defendant could not rely upon a *jus tertii* through which he did not claim. The question at issue was the better right of the parties to possession; and, if this be the issue, such a *jus tertii* is merely irrelevant.

In this respect English and Roman law differ fundamentally. Roman law recognized an absolute *dominium*, so that in Roman law *dominium* and *possessio* can be and are sharply contrasted. In English law we can only compare seisin with seisin, the seisin protected by the writ of right with that protected by the writ of entry, the seisin protected by the writ of entry with that protected by the novel disseisin [1]—the older, in short, with the more recent. English law protects seisin and various rights to seisin of varying dates by different forms of action.

English law, therefore, regarded the person seised as the owner. It gave facilities to the man wrongfully disseised to recover his seisin. But, till he recovered it, he had no more right to the land than any stranger. It is to the man seised that the law gives all the advantages and privileges of ownership. The man disseised has no single one of these advantages and privileges. Let us look at one or two illustrations.

The person seised may make a feoffment and convey an estate in fee simple—a tortious estate, it may be, but still an estate, in fee simple. As Scrope J. said in 1313,[2] 'the disseisor claimeth fee and right and freehold till his tort be proven'. The heir of the person seised will inherit his property; and it is only a person seised who can be a stock of descent.

[1] For these writs see above, pp. 11–16.

[2] Y. B. 6, 7 Ed. II (S.S.) 189.

His widow is entitled to dower. The husband of a woman seised as of wrong is entitled to curtesy. Rights appendant to the estate belong to the disseisor. The fact that there is a person seised of the land will prevent that land escheating to the lord, even though the disseisee—the person entitled—has died without heirs. Similarly, all the ordinary incidents of tenure affect the tenant seised as of wrong just as if he had been the rightful tenant.

The position of the person disseised is the exact converse of this. He cannot alienate because he has nothing which he can alienate. Moreover, to alienate effectually he must make livery of seisin, which he obviously cannot do since he is not seised. Not having seisin, he has only a right of entry or action—a chose in action, which, till 1845, was inalienable.[1] At common law, said Mountague, C. J., in 1553, 'he who was out of possession might not bargain, grant, or let his right or title, and if he had done it, it should have been void.'[2] His right of action will it is true, descend to his heir; but the time will come when, owing to the operation of statutes of limitation, even that right of action will be lost.[3] His wife is not entitled to dower. He, if married to a woman disseised, is not entitled to curtesy. Of a mere right of action, and in the Middle Ages of a right of entry, there could be no escheat; nor did such rights render those entitled thereto liable to any of the other incidents of tenure.

This was the theory of seisin which was worked out by the medieval common lawyers; and much of it

[1] 8, 9 Victoria, c. 106, § 6.

[2] *Partridge* v. *Strange*, Plowden at p. 88. [3] Below, pp. 167–8.

is the accepted theory of the law to-day.[1] Seisin is still prima facie evidence of ownership. The best right to seisin is still the only form of ownership recognized by English law.

> 'The standing proof that English law regards, and has always regarded possession as a substantive root of title, is the standing usage of English lawyers and landowners. With very few exceptions there is only one way in which an apparent owner of English land who is minded to deal with it can show his right so to do; and that way is to show that he and those through whom he claims have possessed the land for a time sufficient to exclude any reasonable probability of a superior adverse claim.' [2]

But it is obvious that some parts of this theory will gradually come to look anomalous in a more orderly state of society, and in a more developed system of law. It will seem anomalous to regard only the rights of the person seised—seised rightfully or wrongfully, and to disregard the rights of the man who is wrongfully disseised. This changed point of view is apparent at the latter part of the medieval period. In most cases the man wrongfully disseised had been given a right of entry; [3] and the omission to pass statutes of limitation extended his rights of action. One or two cases, indeed, were left till 1833, in which the disseised owner had no right of entry—but they remained only as anomalous survivals.[4] The result of this development was not to curtail the advantages possessed by the man seised as against the world at large, nor to give greater powers

[1] *Perry* v. *Clissold*, [1907] A.C. at pp. 79–80; cp. Lightwood, Possession of Land, 151.

[2] Pollock and Wright, Possession, 94–5.

[3] Holdsworth, H. E. L. (3rd ed.), ii. 583–5.

[4] Ibid. 585–6.

of disposition to the man disseised—the man seised could still alienate, and the man disseised was still unable to alienate. The result was to make the seisin of the wrongdoer, and his acts done while wrongfully seised, more easily defeasible by the man who had a better right to get seisin. Moreover, it was still true in the Middle Ages and much later, that the law did not recognize an abstract right of ownership, but only seisin and rights to get seisin. We shall see that it was not till the eighteenth century, and under the influence of ideas which grew up round the action of ejectment, that the disseised owner, who was seeking to recover on the strength of a right to seisin, must prove not merely a better right than the man seised, but an absolutely good right.[1] It is not till then that it can be said that English law recognized an abstract right of ownership; and, even then, it did not depart from its original conception that the man seised, whether rightfully or wrongfully, is prima facie owner, and has therefore all the rights of an owner.[2] No doubt his rights, and his dealings with the land in the exercise of these rights, are defeasible if his prima facie ownership is disproved; but, till it is disproved, he has these rights.

Such in outline is the medieval doctrine of seisin. We must now glance at the manner in which that doctrine was applied to the complex facts of land-holding.

If seisin means possession, and if possession denotes the fact of physical control exercised by a person over a thing, two consequences would seem to follow.

[1] Below, pp. 182–3.

[2] Above, pp. 125–6.

In the first place, two persons cannot at the same time both exclusively possess the same thing. This principle was stated by Coke [1] in the terms of Roman law; it was elaborated by Vaughan, C. J.; [2] and it is recognized by the modern authorities.[3] But, in spite of this theoretical difficulty, the conception of seisin was applied not only to the interest of the tenant who holds in demesne, but also to the interest of the lord who holds in service; and not only to the tenant of the particular estate, but also to the reversioner or remainder-man. As we have seen, it was this extension of the doctrine of seisin which was a principal cause for the evolution of the conception of estates in the land.[4] In the second place, it is difficult to conceive of the possession of an incorporeal thing. But, notwithstanding this difficulty, the conception of seisin was extended to the large and miscellaneous list of incorporeal things known to the medieval common law; and this extension has given rise to some curious and long-lived rules of law.

In the thirteenth century it is quite clear that, for the transference or creation of an incorporeal thing, some act or acts of user, which necessarily varied with the nature of the thing, were as necessary as a livery of seisin in the case of a corporeal thing. These acts were in fact the equivalent of a livery of seisin, for they were the equivalent of that physical apprehension of a corporeal thing which was the essence of such a livery. Thus the attornment of the tenant was necessary to complete the grant of a seignory,

[1] Co. Litt. 368a.

[2] *Holden* v. *Smallbrooke* (1668), Vaughan at p. 189.

[3] Pollock and Wright, Possession, 20.

[4] Above, pp. 50–1.

a reversion, a remainder, or a rent. But, when the nature of an incorporeal thing began to be better understood, the lawyers began to think that these incorporeal things could be created or transferred without the need for these acts, which were the equivalent of a livery of seisin. It was said, first, that a deed would suffice, and then that a deed was necessary, to create or transfer them;[1] and thus we get the modern distinction between corporeal things which lay in livery and incorporeal things which lay in grant. But, in spite of this change in the law, some of the consequences of the old law long remained. The owners of these incorporeal things were protected by real actions, similar in their nature to the real actions by which the owners of corporeal things were protected; and it is for this reason that, though these things could be created or transferred by deed, their owners were insecurely protected till they had done some act by which they got actual seisin. For instance, the grantee of an advowson was not fully protected till he had presented a clerk to the living; and the grantee of a rent had no complete seisin till he had received the first payment thereof.

These rules as to advowsons and rents were altered by Acts of Anne's reign;[2] and we shall see that the statute of Uses and the rise of the action of ejectment modified some of the other rules as to seisin.[3] But we shall see also that, in spite of these modifications, many of the principles of the medieval common law are still at the root of our modern law; and that,

[1] Holdsworth, H. E. L. (3rd ed.), iii. 98–9.

[2] 4, 5 Anne, c. 16; 7 Anne, c. 18. [3] Below, pp. 178, 179–83.

consequently, it is necessary to grasp them if we would understand its theory of ownership and possession.

§ 9. Special Customs.[1]

The common law had created certain types of tenure, certain kinds of estates and interests, certain modes of conveyance, and certain legal doctrines relating to land-holding, which prevailed almost universally within the jurisdiction of the common law courts. If we think of the mass of local customs which made up the land law in the eleventh century we may well admire the universality of its rules. But, in spite of all its efforts, one or two survivals of an older order still remained. The most notable of these survivals are Tenure in Ancient Demesne, Gavelkind, and the Borough Customs.

Ancient Demesne.

The ancient demesne of the crown was the land which belonged to the crown in 1066—'on the day when Edward the Confessor was alive and dead'. To ascertain whether or no a given piece of land was ancient demesne, Domesday Book was the only evidence admitted, and its evidence was conclusive. To these ancient demesnes of the crown many exceptional rules, both of public law and the land law, were applicable. With the former rules we are not here concerned. With respect to the land law, the peculiarity of these manors of ancient demesne was the fact that, in addition to land held by the ordinary free and unfree tenures, there existed land held by a peculiar tenure known as tenure in ancient demesne.

[1] Holdsworth, H. E. L. (3rd ed.), iii. 256–75.

The main characteristic of this peculiar tenure is well described by Blackstone as follows: 'The truth is', he says, 'that these lands are of such an amphibious nature that, when compared with mere copyholds, they may with sufficient propriety be called freeholds; and, when compared with absolute freeholds, they may with equal or greater propriety be denominated copyholds.'[1] They resembled lands held by villein tenure in that the ordinary real actions were not available to the tenant; and, even after villein tenure had become copyhold, and had got the protection of the action of ejectment, that action was never extended to them. They differed from lands held by villein tenure in the fact that these tenants were protected in their holdings by two royal writs—the little writ of right and the writ of monstraverunt. The little writ of right was the writ used by the individual tenant who had been disturbed in his holding: the writ of monstraverunt was the remedy by which the tenants collectively could complain of some infringement of the custom of the manor.

The lawyers never quite made up their minds whether or not these tenants had the freehold. In fact the question whether or not they had the freehold might well have remained a moot point had not their right to the parliamentary franchise turned upon its solution. Blackstone considered the question, and came to the historically correct conclusion that these tenants were neither freeholders nor copyholders, but a *tertium quid*; and his conclusion that they could not be said to have the free-

[1] Law Tracts, 145.

hold has been adopted by the judges.[1] So far as it applied to the parliamentary franchise it was immediately adopted by the Legislature.[2] The changes made by the Common Law Procedure Act, 1852, in effect abolished most of the peculiarities of this tenure.[3] It ceased to differ from ordinary copyhold; and, like copyhold, it is abolished by the Law of Property Act, 1922.[4]

Gavelkind.

The term 'gavelkind' is connected with the old English word *gafol*, which means rent or a customary performance of agricultural services. Originally, therefore, gavelkind land meant land which yielded this rent or these services. In the later common law a different meaning was attached to the term. It came to be used generally as the name for the custom by which lands in Kent were, in the absence of proof to the contrary, presumed to be affected; and sometimes, in later law, to express the fact that lands, whether in Kent or elsewhere, were divided between male heirs on the death of the ancestor.

According to the Kentish custumal, which dates from Edward I's reign, Kentish men were governed by many peculiar customs, and had many privileges, many of which are survivals from the days before the common law. The most notable of these customs and privileges which relate to the land law are the following: Villeinage was unknown in Kent. There was no escheat for felony. A child could alienate

1 *Duke of Portland* v. *Hill* (1866), L. R. 2 Eq. at p. 777.
2 31 George II, c. 14.
3 15, 16 Victoria, c. 76; Williams, Real Property (22nd ed.), 61–2.
4 §§ 128–37.

his land by feoffment at fifteen. The land descended equally to all the sons. Probably the reason for the survival of these customs and privileges is the fact that the geographical position of Kent gave it social and economic advantages which were not enjoyed by the rest of England. It lay on the great highways between England and the Continent; and these highroads are 'the arteries along which flows money, the most destructive solvent of seigneurial power'.[1] For this reason Kent was never subjected to the manorial system of husbandry which was prevalent over the rest of England. Therefore some of the rules of the land law, which that system introduced over the rest of England, were not applied to Kent; and so it retained these survivals of old rules more ancient than the common law.

These customary rules of the land law were very permanent because the presumption was in favour of their application to all the land in the county. Much land, not really subject to them, became subject to them for lack of evidence to the contrary; and the same cause rendered nugatory many of the disgavelling Acts passed from time to time by the Legislature. But modern statutes, culminating in the Property Acts, have swept away the last survivals of these long-lived customs.[2]

The Borough Customs.

Many of the boroughs developed customary rules of land-holding which differed from the common law. There were two main causes for the divergence of

[1] P. and M. i. 166; cf. ibid. ii. 269–70.

[2] Administration of Estates Act, 1925, § 45 (1).

the borough customs from the common law. (1) These customs were in many cases codified in the borough custumal at an early date. Because they were thus stereotyped, they were more able to resist the encroachments of the common law than the uncodified customs of the open country. (2) The borough was a commercial centre, and therefore landowning in the borough tended to diverge at many points from landowning in the country. The rules which suited the knight, the religious house, the serjeant, or the socman, and the manorial rules regulating the humbler classes which cultivated the soil, could not be transplanted in their entirety to the house and the shop of the burgess.

Of these customary rules I need only mention two. (1) In many boroughs there was a custom which permitted land to be devised; and some of the cases in the Year Books, which turn upon these devises, show us that legal doctrines, which later were appropriated by and elaborated in the Chancery, might have been elaborated in the common law, if the common law had not set its face against the will of land. For instance, in the power to sell, which could be given to executors by will,[1] we see what is in substance a power of appointment; [2] and in a case of Edward III's reign we can see a future interest in land which is not a remainder.[3] (2) Some of the rules as to inheritance are old survivals. The best known of these rules is the custom of descent to the youngest son—the 'Borough English' of the common law. The name is derived from the fact that

[1] Below, p. 206. [2] Y. B. 19 Hen. VI, Mich., pl. 47.
[3] 30 Ass., p. 47.

at Nottingham it was the custom of the English as contrasted with the French borough. It was, however, found at other places besides Nottingham, and it was known in manors as well as boroughs, both in England and abroad. Probably its explanation is to be found in the fact that 'the younger son, if he lack father and mother, because of his younger age, may least of all his brethren help himself '.[1]

The custom to devise ceased to be a peculiar custom of the boroughs when this power was given to all landowners; and the custom of Borough English has been abolished by the Administration of Estates Act, 1925.[2]

§ 10. General Conclusions.

Throughout the Middle Ages the land law was the principal branch of the common law. Its main outlines had been drawn by the lawyers and statesmen of the twelfth and thirteenth centuries, and by the legislation of the reign of Edward I. In the fourteenth and fifteenth centuries these outlines had been elaborated by the legal profession; and the rules which they evolved contain some of the oldest and most permanent parts of the law. Though many of them have been modified by the Property Acts, they have not been wholly swept away; and they are still the foundations of large parts of the law. We have seen, for instance, that a few of the consequences of tenure,[3] much of the law as to estates in the land,[4] and much of the law as to seisin and possession,[5] have survived these Acts.

[1] Litt., § 211. [2] § 45 (1). [3] Above, pp. 28, 38.
[4] Above, pp. 73–4. [5] Above, pp. 127, 128.

The medieval land law was summed up at the close of this period in Littleton's Tenures. We can see from his summary, that, though the work of the lawyers had been skilfully done, though some of that work has been very permanent, it suffered from two grave defects.

In the first place, it was so rigid and narrow a system of law that it did not meet the needs of landowners. As the land law came to be more and more purely property law, the incidents and consequences of tenure tended to become burdensome anachronisms; and the restrictions placed by the common law on the landowner's powers of disposition, especially the denial of the power to devise, and the inconvenience of the modes by which he could give effect to his limited powers of disposition, were felt to be irksome and unreasonable. In the second place, the land law was made unreasonably technical by the intricacies of the procedure of the real actions. The age was at once lawless and litigious; and the procedure of the real actions was so technical that it afforded abundant opportunities to the lawless to defeat just claims, and made litigation a useful alternative to violence. That it was largely this system of procedure, as used and misused by the legal profession at the bidding of their clients, which was at fault, is, I think, demonstrated by the fact that the contingent remainder was hardly yet recognized,[1] and that uses were in their infancy.[2] These two topics, which, in the following period, were destined to introduce many complications into the land law, could be neglected by a writer upon

[1] Above, p. 68. [2] Below, pp. 147 seqq.

tenures in the fifteenth century; and yet the law was then almost as complex as it has ever been.

We shall see in the following chapter that it was the development of uses by the Chancellor which helped to meet the first of these defects. This development introduced many new doctrines into the legal system; and when the statute of Uses incorporated much of this doctrine into the common law, and when the Chancellor, starting from the basis of a liberalized common law, introduced new equitable ideas into the land law, we get the conditions in which the modern land law will be constructed upon its medieval basis.

But these developments would not have produced their full effect if the second of these defects—the intricacy of the procedure of the real actions—had not been remedied. At the end of this period we can see the source from which the remedy for this defect will come. Rivalry with the Chancery was inducing the common lawyers to expand the actions of trespass and trespass on the case. The effects of this expansion were almost as notable in the land law as in the law of contract and tort. It was through a development in one of the forms of the action of trespass—the action of ejectment—that the lessee for years [1] and the copyholder [2] had got full protection. In the following period this action of ejectment will, by a series of fictions, be used to do the work of the real actions; and it will be adapted so successfully to this new sphere of activity that it will gradually reduce the real actions to the rank of antiquarian curiosities.[3]

[1] Above, pp. 72–3. [2] Above, p. 43. [3] Below, pp. 169–74.

In the next chapter I shall deal with the history of the manner in which the doctrine of uses, the treatment of uses by the Legislature, and the equitable doctrines of the Chancellor, introduced the new ideas into the land law, which were needed to enable it to meet the demands of a new age. I shall also show how the provisions of other statutes of the sixteenth and early seventeenth centuries, and the rise of the action of ejectment, created the conditions precedent for the development of the modern land law.

CHAPTER II

THE SIXTEENTH AND EARLY SEVENTEENTH CENTURIES (1485–1660)

It was during these centuries that the rise of Uses and Trusts, and the treatment by the Legislature of the problems raised by their development, created the conditions under which the courts of common law and the court of Chancery could begin to construct the modern land law upon its medieval basis. I shall relate the history of these developments under the following heads: § 1 The Medieval Development of Uses and Trusts; § 2 The Statutes of Uses and Wills; § 3 The Effects of these Statutes on the Land Law; § 4 Other Developments in the Land Law.

§ 1. The Medieval Development of Uses and Trusts.[1]

'The term "use"', says Maitland,[2] 'is a curious one; it has, if I may say so, mistaken its own origin. You may think that it is the Latin *usus*, but that is not so; it is the Latin *opus*. From remote times—in the seventh and eighth centuries in barbarous or vulgar Latin you find "ad opus" for "on his behalf". It is so in Lombard and French legal documents. In Old French this becomes *al oes, ues*. In English mouths this becomes confused with "use". In record Latin it remains *ad opus*.' The trusts of our modern law are the lineal descendants of this medieval

[1] Holdsworth, H. E. L., iv. 407–49.
[2] Equity, 24.

opus or *use*. We shall see that legislation, especially the famous statute of Uses of 1535,[1] and later developments of equity after the passing of that statute,[2] have created differences between the use and the trust. But in the most important essentials the use and the trust were and are identical. In this section, which deals only with their medieval development before the passing of the statute of Uses, the two terms can be used convertibly.

Early writers on the use had no hesitation in looking to Roman law for its origin. They all dwell upon the analogy which exists between the position created by the grant of a *usus* or *usufructus* or *fidei commissum*, and the position created by the gift of property to *A* to the use of or in trust for *B*.[3] But the existence of an analogy is one thing: the proof that the later in date of these two analogous things is derived from the earlier is quite another. Every one is now agreed that these institutions of Roman law are merely analogies of a superficial kind; and that, though some of them may have had some slight influence on the development of the use in the thirteenth and fourteenth centuries, we must look elsewhere for its origin. Mr. Justice Holmes was the first to point out that the root idea underlying the conception of the use is to be found among the Germanic tribes.[4] That root idea

[1] Below, p. 161. [2] Below, pp. 201–3.

[3] Gilbert, Uses, 3; Sanders, Uses, 1–8; Bl. Comm. ii. 327–8; Spence, Equitable Jurisdiction, i. 436; Digby, History of the Law of Real Property (4th ed.), 314–16. But note that Bacon in his Reading on the Statute of Uses, Works (ed. Spedding), vii. 407–8 treats these Roman law analogies merely as analogies.

[4] L. Q. R. i. 162; Essays in Anglo-American Legal History, ii. 705–16.

consists in the recognition of the duty of a person to whom property has been conveyed for certain purposes, to carry out those purposes; and early Germanic law found in the 'Salman' or 'Treuhand' the machinery by which effect could be given to this duty.[1] Germanic law, therefore, was familiar with the idea that a man to whom property has been conveyed to the use of or in trust for another was bound to fulfil his trust. And there are many illustrations, both in England and on the Continent, of the extensive use made of this idea.[2] Thus, Frankish formulae of the Merovingian period speak of property given to a church *ad opus sancti illius*; Mercian land books of the ninth century convey land *ad opus monachorum*; and Domesday Book speaks of geld or money, or sac and soc, held *ad opus regis* or *reginae* or *vicecomitis*.

But, till the law develops into a regular system, the place which this vague idea will take in relation to its various parts is necessarily uncertain. This development began with the legal renaissance of the twelfth and thirteenth centuries; and it is the very different effect of that legal renaissance upon the development of English and continental law which accounts for the peculiar development of uses and trusts in England. The continental legal development was much more directly affected than the English by a Roman law, adapted to medieval conditions by the schools of the glossators and the post-glossators, and to modern conditions by the jurists of the age of the

[1] See Caillemer, L'Exécution Testamentaire, 124 n. 2, 561–4; Goffin, The Testamentary Executor, 24, 26–7.

[2] See the instances collected in P. and M. ii. 231–2.

Reception and their successors.[1] The result was that many primitive legal ideas disappeared, and were replaced by rules drawn from a Roman law which had been thus adapted to modern conditions. In England, in the twelfth and early thirteenth centuries, the influence of Roman law exerted through a strong central court, and by literate lawyers of the school of Glanvil and Bracton, had created a native body of law which was capable of standing alone, and of developing along its own insular lines;[2] but at the end of the thirteenth century that influence ceased.[3] The result was that many primitive ideas, which were gradually eliminated from continental systems of law, were developed by English lawyers into quite peculiar and quite original institutions and bodies of legal doctrine. Well-known illustrations in other branches of the law are the English jury system,[4] the English system of pleading and of criminal procedure,[5] the English system of local self-government,[6] and the manner in which the pervading medieval idea of the supremacy of law was converted into the fundamental constitutional doctrine of the supremacy of the common law.[7] It was the same with this trust concept. It was preserved, and so developed that it became a unique body of doctrine.

We have seen that the Salman was the institution by means of which effect could be given to the broad principle, that a person to whom property had been given to the use of or on trust for another ought to

[1] For these continental developments see Holdsworth, H. E. L. iv. 220–8.

[2] Holdsworth, H. E. L. (3rd ed.), ii. 202–6, 267–86.

[3] Ibid. 287 and n. 4.

[4] Ibid. i. 314–20.

[5] Ibid. iii. 622, 632.

[6] Ibid. ii. 404–5.

[7] Ibid. 252–5, 441–2, iv. 187–9, 209.

fulfil his trust. Now the breadth of this principle made it capable of the most diverse applications. The Salman could be used as a testamentary executor, or as a bailee, or as an agent, or as a feoffee to whom land is conveyed on trust. But the position which the idea embodied in the institution of the Salman took in the developed common law was necessarily conditioned by the accidents of the history of the common law. That part of the law relating to the testamentary executor which was concerned with his duty to the legatee was turned over to the ecclesiastical courts. The ecclesiastical lawyers naturally adopted Roman analogies and spoke of him as a *heres* ; and in later days, when the court of Chancery had ousted the ecclesiastical courts, that court naturally applied to him many of the rules which it had evolved for the trustee. The duties of a bailee and an agent to their bailor, principal, or third parties, were enforced by the common law by means of developments in the personal actions. If, for instance, *A* handed chattels to *B* to the use of or for the benefit of *C*, and *B* did not hand them to *C*, *C* had a remedy. Blackstone saw that this was an application of the trust concept. After remarking that trusts were peculiarly within the province of the court of Chancery, he says,[1] 'There are other trusts which are cognizable in a court of law: as deposits and all manner of bailments; and especially that implied contract . . . of having undertaken to account for money received to another's use, which is the ground of an action on the case almost as universally remedial as a bill in equity.'

But by far the commonest of these uses and trusts

[1] Comm. iii. 432.

in the Middle Ages were uses and trusts of land. There were two main reasons for this. The first and most important was the fact that in the Middle Ages chattels consisted of such things as cattle, furniture, armour, or books, which are of a destructible character. Mainly for this reason permanent trusts of these things are not very common even at the present day. It was not until the seventeenth century, when we begin to see accumulations of capital invested in the form of transferable stock, that we get forms of personal property which partake of the permanent character of land. It was not till then that trusts of personalty became as general and important as trusts of realty. Secondly, in the Middle Ages the land law was the most important and the most highly developed branch of the common law. We have seen that it covered many relationships which, in later law, were taken over by the law of obligations.[1] As we might expect, the habit of conveying land to the use of or on trust for another was common;[2] and it was by no means certain in the age of Bracton that the common law would not recognize the interest of the person to whose use another held.[3] But, in 1379, all the judges were consulted by Parliament as to whether a request made by Edward III to his feoffees to uses could be recognized and enforced by the common law; and they replied unanimously that it could not, unless it complied with the strict rules relating to common law conditions.[4] Thus uses or trusts of land were banished from the common law.

[1] Above, p. 90. [2] P. and M. ii. 233.
[3] Bracton's Note Book, cases 641, 754, 999, 1244, 1683, 1851.
[4] Rot. Parl. ii. 61 (2 Richard II, no. 26).

But the use or trust of land was too convenient and too widespread an arrangement to disappear in consequence of this attitude of the common law. The attempt of the Franciscans to live without property illustrated its power on a European stage.[1] In England, as elsewhere, the friars soon found themselves in the position of *commodatarii*, or *usufructuarii*, or the beneficiaries of an 'opus' or 'usus'; and in 1279 the bull *Exiit qui Seminat* declared that this 'usus' was not property. But an arrangement which makes the legal owner of property the executor of the wishes of the beneficiary with regard to it, will enable the beneficiary to deal freely and easily and secretly with the property either in his lifetime or after his death. It will give the beneficiary all the advantages of property, and yet leave him subject to none of the legal liabilities which property entails. So valuable a device was not likely to be abandoned by owners of property because the common law declined to recognize it. But its adoption raised serious problems for the state. To ignore it wholly was to put a premium on fraud, which was quite contrary to the medieval idea that the ultimate purpose of the law was the maintenance of justice and equity. On the other hand, its protection might easily lead to frauds and evasions of legal liability, injurious both to individuals and the state. The way in which the problem was solved is the key to the reason why English law has developed its peculiar doctrines of uses and of trusts. On the one hand the interest of the beneficiary of the use was protected by the court of Chancery: on

[1] Lea, History of the Inquisition, iii. 5–8, 27–30, 130–46; P. and M. ii. 229, 235–6.

the other hand that interest was controlled by the Legislature. Let us examine briefly the effects of this protection and this control.

(1) We must, as we have seen, look to the Salman for the origin of the idea that property could be entrusted by its owner to a person who was bound to deal with it according to the wishes of the owner. But by far the most important application of that idea in English law arises from the manner in which the court of Chancery protected the interests of the person who had conveyed the property on trust, and of third persons for whose benefit it was thus conveyed on trust. The use or trust of to-day is the product of the equitable jurisdiction of the Chancellor.[1] Just as the original conception of equity—the conception that justice ought to be done even at the cost of non-compliance with the strict letter of the law—obtained in England a unique technical meaning because, owing to the rigidity of the common law, a separate court was entrusted with its administration;[2] so, for the same reason, the interest of the persons, to whose use another held property, acquired in English law a unique character. This will be apparent if we look at the manner in which the position, first of the feoffees to uses or trustees, and secondly of the *cestui-que* use or beneficiary was defined.

(i) At law the feoffees to uses or trustees were the absolute owners of the property of which they had been enfeoffed, and they were subject to all the liabilities of ownership. In equity they were compelled to

[1] Ames, Essays in Anglo-American Legal History, ii. 742.
[2] Holdsworth, H. E. L. (3rd ed.), i. 446–9.

use their powers as legal owners for the benefit of the *cestui-que* use. They must suffer him to take the profits of the land ; they must convey the land in accordance with his directions ; and they must take all necessary legal proceedings to defend the title to the land.

(ii) It thus appears that the rights of the *cestui-que* use or beneficiary was a right, not to the property, but against the feoffees to uses or trustees. In early days, it would seem, this right was of a strictly personal character, and that there was no remedy even against the heir of a foeffee. But in the course of the fifteenth century his rights were gradually enlarged by giving him a remedy against other persons. The Chancellor laid it down that the conscience of any one was affected by the use or trust who had taken the property with notice, actual or constructive,[1] of the use or trust, or who had taken the property gratuitously, whether or not he had notice of the use or trust. It was only if a person took the property for value and without notice, or by a title paramount to that of the foeffees or trustees, that he was not bound by the use or trust. Thus the interest of the beneficiary had become almost property—a right which was valid as against almost the whole world ; and this is the essence of the equitable ownership of our modern English law.

In moulding the incidents of this new equitable ownership the Chancellor started from the basis of the

[1] Broadly speaking, constructive notice means that knowledge which a man would have acquired, if he had taken care to make proper investigations ; for the technical rules which have resulted from the working out of this general idea see Cheshire, Real Property (3rd ed.), 56–7.

legal ownership of the common law. But he followed the law very critically—amending and supplementing it. In fact he compelled the feoffees to uses to carry out any directions given by the *cestui-que* use which were not positively illegal. Thus the *cestui-que* use got a large number of powers over the property which were denied to the legal owner by the strict rules of the common law. He got, for instance, a testamentary power; and there is no doubt that this was the chief cause for the popularity of uses.[1] He could create future estates in the land (shifting and springing uses) unknown to the common law;[2] and these shifting and springing uses were not subject to the strict rules applicable to remainders.[3] He could found charitable institutions and give directions for their management.[4] He was freed from the restraints of form which the common law imposed upon dispositions of property.[5] Above all he could escape from all the burdensome incidents of feudal tenure.[6] But, in thus moulding the incidents of the estate of the *cestui-que* use, the Chancellor had concentrated his attention upon the rights and powers of the *cestui-que* use. The question of his legal liabilities never

[1] Doctor and Student, ii. c. 22; Bacon, Reading on the Statute of Uses, Works (Ed. Spedding), vii. 409.

[2] Doctor and Student ii, c. 22.

[3] For remainders see above, pp. 67–8; below, pp. 189–97.

[4] Testamenta Eboracensia (Surt. Soc.) iii. 25, 158.

[5] As Bacon picturesquely put it, Reading at p. 420, 'Conveyances in uses were like privileged places or liberties; for as there the law doth not run, so upon such conveyances the law could take no hold.'

[6] The feoffees to uses were a body of joint tenants; if one died the property survived to the others, so that no relief was payable, there could be no escheat, and no wardship or marriage.

arose, as they were annexed to the legal estate. But some of the results of the wholesale evasion of legal liability, thereby rendered possible, were serious ; and so, very soon after the Chancellor had begun to convert the interest of the *cestui-que* use into a form of property, the Legislature found it necessary to intervene in the interests both of honest dealing and of public policy. Let us now turn to this legislative control which has had some though not nearly so great an influence as the action of the Chancellor in shaping the law of trusts.

(2) In the Middle Ages the Legislature intervened to prevent these uses or trusts from being used for purposes of fraud. As early as 1377 it interfered to prevent frauds upon creditors ;[1] in 1392 to prevent evasions of the statutes of mortmain ;[2] and in 1378 to prevent conveyances to the use of great lords, that they might maintain the doubtful title of the conveyor.[3] But it did little else. In particular it did nothing to prevent the evasion of the incidents of feudal tenure rendered possible by the use. It is clear that, long before the fifteenth century, any meaning which these incidents of tenure had once had, had departed. They were merely pecuniary exactions, profitable to the king or other lord entitled, and very burdensome to the tenant. Both the king and other lords lost by their evasion. But while the lords on the whole gained, because, though lords in respect of some parts of their possessions, they were tenants in respect of others, the king always lost. He alone was

[1] 50 Edward III, c. 6 ; cp. also 2 Richard II, st. 2, c. 3 ; 3 Henry VII, c. 5 ; 19 Henry VII, c. 15.

[2] 15 Richard II, c. 5.

[3] 1 Richard II, c. 9 ; cp. also 4 Henry IV, c. 7 ; 11 Henry VI, c. 3.

always lord and never tenant. To the medieval king who must not only live of his own, but also pay the expenses of government from the same source, this evasion of the incidents of tenure was a serious matter. The revenue of the state was gravely diminished. But, till the strength of the monarchy was restored by the House of Tudor, no king was strong enough to prevent this evasion. It was not till the reign of Henry VIII that any serious attempt was made to deal with this question; and, as we shall see, even Henry VIII found it no easy matter to induce Parliament to legislate upon it.

Thus, at the close of the medieval period, the development of uses and trusts had given rise to the equitable ownership of English law. Through the medium of trustees landowners had gained a large new series of powers over their property; and they could use these powers by the simple machinery of a direction to the feoffees to uses or trustees, which might be quite informal. Some of the problems, to which the rise of this new form of ownership had given rise, had been dealt with by the Legislature. We shall now see that it was its fiscal consequences which, in 1535, were the chief cause for the passing of the statute of Uses—the statute which has shaped the whole future history of uses and trusts of land.

§ 2. The Statutes of Uses and Wills.[1]

The statute of Uses[2] was perhaps the most important of all the statutes dealing with the law of real property. The need for a statute of Wills[3]

[1] Holdsworth, H. E. L., iv. 449–73.

[2] 27 Henry VIII, c. 10.

[3] 32 Henry VIII, c. 1.

was caused by the passing of the statute of Uses. We must therefore deal with these two statutes together; and, as the cause is greater than the effect, devote our chief attention to the statute of Uses.

Without a considerable knowledge of the legal history of the sixteenth and early seventeenth centuries we cannot understand the real meaning of the statute of Uses; and, in consequence of the absence of this knowledge, no statute has been more misunderstood. The causes for its enactment, the objects of its framers, the extent to which those objects were attained, and the far-reaching and permanent effects, direct and indirect, which it has had on all branches of the law of property, have been from time to time most diversely and, generally, most inaccurately estimated. Because at later periods in the history of the law some of the objects of the statute were frustrated, either by the new development of equitable doctrine which were called for by altered legal and social conditions, or by the ingenuity of conveyancers, its effects have been sometimes unduly minimized. The student is told almost in one breath that the only effect of the statute was to add three words to a conveyance, and that it is the foundation of the modern system of conveyancing. We can only avoid these paradoxes if we look at the matter historically and examine (i) the political causes which shaped the statute of Uses; (ii) the provisions of the statute and its immediate consequences; and (iii) the extent to which the framers of the statute succeeded in fulfilling the objects with which it was framed.

(i) The Political Causes of the Statute of Uses.

The immediate cause for the passing of the statute of Uses must be looked for in Henry VIII's fiscal necessities—just as the immediate cause for his Reformation legislation must be looked for in his matrimonial necessities. He wanted money badly, and the restoration of his feudal revenue (which was after all his own property) seemed to promise a permanent increase in the royal revenue. His earlier measures, proposed to attain this object, failed to pass the House of Commons, since they aroused the hostility of two very powerful interests in that House—the interest of the landowners and the interest of the lawyers. The statute of Uses of 1535 was a new and different attempt to tackle the problem. Henry won over the common lawyers to his side by playing upon the jealousy which they felt for the Chancery, and by producing a scheme for annexing the legal estate to certain uses of land, which gave their courts jurisdiction over the uses to which the legal estate had been thus annexed. By these means Henry got the statute through Parliament. At the same time he tried to induce Parliament to pass an elaborate bill for the registration of conveyances. If it had been passed, and had been efficiently carried out, we should have had to-day a series of county registers which would have considerably simplified the land law. We should not have been faced with the difficulty of fitting a scheme of registration on to a system which the large powers of landowners, and the ingenuity of conveyancers, have made more complex than any other modern system. But this bill failed to pass. Instead,

Parliament passed a short bill to provide for the enrolment, either in the courts at Westminster or in county registeries, of bargains and sales of freehold interests in land. We shall see that later this statute was evaded by the ingenuity of the conveyancers.[1]

This history of the political causes which shaped the statute of Uses enables us to appraise the preamble to the statute at its true historical value. Like the preambles to other statutes of this period, it is far from being a sober statement of historical fact. Rather it is an official statement of the numerous good reasons which had induced the government to pass so wise a statute—the sixteenth-century equivalent of a leading article in a government newspaper upon a government measure. It bears upon it the traces of the alliance between the king and the common lawyers by means of which the statute was carried through the House of Commons. It contains all the objections to uses which were the commonplaces of these lawyers —'the fraudulent feoffments, fines, recoveries, and other assurances craftily made to secret uses, intents and trusts'; the testaments made by dying men under the influence of greedy and covetous persons; the insecure titles of purchasers; the loss of dower and curtesy; the perjuries committed in the legal proceedings arising out of these secret uses. Skilfully insinuated among these objections, and holding by no means a prominent place, are those which the king felt so keenly—the loss of the incidents of tenure, of the lands of traitors, of land given to aliens, of the escheats of the lands of felons, and of the rights to year day and waste from the same lands.

[1] Below, pp. 159–60, 294–5.

Maitland has truly said that the statute of Uses 'was forced upon an extremely unwilling Parliament by an extremely strong-willed king'.[1] But I think that the evidence shows that this strong-willed king was obliged to conciliate the common lawyers in order to get the statute through the House of Commons; and that probably their opposition caused the failure of his well-considered scheme for the registration of conveyances. If this be so, the action of the common lawyers has had a large effect upon the form which the statute of Uses and the statute of Enrolments finally assumed, and, consequently, upon the whole of the future history of the law of real property.

(ii) The Statute and its Immediate Consequences.

The governing idea of the statute was to take the seisin or legal estate from the feoffees to uses, and vest it in the *cestui-que* use for the estate which he had in the use. The first clause in substance provides that when any person or persons were or should be seised of any lands or other hereditaments to the use of any other person or persons, or to the use of any body politic, for estates in the use in fee simple, fee tail, for life, or for years; then these other persons or bodies politic should be seised for the like estates which they had in the use; and the estates of which the feoffees were seised were, to the extent of these estates thus vested in the *cestui-que* use, to be taken from them. Thus if land were given to *A* and his heirs to the use of *B* and his heirs, *A*'s fee simple estate was by the statute taken from *A* and vested in *B*. But, as it was the estate of the feoffees which was taken from

[1] Equity, 35.

them, and vested in the *cestui-que* use, it was necessary to give the feoffees an estate sufficient to execute the use. If, for instance, land were given to *A* to the use of *B* and his heirs, *A*'s life estate was all that could pass to *B*, so that *B* would get, not a fee simple, but an estate *pur autre vie.* Conversely if the uses declared did not exhaust the feoffees' estate, they took beneficially what was left. Thus if land were given to *A* and his heirs to the use of *B*, *B* would get a legal life estate, with remainder in fee simple to *A*.

The words of the statute of Uses make it clear that there was no intention to abolish uses. As Bacon points out in his Reading on the statute,[1] both this statute and the statute of Enrolments provide not only for uses then existing, but also for uses that shall be hereafter. What it did intend to do was to execute or turn into legal estates the uses to which it applied, in order that the various evils, which the preamble attributed to the division between the legal and equitable ownership, might be avoided. It is also reasonably clear that the statute did not apply to all uses. (1) The first clause deals only with the case where one is *seised* to the use of another. Seeing that when the statute was passed the word ‘ seisin ’ had come to be exclusively applicable to hereditaments,[2] it could not apply when one was *possessed* of chattels real or personal to the use of another. Though the words of the first clause made it clear that it applies where *A* is seised to *B*'s use for a term of years, it does not apply where *A* is possessed of a term to the use of *B*. (2) The words of the first clause are applicable only to the case where *A* is seised to the use of *B*, i.e. where *A* is

[1] Works (Ed. Spedding), vii. 422.

[2] Above, p. 122.

under the merely passive duty of allowing *B* to occupy the land for the estate limited to him by the instrument settling the uses, or by other directions given to the feoffees. It was in such cases that the evils mentioned in the preamble arose. *B* was in possession of the land and apparently owner; but he escaped all the liabilities of ownership, and had great opportunities for the defrauding of purchasers. It is quite another case where the feoffees are in possession and have active duties to perform. The evils of divided ownership do not arise in such a case; and to have taken away from the feoffees their legal estate would have made it impossible for them to carry out their trust.

But though the statute did not take away the power of creating uses, though it did not even execute all uses, it certainly executed what was the most numerous class of uses. It therefore subjected landowners, entitled to the benefit of these uses, to all the liabilities and disabilities of legal ownership; and, worst of all, it took away from them the power of devising their lands.

Naturally the statute was not popular with the landowners. In fact, so much hostility did it arouse that it was a factor in aggravating the danger of the rebellion known as the Pilgrimage of Grace. That rebellion was no doubt caused chiefly by the religious changes; but it would seem that the abolition of the power to devise was the cause which induced the landed gentry to side with the rebels. Henry was never under any illusions as to the limitations upon his own powers. He knew how important it was to secure the adhesion of a class upon whom the working of the local government depended. Five years later, therefore, he restored in a large measure the power to devise lands. The Wills Act of 1540 [1] in substance allowed landowners to dispose by will of all their lands held for an estate in fee simple [2] by socage tenure, and of two-thirds of their land held for an estate in fee simple by knight service. Hence, when tenure of knight service was abolished in 1660,[3] all restrictions upon the power to make a will of lands held by a free tenure for an estate in fee simple disappeared.[4]

The statute of Wills was the direct result of the statute of Uses. The king got back some part of those rights of which the practice of settling lands to uses had almost entirely deprived him; and the permanent settlement of these rights, by the Act of 1540, was marked by the establishment, in the same year, of a new court—the Court of Wards—entrusted with the duty of seeing that they were duly enforced.[5] On the other hand the landowners retained a large part of the power to devise which they had enjoyed for upwards of a century. The breadth of the terms in which that power was conferred created a new kind of future interest in the land—the executory devise—which differed entirely from legal remainders, and in some respects from future interests created by way of shifting and springing use.

[1] 32 Henry VIII, c. 1.

[2] 34, 35 Henry VIII, c. 5.

[3] Above, pp. 36–7.

[4] Land held by copyhold tenure did not come within these statutes; but in the sixteenth century a custom had become general, though not quite universal, to allow a copyholder to surrender his land to the use of his will, see Holdsworth, H. E. L. vii. 366–7.

[5] 32 Henry VIII, c. 46.

(iii) To What Extent did the Statute fulfil its Objects?

The objects of the statute of Uses can be grouped under the four following heads: (1) the restoration to the king of his revenue from the incidents of tenure; (2) the abolition of the power to devise; (3) the restoration of publicity of conveyance; (4) the abolition, in the case of uses to which the statute applied, of the separation between legal and equitable ownership.

We have seen that the statute accomplished the first two of these objects so effectually that it helped to cause rebellion; and that the king found it expedient to restore partially the power to devise, and to suffer the consequent diminution of his revenue from the incidents of tenure. The third object was attained because the statute of Enrolments, which must be regarded as an integral part of the statute of Uses, required the enrolment of all bargains and sales of freehold interest in land. It is true that the statute made no provision for covenants to stand seised;[1] nor did its framers foresee that ingenious conveyancers would evade the statute of Enrolments by the devise of a bargain and sale for a term of years followed by a release. But we cannot expect the framers of any statute to possess prophetic foresight. The covenant to stand seised was not a recognized form of conveyance at the time that the statute was passed;[2] and it was not till many years later that the validity of the method of evading the statute of Enrolments,

[1] For this conveyance see below, pp. 292–3.

[2] See Holdsworth, H. E. L. iv. 425–6.

by means of a bargain and sale for a term of years, was finally established.[1]

The question whether the statute succeeded in accomplishing the fourth of these objects, by abolishing the separation between the legal and the equitable ownership, is rather more complicated. In the first place, we must remember that the statute did not attempt to abolish this separation in all cases. We have seen that it did not apply either to the case where *A* is possessed of chattels real or personal to the use of *B*, or to the case where the trustee has active duties to perform. The question is, did it succeed in attaining its object in the case to which it did apply, i.e. where *A* is seised of hereditaments to the use that he permits *B* to enjoy the property. The answer is that it did succeed for about a century, because both the courts of common law and the court of Chancery set their faces against any attempt to evade the statute by the limitation of a use upon a use.

The technical reason for this decision, which is generally known as the rule in *Tyrrel's Case*,[2] was that the second use, being inconsistent with the first, was on that account void. If, for instance, *A* were seised to the use of *B* to the use of *C*, *B* took the legal estate by the effect of the statute and *C* took nothing. The substantial reason for the decision was that if *C* had been allowed by the court of Chancery to take an equitable estate, the king would again have been defrauded of his feudal revenue. The Chancellor, being a great officer of state, was the last person to coun-

[1] The validity of this device was upheld in *Lutwich* v. *Mitton* (1621) Cro. Jac. 604; see below pp. 293–5.

[2] Dyer 155a; Benloe 61; 1 And. 37, pl. 96.

tenance such a device. It is true that, early in the seventeenth century, there are some hints that in a case of fraud the Chancellor would enforce the second use as a trust.[1] But it is not till after 1660, when the feudal incidents had been abolished, that the court of Chancery finally decided to enforce the second use as a trust in all cases.[2] It was not till this result had been achieved, more than a hundred years after the passing of the statute, that it can be said that it had failed to effect a union between the legal and equitable estate in the cases to which it applied.

We must now consider the general effects of these statutes on the land law.

§ 3. THE EFFECTS OF THESE STATUTES ON THE LAND LAW.

The uses executed by the statute of Uses, and thus brought within the sphere of common law jurisdiction, gave a much-needed elasticity to the land law, and enabled this essentially medieval body of law to be adapted to the changed commercial, industrial, and agricultural conditions of the sixteenth and seventeenth centuries. With the history of the technical developments in the law, by means of which they produced this result, I shall deal in the following chapter. Here I shall only indicate in brief outline the manner in which they influenced the future development of the land law.

The broad result of the conversion of the uses affected by the statute into legal estates was a large addition to the powers of the landowner, and an im-

[1] *Sambach* v. *Dalston* (1633–4), Tothill 188; cp. Holdsworth, H. E. L. v. 307–9.

[2] Ibid. vi. 641–2.

provement in the means by which these powers were exercised. Since the statute was not accompanied by any large reforms of the land law, landowners retained all their existing powers of dealing with their property, and, in addition, gained the new powers and the improved modes of exercising them, which were rendered possible by the machinery of the use. The skill with which the conveyancers availed themselves of the position, which the statute had created, enabled landowners to make full use of their opportunities; and they used them with very little interference on the part of the Legislature. The chief limitation on their freedom of action came, not from the Legislature, but from the courts.

We have seen that, from an early period, the courts had been astute to prevent any direct restrictions upon freedom of alienation.[1] The readiness with which they had allowed the estate tail to be barred by the device of a common recovery, showed that they were equally astute to prevent the indefinite fettering of that freedom by the means of unbarrable entails,[2] even when the creation of these entails had the sanction of the Legislature; and the restrictions which they placed upon contingent remainders were inspired by the same policy.[3] It was soon seen that the limiting of land in perpetuity to a successsion of limited owners could be very easily effected by the machinery of the use. But we shall see that, from the latter part of the seventeenth century, the courts, by applying to some of these interests the rules applicable to legal contingent remainders, and by applying to others principles which eventually developed into the

[1] Above, p. 108. [2] Above, pp. 57–60. [3] Below, pp. 221–2.

modern rule against perpetuities, prescribed the utmost length of time for which future limited interests in all kinds of property could lawfully be made to endure.[1]

Subject to this restriction, landowners were able to use the new facilities which were now at their disposal very much as they pleased. We get therefore, in the first place, a much greater variety in the nature of the interests which could be created in the land, and, in the second place, a development in the machinery by which both these and other interests could be created or transferred.

(i) At common law a man could not convey an interest to himself or his wife. This was quite possible by means of the machinery of the use; and it was found to be convenient when it was wished to change trustees or to settle property on marriage. At common law the only future interests in land which it was possible to create were reversions, and remainders vested or contingent; and, as we shall see, the liability of the contingent remainder to failure or destruction rendered it a precarious estate.[2] But future legal estates could now be created by means of shifting and springing uses and executory devises. It was ultimately held that they were not liable to failure or destruction in the same manner as legal contingent remainders; and the rules affecting their creation were not so rigid. At common law it was not as a rule possible to separate the power of disposition over land from the estate in the land. It was not possible to give to *A* a limited interest, and to give either to *A* or to some third person, who had no estate in the land,

[1] Below, pp. 223–7.

[2] Below, pp. 194–5.

a disposing power over the fee simple. But such powers of appointment could be created by means of uses.[1] Moreover a settlor of property could give a power to revoke the uses declared, and to appoint to fresh uses. When the appointment was made the feoffees stood seised to the use of the appointee, the statute executed the use in his favour, and so gave him the legal estate. The best illustration of the manner in which the conveyancers made use of these new facilities was the modern strict settlement of land. A person seised in fee simple was able to convey the property to trustees to the use of himself and his heirs till marriage, and from and after marriage to the use of himself for life, with remainder to the use of his eldest and other sons successively in tail, with remainder to his right heirs. The claims of his widow and younger children could be met by rent charges on the property, secured by limiting long terms of years to the use of the trustees, in priority to the estates tail; and, if it was desired to give larger powers over the property either to the life tenant or the trustees, in the interest either of the family or of the needs of estate management, this could be accomplished by means of powers of appointment.

(ii) The methods by which lands could be settled or conveyed were simplified. The law will not, for three hundred years, allow that corporeal hereditaments lie in grant;[2] but a long step in that direction was taken when it became possible to limit a use by deed, and when the statute annexed the legal estate to the person in whose favour the limitation was made. When the ingenuity of the conveyancers evaded the

[1] Below, pp. 207–8.
[2] 8, 9 Victoria, c. 106, § 2.

requirement of enrolment,[1] the landowner acquired not only a convenient, but also a secret method of conveyance.

These new powers acquired by landowners had both their strong and their weak points. They enabled land to be settled in such a way that, while it devolved as one estate upon the eldest son, provision could be made out of it for other members of the family. Thus a succession of substantial landowners was created, who, in the seventeenth and eighteenth centuries, did good service in administering the local government of the country, in improving its agricultural condition, and in imparting an element of social stability. On the other hand, these large powers of disposition, coupled with secret modes of exercising them, caused inevitably a large amount of complication in the law. The manner in which the new law was pieced on to the old added to the complication thus caused. It made dealings in land expensive, because the whole history of the property must, on the occasion of each purchase, be critically examined by an expert. In the sixteenth, seventeenth, and eighteenth centuries the political and social advantages of the large powers acquired by the landowners probably outweighed the evils arising from the necessary complications in the land law which resulted therefrom. But changes in economic conditions, and in the political and social organization of the state, have gradually destroyed these compensating advantages. They have created a demand for simplification, which the legislation of the nineteenth and twentieth centuries, culminating in the Property Acts, has attempted to meet.[2]

[1] Above, pp. 159–60; below, p. 294. [2] Below, pp. 310–24.

The influence of equitable trusts on the land law in the latter part of the seventeenth and in the eighteenth centuries has been as great as the influence of the uses executed by the statute of Uses. They were designed to suit modern needs, and they were free from many of the technical defects of the medieval use. It is for this reason that the equitable trust has, as the result of the Property Acts, swallowed up both the use and the remainders and reversions recognized by the common law.[1] The statute of Uses has been repealed; and the only two legal estates in the land are a fee simple absolute in possession and a term of years absolute. But the Law of Property Act 1925 provides that ' interests in land validly created or arising after the commencement of this Act, which are not capable of existing as legal estates, shall take effect as equitable interests, and . . . interests in land which under the statute of Uses or otherwise could before the commencement of this Act have been created as legal interests, shall be capable of being created as equitable interests.' [2]

§ 4. OTHER DEVELOPMENTS IN THE LAND LAW.

The other developments in the land law can be grouped under two main heads. First, there are several statutory changes in the law ; and, secondly, there is the development by the courts of the action of ejectment—a development which, as we shall see in the next chapter,[3] had most important effects on the substantive law as to the seisin and possession of land.

[1] Law of Property Act, 1925, § 1 (3) and (8).

[2] § 4 (1).

[3] Below, pp. 179–83.

Statutory Changes.

The statute of Uses was designed to suppress a mode of defrauding creditors and purchasers by putting an end, in the cases to which the statute applied, to the separation of the legal from the equitable estate. But further legislation was found to be necessary. A statute of 1571 [1] made void gifts of lands or goods with intent to defraud creditors; and a statute of 1584–5 [2] provided for the case of conveyances of land made with intent to defraud subsequent purchasers. The construction put upon the latter statute was remarkable. The courts, faced with the difficulty of proving a fraudulent intent, adopted the device of inferring fraud from the existence of certain specified circumstances.[3] They laid it down that if *A* made a voluntary conveyance to *B*, and then afterwards, at however great a distance of time, attempted to convey the same proprety to *C* for value, the conveyance to *B* must be deemed to have been made with intent to defraud a subsequent purchaser, and so was void. This construction was overruled by the Voluntary Conveyances Act 1893.[4] Both these statutes of Elizabeth's reign are repealed, and re-enacted with some modifications by the Law of Property Act 1925.[5]

A statute of 1540 fixed definite periods for the limitation of certain of the real actions; [6] and in 1623 a statute fixed the period of twenty years for the exercise of a right of entry.[7] As no action of ejectment lay unless the claimant had a right of entry,

[1] 13 Elizabeth, c. 5.
[2] 27 Elizabeth, c. 4.
[3] Holdsworth, H. E. L. iv. 481.
[4] 56, 57 Victoria, c. 21.
[5] §§ 172, 173; see Cheshire, Real Property (3rd ed.), 730–6.
[6] 32 Henry VIII, c. 2.
[7] 21 James I, c. 16.

and as the action of ejectment was rapidly superseding the real actions, this statute was of far greater practical importance than the statute of 1540.[1]

Two statutes gave further protection to the lessee for years. We have seen that, by the beginning of the fifteenth century, the interest of the lessee for years had gained adequate protection by the development and improvement of the action of ejectment.[2] But he was still liable to be ousted by a fictitious recovery of which he had no notice. A statute of 1529 [3] allowed him to falsify these recoveries in the same way as a freeholder was already able to do. But the practice of settling lands in such a way that the freeholder in actual possession had only a limited interest exposed him to another danger. On the determination of the freeholder's interest his lessee was liable to be ejected by the heir or other person entitled in succession. To permit this was quite contrary to the policy of the statutes for the encouragement of tillage; [4] and so a statute of 1540 [5] gave the lessee some protection by providing that, under certain conditions, certain leases made by certain limited owners should be good as against their heirs and successors, as if made by a tenant in fee simple. We must wait till the nineteenth century before we get any large extension of the policy of this statute.[6]

In the law of landlord and tenant the most important change was made by a statute of 1540,[7] which permitted certain covenants in leases to run with the

[1] Holdsworth, H. E. L. iv. 484–5.
[2] Above, p. 72.
[3] 21 Henry VIII, c. 15.
[4] Above, pp. 43, 72–3.
[5] 32 Henry VIII, c. 28, amended by 34, 35 Henry VIII, c. 22.
[6] Below, pp. 210–12.
[7] 32 Henry VIII, c. 34.

reversion. It was passed in consequence of the large transfer of reversionary interests which resulted from the dissolution of the monasteries. I shall deal with its effects in the following chapter.[1]

None of these statutes covers any very large amount of ground. But taken together they effect some very practical and valuable reforms. From the end of the seventeenth century until the beginning of the nineteenth century the development of the land law was left almost entirely to the courts, with very little help or hindrance from the Legislature. And so these statutes long retained their importance. Some of them have only been repealed by modern statutes which carry out their policy more completely. Without their assistance it would hardly have been possible for the courts to develop our modern law of real property from its medieval basis.

The Action of Ejectment.[2]

We have seen that the action of ejectment was a form of the action of trespass, which was used to protect the tenant for a term of years; that at first only damages could be recovered in this action; but that in the year 1499 it was finally settled that the term itself could be recovered.[3] The action had thus come to possess the leading characteristic of the real actions; and, in the course of the sixteenth and the following centuries, its machinery and incidents were so skilfully adapted to the performance of the functions of these real actions, that it almost entirely superseded them. As early as 1601 Coke was able to say that 'at

[1] Below, pp. 250–3.

[2] Holdsworth, H. E. L. vii. 4–23.

[3] Above, p. 72.

this day all titles of lands are for the greatest part tried in actions of ejectments'.[1]

There were three main reasons why the action of ejectment superseded the real actions. First, the procedure in these actions was lengthy, technical, and tricky. The action of ejectment, because it was a form of the action of trespass, was relatively speedy and free from technicality. Secondly, the real actions were numerous and narrow in their scope—it was easy to fail because the wrong form of action had been chosen. The form of the action of ejectment was always the same, and it applied to all forms of land holding—copyhold and leasehold as well as freehold.[2] Thirdly, the courts favoured the action of ejectment. The real actions were the monopoly of the court of Common Pleas, but the action of ejectment could be brought in any of the common law courts. In fact the marked declension of the court of Common Pleas as compared with the King's Bench, dates from the virtual supersession of the real actions by the action of ejectment.[3]

The conversion of an action, which was originally designed to protect a lessee for years from unlawful ejectment, to an action which was capable of settling questions of title to the freehold, obviously required from the courts which controlled it much skilful management. Both the machinery and the character and incidents of the action needed to be manipulated; and, during the course of the sixteenth, seventeenth,

[1] *Alden's Case* (1601), 5 Co. Rep. at f. 105 b.

[2] Land held in Ancient Demesne, above, pp. 131–3, was the only land to which it did not apply.

[3] Holdsworth, H. E. L. (3rd ed.) i. 199–200.

and eighteenth centuries, they were so skilfully manipulated that the cases in which the action would not serve all the purposes of landowners were quite exceptional.

The procedure in the action was as follows: The person claiming the freehold entered upon the land, and, being thus in possession, he made a lease to a lessee and left him in possession. The lessee remained in possession till the tenant of the land or any other person ejected him. The lessee could then bring the action of ejectment against the tenant, or any one else who had ejected him. Such other person, who might be wholly unconnected with the land, was known as the 'casual ejector'. But it soon became clear that the casual ejector, the lessor of the plaintiff lessee, and the lessee might all be conspiring to deprive the actual tenant of his land. To obviate this abuse, the courts made a rule that a plaintiff could not recover land against a casual ejector without giving notice to the tenant, by delivering to him a copy of the declaration [1] in the action. The tenant was thus enabled to intervene if he wished to do so.

The plaintiff, in order to succeed in his action, must prove four things: first the lease under which he claimed, secondly his entry under the lease, thirdly his ouster by the defendant, and fourthly the title of his lessor to grant the lease. It was the need to prove this fourth point which brought in the question of the title to the freehold; and, when the action was used to try title, it was the only real point in the case. The preliminary lease, entry, and ouster were merely machinery. But they were necessary machinery;

[1] The declaration is the plaintiff's statement of claim.

and the whole complicated process was gone through till the time of the Commonwealth, when a method was invented which rendered it unnecessary in almost all cases. This new method was soon generally adopted; and it continued to be used till the reforms of the nineteenth century. It depended, as Blackstone says,[1] 'upon a string of legal fictions'.

A lease for years was stated to have been made by the person claiming title (whom we will call Smith) to a lessee—John Doe. John Doe was stated to have entered, and Richard Roe—the casual ejector—was stated to have ejected him. For this ejectment John Doe brought his action against Richard Roe; but, so soon as the action was begun, and the declaration delivered, Richard Roe sent a written notice to the tenant in possession of the lands (whom we will call Saunders), signed 'your loving friend Richard Roe', stating that an action had been brought against him by John Doe and that he did not intend to make any defence, and therefore advising Saunders to appear in court and apply to be made defendant in the action. Upon Saunders making this application, he was allowed to come in and defend, upon the terms of admitting the fictitious lease by Smith to Doe, the fictitious entry by Doe, and Doe's fictitious ouster by Roe. Thus the real point at issue, namely, whether Smith the plaintiff or Saunders the defendant had the better title, was the only point left to be decided by the court. The action to try this point was entitled *Doe d.*[2] *Smith* v. *Saunders*.

The one respect in which the real actions were superior to the action of ejectment was the fact that

[1] Comm. iii. 203.

[2] i.e. on the demise of.

they did, and the action of ejectment did not, finally settle the question of title between the parties and their representatives. Since the action of ejectment was only an action of trespass, a verdict in one action was no bar to another action for a new and different trespass. This defect was remedied by the combined action of the court of Chancery and the courts of common law. In the earlier half of the seventeenth century, the court of Chancery issued injunctions against persons who brought repeated actions of ejectment to try the same title ; and the legality of the issue of these injunctions, for the purpose of preventing such vexatious litigation, was upheld by the House of Lords in 1709 in the case of *Earl of Bath* v. *Sherwin*.[1] A better remedy was devised by the courts of common law themselves in the latter half of the seventeenth century. They refused to allow a second action between the same parties till the costs of the first action were paid ; and, in the eighteenth century, they refused to allow a second action till the costs of the first were paid, whether or not it was between the same parties, if 'the second ejectment was in substance brought to try the same title'.[2] The rule in this form seems to have succeeded in stopping most litigants from trying to bring repeated actions on the same facts. Thus the action of ejectment got the two most characteristic features of the real actions—a capacity for giving the plaintiff specific recovery, and a certain measure of finality.

There were, however, certain limitations on its sphere. It was a common law action ; and, in spite of

[1] 4 Bro. P.C. 373.

[2] *Kene d. Angel* v. *Angel* (1796), 6 T.R. 740.

the attempt of Lord Mansfield to anticipate the Judicature Acts by recognizing equitable titles, no account could be taken of these titles. It did not lie for purely incorporeal hereditaments;[1] and there were certain cases in which a plaintiff, because he had no right of entry, was thrown back on to the real actions. But, in spite of these defects, it is clear from the report of the Commissioners who reported on the law of real property in 1829, and of the Commissioners who reported on the courts of common law in 1830, that the real actions were dead. They were abolished in 1833,[2] so that the action of ejectment was left as the only action for the recovery of interests in land. The procedure in this action was simplified in 1852;[3] but it was not till the forms of action were abolished by the Judicature Act of 1873 that the rule that ejectment would not lie for a purely incorporeal hereditament became meaningless;[4] and it was not till the fusion of courts created by that Act that Lord Mansfield's ideal was realized, and that effect could be given in one action—now called 'an action for the recovery of land'—to both the legal and the equitable rights of landowners. The result of these changes is that the only limitation on the sphere of the action for the recovery of land is one which it has in

[1] It was thought that as there could be no physical possession of an incorporeal thing there could be no entry upon it; as there was no right of entry ejectment did not lie; this defect was remedied by another application of the action of trespass on the case, see Holdsworth H. E. L., vii. 21–2.

[2] 3, 4 William IV, c. 27, § 36; for the three exceptional cases in which they were not abolished see Holdsworth, H. E. L. vii. 22 n. 5; Maitland, Forms of Action, 301–2.

[3] 15, 16 Victoria c. 76, §§ 168–221.

[4] Maitland, Forms of Action, 354–5.

common with all other actions—liability to be barred by the statutes of limitation.

The changes and developments which had been made by the Legislature and the courts during the sixteenth and early seventeenth centuries were the foundation upon which the modern land law was developed, from its medieval basis, during the latter part of the seventeenth, the eighteenth, and the early nineteenth centuries. To the history of its development during these centuries we must now turn.

CHAPTER III

THE DEVELOPMENT OF THE MODERN LAND LAW (1660–1833)

On the basis of the medieval land law, and of the new developments made by the Legislature and the legal profession in the sixteenth and early seventeenth centuries, the lawyers of the late seventeenth, the eighteenth, and early nineteenth centuries built up the fabric of the modern land law. I shall relate the history of their achievement under the following heads: § 1 Seisin, Possession, and Ownership; § 2 Future Interests; § 3 Powers of Appointment; § 4 The Rules against Perpetuities; § 5 Landlord and Tenant; § 6 Mortgages; § 7 Incorporeal things; § 8 The Statutes of Limitation and Prescription; § 9 Conveyancing; § 10 General Conclusions.

§ 1. Seisin, Possession, and Ownership [1]

Throughout the sixteenth, seventeenth, and eighteenth centuries the medieval rules as to seisin and disseisin [2] were being modified; but they were still the basis upon which the law on this topic rested; they might have very important consequences; and they made the law very complex. At the same time a new body of rules as to possession and ownership was growing up round the actions of trespass *quare clausum fregit*, and ejectment. These rules were in some respects the same as the medieval

[1] Holdsworth, H. E. L. vii. 23–81.

[2] For these rules see above, pp. 121–31.

rules as to seisin and disseisin, and in other respects they were very different. But they were a far more generalized body of rules than the medieval rules, because they were, from the first, applicable to copyholds and terms of years as well as to freeholds, and because they came to be applied to equitable as well as to legal estates.

I shall deal with this topic under the following heads: (1) The medieval rules and their modification; (2) The new rules which grew up round the actions of trespass *quare clausum fregit* and ejectment; (3) The application of these rules to equitable estates; (4) The effect of the statutory changes of the nineteenth century.

(1) The medieval rules and their modification.

I have already said something of the powers of the disseisor and the disabilities of the disseisee in the medieval period.[1] We have seen that in the medieval period modifications had been made in the law in favour of the disseisee. Further modifications were made during these centuries.[2] The tendency, which was beginning to be apparent at the close of the medieval period, to regard seisin not merely as physical possession, but as a physical possession to which a person had a right—to connect seisin with title—became more pronounced. Thus a person who had a right to get physical possession (e.g. an heir on the death of an ancestor), but who had not yet entered on the property, was said to have a seisin in law; and, because he had a seisin in law, he was given some of the rights of the person actually seised—e.g. his

[1] Above, pp. 125–6. [2] Holdsworth, H. E. L. vii. 31–46.

wife was entitled to dower.[1] Again, under the statute of Uses, seisin could be acquired or transferred without any physical delivery of possession.[2] This helped to differentiate seisin from physical possession,[3] and to give it some of the characteristics of a right. It is not surprising, therefore, that Coke should be able to say that the disseisee 'had the land to many purposes'.[4]

But, in spite of these developments, the medieval principle was still the governing principle of the common law. In the first place, though there had been some curtailment of the disseissor's rights as against the disseisee, his rights as against the world at large remained unimpaired. It was still true that the disseisor gained a tortious fee simple. It was a fee simple because a wrongdoer cannot qualify his wrong; and, being a fee simple, he could create estates out of it which disabled the owner, when he recovered his property, from bringing actions of trespass against the alienees of the disseisor, because these alienees had come in by title. In the second place, the disseisee could not alienate his property,[5] and his widow was not entitled to dower.[6] It is true that the disseisee had a right of action, unless that right was barred either by the levying of a fine, or by the statutes of limitation. It is true that he had in most cases a right

[1] Holdsworth, H. E. L. vii. 28. [2] Above, p. 164; below, p. 290.

[3] Seisin thus acquired by force of the statute of Uses is distinct from the physical possession needed to support an action of trespass, *Cook* v. *Harris* (1699), 1 Ld. Raym. at p. 367; *Harrison* v. *Blackburn* (1864), 17, C. B. N. S. at p. 691.

[4] *Butler and Baker's Case* (1591), 3 Co. Rep. 35a.

[5] Above, p. 126; Holdsworth, H. E. L. vii. 48, 50–1.

[6] Ibid. 48.

of entry; and, when he had a right of entry, the right to bring the action of ejectment. But there still survived certain anomalous cases in which he had no right of entry.

Lord Mansfield, in the famous case of *Taylor* v. *Horde*,[1] tried to curtail the powers of a disseisor, and to enlarge the rights of the disseisee, by a new definition of seisin and disseisin. Though his views on this matter were proved not to be law, he interpreted rightly the trend of legal development; and we shall see that, in the nineteenth century, the Legislature has effected all and more than all that he desired to effect by his decision in *Taylor* v. *Horde*. That it was able easily to effect these reforms was due largely to the developments in the law of ownership and possession, which had been effected by the working of the actions of trespass *quare clausum fregit* and ejectment.

(2) *The new rules which grew up round the actions of trespass* quare clausum fregit *and ejectment.*

The working of the action of trespass and its offshoots has played a large part in the creation of our modern common law. The action of assumpsit created our modern law of contract and quasi-contract; the action of trover and conversion created our modern law as to the possession and ownership of chattels personal; and, similarly, the actions of trespass *quare clausum fregit* and ejectment created a large part of our modern law as to the possession and ownership of interests in land. In all three cases the newer action

[1] (1757) 1 Burr. 60. For the facts see Holdsworth, H. E. L. vii. 55–6; for Lord Mansfield's views see ibid. 43–6.

almost superseded the older forms of action. Just as assumpsit superseded debt, and trover detinue, so trespass *quare clausum fregit* and ejectment superseded the real actions. But the new law as to ownership and possession of land, which grew up around the actions of trespass and ejectment, did not supersede the old law, which had grown up round the real actions, as completely as the new law as to contract and the ownership and possession of chattels, which grew up round the actions of assumpsit and trover, superseded old law which had grown up round the actions of debt and detinue. This was mainly due to two causes. First, the law which had grown up round the real actions was a far fuller and more elaborate body of law than that which had grown up round the older personal actions ; and, secondly, the real actions were not so completely superseded. There were cases in which it was still necessary to have recourse to them. The medieval principles, therefore, continued to lead an active existence side by side with the modern principles ; and this combination of medieval and modern principles made the law on these topics very complicated. The legislation of the nineteenth century simplified it by eliminating the medieval principles, and adopting the modern principles, which had grown up round the two actions of trespass *quare clausum fregit* and ejectment. These modern principles, shortly stated, are as follows :

(i) The medieval principle that seisin or possession was title as against all the world, except as against those who could show a better title,[1] was a principle as well recognized in the action of trespass as in the

[1] Above, p. 125 seqq.

real actions. This principle is the foundation of the decisions in the modern cases, which lay down in perfectly clear terms that mere possession is sufficient to enable a possessor to bring trespass against a wrongdoer.[1] Exactly the same principle is applicable to the possession of chattels. Whether mere possession was also sufficient to enable a possessor without title to sue a trespasser by action of ejectment was not clearly settled till the nineteenth century; but the better opinion was that it was sufficient; and this is now the law.[2] Here, too, the same principle is applied to an action for the conversion of a chattel brought against a trespasser who has converted it. Thus the medieval principle that possession is ownership as against all the world, except as against those who can show a better title, having been maintained in the law of this period, remains part of our modern law.[3]

(ii) If, on the other hand, a disseised or dispossessed owner were suing a person in possession of his property, who had not got possession of it by a trespass committed against him, he must bring the action of ejectment; and to succeed in this action he must show a legal right to enter and take physical possession, which is not barred by the statutes of limitation. In other words, though possession is title as against those who can show no better title, any one who can show a better legal right to enter, which is not barred, can successfully sue the possessor. Here again the land law and the law as to chattels run on parallel lines.

[1] *Graham* v. *Peat* (1801), 1 East 243.

[2] *Davison* v. *Gent* (1857), 1 H. and N. 744.

[3] *Perry* v. *Clissold*, [1907] A. C. 73.

(iii) The question now arises what sort of right must the plaintiff prove? Is it merely a better right than the defendant's, such as the demandant in a writ of right or writ of entry must prove as against the tenant? Or, must he prove a right good as against all the world? This is a very fundamental question, because, upon the answer to it depends the nature of the right asserted in this action, and, therefore, the nature of the ownership of land recognized by English law. If the plaintiff need only prove a better right than the defendant's, then modern English law would, like the medieval law,[1] have continued to refuse to recognize anything like an abstract *dominium* or ownership which is good as against all the world. It would only have recognized relatively good or relatively bad rights to possession. If, on the other hand, the plaintiff, in order to succeed in this action, must prove an absolutely good right, then it would be true to say that through this action the conception of an abstract *dominium* or ownership, which is good as against all the world, has come into modern English law.

After some hesitation it was settled that the plaintiff in ejectment must show an absolutely good right.[2] In this way, and by this road, English law has acquired a conception of an abstract right of absolute ownership which is good as against the whole world. It follows that a defendant can resist the claim of a plaintiff by showing that this right belongs to a third person; for, if it belongs to a third person, it cannot belong to the plaintiff. In other words, a *jus tertii* is a good defence to an action of ejectment when the

[1] Above, pp. 125, 128. [2] Holdsworth, H. E. L. vii. 62–4.

plaintiff is suing a defendant who has committed no trespass against him.[1]

These principles of the modern law were all elucidated during the eighteenth and nineteenth centuries by decisions in actions of trespass and ejectment. We shall now see that they were applied by the Chancellors to equitable estates.

(3) The application of these rules to equitable estates.

Lord Mansfield's attempt to give effect to equitable rights in the common law action of ejectment deservedly failed.[2] The courts of law refused to recognize the title of the equitable owner. The trustee was, in their view, the owner; and the *cestui-que* trust a person who had a merely precarious and permissive enjoyment at the will of the trustee. Therefore the principles of the law as to the ownership and possession of equitable estates were shaped by the court of Chancery. In constructing these principles equity did what it had done before the passing of the statute of Uses—it followed the law. But it found itself able to follow the more reasonable rules of the modern common law more closely than the rules of the medieval common law. The medieval common law had concentrated its attention on the fact of seisin and had given all the rights and privileges of ownership to the person seised. Equity, on the other hand, concentrated its attention on the rights of the equitable owner. There was little in common between points of view which were so diverse.

But, by the beginning of the eighteenth century, we can see signs of an approximation between the

[1] Ibid., 65–6. [2] Above, pp. 173–4.

legal and equitable conceptions of ownership and possession. Through the working of the action of ejectment the common law was beginning to acquire the conception of an abstract right of ownership.[1] On the other hand, equity was beginning to be faced with the problem of settling the position of the possessor of an equitable estate who had no title thereto. Suppose that the legal estate was outstanding in the possession of a trustee who had no active duties to perform, the equitable estate might be in the possession of a *cestui-que* trust who had no title to it.[2] In a case of this kind equity found it necessary to recognize not only the rights of the owner, but also the rights of a possessor—just as the common law had found it necessary to recognize not only the rights of the person seised, but also the rights of the owner.

In 1821, in the case of *Cholmondeley* v. *Clinton*,[3] equity decided that it would apply to the possessors of equitable estates the common law rules as to possession ; and that, by virtue of James I's statute of limitation,[4] such possessors would gain a good equitable title by twenty years' possession. Equity thus got a doctrine of possession ; and English law thus gained a body of principles applicable both to legal and equitable estates.

[1] Above, pp. 182–3.

[2] This question could not arise when the trustee had active duties to perform for his *c.q.* trust ; for, in this case, the trustee would be in possession ; and his possession would enure for the benefit of the *c.q.* trust entitled. It could never arise as between trustee and *c.q.* trust ; for, in this case, even the common law courts recognized that the trustee's possession was held on account his *c.q.* trust, and could therefore give him no title.

[3] 2 Jac. and W. 1 ; 4 Bligh 1 ; see Holdsworth, H. E. L. vii. 76–7.

[4] 21 James I, c. 16, § 1 ; above, p, 167.

Throughout the eighteenth century the tendency of the development of the law as to the ownership and possession of legal and equitable interests in land had been in the direction of assimilation. On the one hand, the common law was beginning to acquire a conception of ownership based on an absolutely good right to possession, which, though it differed somewhat from equitable ownership, yet had many more affinities with this ownership than with the medieval conceptions of seisin and disseisin. On the other hand, equity was developing conceptions of ownership and possession similar to those which were being developed by the working of the action of ejectment; and when, at the beginning of the nineteenth century, it accepted the common law and statutory rules as to the position of possessors, the similarity between the two sets of principles became far more marked than their dissimilarity. Therefore a possibility of ultimate fusion came into sight. This possibility was realized by the legislation of the nineteenth century.

(4) The effect of the statutory changes of the nineteenth century.

The legislation following upon the Reform Act of 1832 got rid of those survivals of the medieval law as to seisin and disseisin, which limited the application of the modern principles of law as to ownership and possession, which had been developed by the working of the actions of trespass and ejectment. The Act of 1833, which abolished the real actions, got rid of the anomalous cases in which a disseised owner was denied a right of entry.[1] Fines were abolished in the

[1] 3, 4 William IV, c. 27, § 39.

same year;[1] and that meant that the power of a disseisor to bar a disseisee's right by the levying of a fine disappeared. The Act of 1845 made it impossible for a disseisor to convey a tortious fee simple;[2] and made it possible for a disseisee to convey his rights to the property.[3] Thus the theory of ownership and possession, which had grown up round the actions of trespass and ejectment, became the theory of our modern law. But the principles of the law of ownership and possession as thus developed bore marks of the three chief periods in the history of that law. From the medieval period it derived the principle that the person seised or possessed is *prima facie* the owner in fee simple—that ownership is in effect a seisin or possession which none can dispute. From the period of the sixteenth, seventeenth, and eighteenth centuries it derived the ideas, first, that an owner ought generally to be able to recover his possession by entry or action of ejectment against the possessor; and, secondly, that as ownership is a true *jus in rem*—a right as against all the world—a person who wishes to recover against the possessor must show, not merely a better right than the possessor, but an absolutely good right. From the legislation of the nineteenth century came the completion of the development made in the preceding period. That legislation has abolished the surviving medieval rules which, in some cases, still made it possible for a possessor to recover his possession by entry or action of ejectment from an owner who had ejected him—'practically,' said Maitland,[4] writing in 1888, 'for the last three

[1] 3, 4 William IV, c. 74.
[2] 8, 9 Victoria, c. 106, § 4.
[3] § 6.
[4] Coll. Papers, i. 456–7.

hundred years and more, theoretically as well as practically for the last fifty years and more, we have had no action in which an ejected possessor could recover possession from the owner who ejected him.' It has simplified the law in two ways. First, it gives every owner the power to assert his rights by entry or action of ejectment as against all possessors. Secondly, it takes away from every owner, not only his right of entry or action, but also his title to the property, if another has been in possession of it, without acknowledging his title, for the period fixed by the Real Property Limitation Act.[1] Thus the law as to the ownership and possession of land, as is stands to-day, is a true *jus tripertitum*, for its principles are derived from all these three epochs in the history of the common law.

These developments not only simplified the law, they tended also to bring the principles of the law as to the ownership and possession of land into conformity with the law as to the ownership and possession of chattels. One of the chief reasons why the law as to the seisin and disseisin of hereditaments had fallen apart from the law as to the possession and dispossession of chattels was the fact that the first was moulded by the real and the second by the personal actions.[2] In spite of this, there were, even in the Middle Ages, fundamental similarities.[3] But the resemblance is closer in the modern common law by reason of the similarity of the actions round which that modern law has grown up. Just as the modern law as to the ownership and possession of

[1] For this Act see below, pp. 276–9. [2] Above, p. 122.

[3] Pollock and Wright, Possession, 50; above, p. 122.

land has grown up round the actions of trespass and ejectment, so the modern law as to the ownership and possession of chattels has grown up round the actions of trespass and trover; and both ejectment and trover were varieties of the action of trespass. It was only natural, therefore, that, when the law as to the ownership and possession of both land and chattels passed under the sway of these closely related actions, the legal principles underlying these kindred branches of law should tend to approximate.

These principles of the law as to the ownership and possession of land are not affected by the Property Acts. They are assumed by these Acts, and they govern our modern law.

§ 2. Future Interests

The number and variety of the future or executory[1] interests in the land recognized by English law were large. This fact can only be accounted for by the length and accidents of the history of this branch of the law; and it is only history which can explain the complicated rules which regulated the nature of these interests, and their relations to one another. These future interests in the land could, from the point of view of their historical origin, be divided into three great classes. First, there were the future interests recognized by the medieval common law—reversions and vested and contingent remainders. Secondly, there were the future estates which were, so to speak, brought into the common law, and made

[1] The term 'executory interest' means any kind of future interest; but it is sometimes used to mean interests other than common law remainders and reversions.

legal estates by the operation of the statutes of Uses and Wills. They were shifting and springing uses and executory devises. Thirdly, there were the purely equitable estates, which were mainly due to developments in the principles of equity which took place after the passing of the statutes of Uses and Wills. The Property Acts have simplified the law by limiting future freehold interests in the land to the third class. The statute of Uses and Henry VIII's statute of Wills are repealed; and the law now recognizes as legal estates only an estate in fee simple absolute *in possession*, and a term of years absolute.[1] A term of years absolute may, as we shall see, be granted so as to take effect either in possession or in reversion.[2] The grant of such a reversionary term creates a legal future estate; [3] but, with this exception, all future estates and interests in the land are equitable.

For some considerable period, however, it will be necessary to know something of the nature and incidents of all these classes of future interests in the land. I shall, therefore, give a very brief account of the growth of these three classes of interests.

Reversions and Remainders.

I have already said something of reversions and vested remainders, and of the difference between vested and contingent remainders.[4] It was during this period that the validity of contingent remainders was established, that the conditions under which they

[1] Law of Property Act, 1925, § 1 (1).

[2] Ibid, § 205 (1) (xxvii); below, p. 233.

[3] Cheshire, Real Property (3rd ed.), 460.

[4] Above, pp. 65–8.

could be limited were ascertained, and that the nature and incidents of the interest conferred by them were defined.[1]

(1) Their validity. We have seen that towards the end of the medieval period the validity of a contingent remainder was recognized, but only if the contingency upon which it was limited was the death of a living person—e.g. an estate to *A*, remainder to the heir of *B* a living person.[2] But, by the middle of the sixteenth century, remainders which depended upon other contingencies were recognized as valid, provided that the contingent event was not illegal or legally impossible. The idea, held at one period, that the contingency must not be too remote was rejected at the end of the seventeenth century.[3]

(2) Conditions under which they could be limited. Before the Property Acts three principles applicable to remainders, both vested and contingent, and two principles applicable only to contingent remainders, were recognized by English law.

The following three principles were applicable to remainders both vested and contingent.

In the first place, a remainder must await the regular ending of the precedent estate. If *X* conveyed an estate to *A* for life, remainder to *B*, the death of *A* operated as a limitation which fixed the time for the beginning of *B*'s estate, and *B*'s estate at once began, even though he had not entered. On the other hand, if *X* conveyed an estate to *A* for life,

[1] Holdsworth, H. E. L. vii. 81–116. [2] Above, p. 68.

[3] Holdsworth H. E. L. vii. 97–8; this idea was one of the applications of the supposed rule against double possibilities; for this supposed rule and its applications see below, p. 222, n. 6.

remainder to *B*, and inserted in the conveyance a proviso that, if *A* failed to pay the rent reserved, *B*'s remainder should take effect, this proviso was void. It was in effect, not a limitation which fixed the duration of *A*'s estate, but a condition which gave a right of re-entry on the breach of it; and it was only the grantor or his heirs who could take advantage of such a condition. Since *B* was a stranger he could not take advantage of it.

In the second place, the freehold could not be limited *in futuro*. This was the most fundamental of all the common law rules as to the limitation of estates. It applied to all limitations of estates, whether derived out of an estate in possession or out of an estate in remainder or reversion. It follows from this principle that 'no remainder may be limited to take effect upon the expiration of an interval of time after the determination of the precedent estate';[1] for otherwise the freehold would in effect be limited *in futuro*, and, during the interval, would be placed in abeyance. It is clear that if a remainder is vested, and limited to take effect as soon as the precedent estate determines, there can be no abeyance of the freehold. But if a remainder is contingent, there may be such an abeyance if it is not vested during the duration of the precedent estate or at the same instant as it determines. Therefore, when the validity of a contingent remainder to the heirs of a living person was admitted, it was only allowed to take effect if the heir was ascertained by the death of such living person during the duration of the precedent estate.[2]

[1] Challis, Real Property (3rd ed.), 82.

[2] Above, p. 68.

In the third place, the remainder must pass out of the grantor at the time when the livery of seisin of the particular estate was made—'the growing and being of the remainder is by the livery of seisin to him that shall have the freehold.'[1] Thus, if a man lets land for years with remainders over for life or in tail or in fee, 'it behoveth that the lessor make livery of seisin to the lessee for years, otherwise nothing passes to them in remainder.'[2] Livery of seisin made to the lessee 'enures for the benefit of them in remainder'.[3] If livery of seisin is not made to the lessee 'then is the freehold and also the reversion in the lessor'.[4] In other words, the remainder cannot take effect.

The following two principles are applicable only to contingent remainders.

In the first place, though the particular estate upon which a vested remainder depends may be a term of years, because the seisin in such cases is vested in the remainderman, the particular estate upon which a contingent remainder depends must be an estate of freehold, because, pending the contingency, there is no person in whom the seisin can vest; and, therefore, if the precedent estate was not an estate of freehold, the freehold would be in abeyance.

In the second place, if an estate were limited to *A* for life, and a remainder in fee simple to the heirs of *B*, a living person, the question arose, what became of the fee pending the contingency? The feoffee in such a case had alienated the whole fee simple, and, pending the contingency, there was no one ready to take it. In such a case the better opinion was that the common

[1] Litt. § 721; Bl. Comm. ii. 168. [2] Litt. § 60.
[3] Co. Litt. 49 a. [4] Litt. § 60.

law made an exception to its rule, and permitted the freehold to be in abeyance.[1] With certain other rules as to the limitation of contingent remainders, which were aimed at the prevention of the creation of a perpetuity by their means, I shall deal when I come to consider the history of the rules against perpetuities.[2]

(3) The nature and incidents of the interest conferred by a contingent remainder.[3] At the outset a contingent remainder was regarded, not as an estate in the land, but merely as a possibility that an estate might at some future time arise. Therefore it could neither be alienated *inter vivos* nor devised. The common law judges were the more ready to come to these conclusions, partly because they thought that a permission to alienate contingent remainders might encourage maintenance—they applied to the contingent remainders the same reasoning as they applied to choses in action; and partly because they thought that a permission to alienate would complicate titles. But, in the eighteenth century, the common law judges permitted them to be devised; and the court of Chancery recognized the validity of their assignment. By the Wills Act of 1837 [4] and the Real Property Act of 1845 [5] they were made freely devisable and assignable.

We shall see that in the sixteenth and early seventeenth centuries the judges were faced with the problem of preventing the creation by landowners of perpetuities, that is, settlements of their property by

[1] Holdsworth, H. E. L. vii. 86. [2] Below, pp. 220–3.

[3] Holdsworth, H. E. L. vii. 101–4.

[4] 7 William IV and 1 Victoria, c. 26, § 3.

[5] 8, 9 Victoria, c. 106, § 6.

virtue of which the land was given to an indefinite succession of limited owners, no one of whom had a complete power of alienation.[1] One of the means by which landowners sought to effect this object was the use of contingent remainders. But, as a contingent remainder was a mere possibility, it was easily destructible. Obviously to emphasize its destructibility was an easy way to prevent it from being used to create a perpetuity. The judges took this line, with the result that the destructibility of a contingent remainder was one of its leading characteristics.

The ways in which a contingent remainder could be destroyed depended (i) on the rules regulating the limitation of remainders, and (ii) on the common law rules as to merger and forfeiture.

(i) From the earliest times a contingent remainder was only allowed to take effect if it became vested during the duration of the precedent estate, or at the same instant as that estate determined;[2] because, if the rule had been otherwise, the freehold would in effect have been limited *in futuro*, and, pending the contingency, would have been in abeyance. This rule was the more rigidly adhered to, because the judges soon perceived that adherence to it was a principal safeguard against the creation of a perpetuity by means of contingent remainders.

(ii) The operation of the law of merger likewise destroyed a contingent remainder. Thus, in the case of *Purefoy* v. *Rogers*,[3] a married woman was tenant for life, with remainder to her son if one should be born. The reversioner in fee, before the birth of a son, conveyed

[1] Below, pp. 218–19.

[2] Above, p. 68.

[3] (1671), 2 Wms. Saunders 380.

his reversion to the married woman and her husband. It was held that her life estate was merged in the fee simple, and that the contingent remainder was therefore destroyed. The same result followed in the converse case, that is, if the tenant of the particular estate surrendered his estate to the reversioner in fee, or to a vested remainderman in fee. The case of *Thompson* v. *Leach*[1] is an illustration of the working of this rule. S. Leach was tenant for life, with contingent remainders in tail, remainder to Sir Simon Leach in tail, remainder in fee to N. Leach. Before the contingency happened, the tenant for life surrendered his estate to Sir Simon Leach. It was held that but for the fact that the surrender was void because the tenant for life was a lunatic [2] the contingent remainders would have been destroyed by this surrender. The same result followed if, before the contingent remainders vested, the tenant of the precedent estate incurred a forfeiture.[3]

This liability of contingent remainders to destruction was modified in two ways.

In the first place, the liability of contingent remainders to be destroyed by the operation of the rules of merger and forfeiture was got rid of by means of the device of trustees to preserve contingent remainders. After the estate to the tenant for life an estate was limited to trustees and their heirs during the life of the tenant for life, in case his estate determined by forfeiture or otherwise in his lifetime, in trust for him,

[1] (1691), 2 Vent. 198 ; S. C., 1 Ld. Raym. 313 ; 3 Mod. 296.

[2] 3 Mod. at p. 301. For an exceptional case in which the doctrine of merger was not allowed to operate so as to destroy a contingent remainder see Holdsworth, H. E. L. vii. 110–11.

[3] Challis, Real Property (3rd ed.), 135–6.

and to preserve the contingent remainders. This device was perfected by Sir Orlando Bridgman and Sir Geoffrey Palmer—two famous conveyancers of the Commonwealth period. Its efficacy depended on the fact that this remainder to the trustees was a vested remainder. In spite of some opinions to the contrary, it was held to be a vested remainder by the court of Common Pleas in 1697,[1] and by the House of Lords in 1740.[2]

In the second place, the Legislature intervened. In 1845 the device of trustees to preserve contingent remainders was rendered unnecessary by an enactment that a contingent remainder should be able to take effect 'notwithstanding the determination by forfeiture surrender or merger of any preceding estate of freehold.'[3] Two other statutes dealt with the liability of a contingent remainder to fail, by reason of the natural determination of the precedent estate before the remainder vested. In 1695 the House of Lords had held, in the case of *Reeve* v. *Long*,[4] that, if an estate was limited to *A* for life, with remainder to his unborn son, and a posthumous child was born, that child could take. But the correctness of this decision was so doubtful that in 1698 a statute was passed to confirm it.[5] In 1877, in consequence of the observations of the Court of Appeal in the case of *Cunliffe* v. *Brancker*,[6] the Contingent Remainders Act provided in substance that a contingent remainder was not to fail by reason of the determination of the precedent

[1] *Duncomb* v. *Duncomb*, 3 Lev. 437.

[2] *Dormer* v. *Parkhurst*, 6 Bro. P.C. 351.

[3] 8, 9 Victoria, c. 106, § 8.

[4] 3 Lev. 408 ; S.C. 1 Salk. 227 : 4 Mod. 282.

[5] 10 William III, c. 22.

[6] (1876), 3 C. D. at p. 407.

estate if it would have been valid as a shifting use or executory devise.[1] We shall see that this in effect meant that a contingent remainder which complied with the rule against perpetuities was preserved by this Act; but that a contingent remainder which did not so comply was not preserved.[2]

Shifting and Springing Uses and Executory Devises.[3]

These varieties of future interests in land were brought within the purview of the common law by the statutes of Uses and Wills.

We have seen that, as the result both of the statute of Uses and the statute of Wills, it became possible to create a number of executory interests, wholly unknown to the common law, which conferred legal estates in the land upon those entitled to them. I have already explained the manner in which this result was produced by the operation of the statute of Uses. We have seen that, as soon as the seisin of land or other hereditaments was transferred to feoffees to the use of another, or as soon as by implication or by operation of law a use was created on the seisin of the legal owner, that use was turned into a legal estate; and that therefore all the methods formerly applicable to the creation of uses now became applicable to the creation of legal estates.[4] Similar results were produced by the operation of the statute of Wills.[5] But it should be noted that this statute could be called into operation in one of two ways. A testator might

[1] 40, 41 Victoria, c. 33; for a somewhat different and a more restrictive construction of this Act see Strahan, Conveyancing (2nd ed.), 180.

[2] Below, p. 221.

[3] Holdsworth, H. E. L. vii. 116–49.

[4] Above, pp. 163–4.

[5] Above, p. 158.

directly devise his land, and the executory devises created by him took effect by virtue of the provisions of the statute of Wills which authorized such devises. Or a testator might, by the form of his devise, show that he intended to make use of the machinery of the statute of Uses to effect his purposes. In that case, by reason of the intention expressed by the testator, the estates created by the will took effect as legal estates by virtue of the statute of Uses.

The difference between a shifting and a springing use turns upon the question whether the use does or does not 'defeat an estate previously limited by the same instrument'. Thus if an estate be limited to the use of *A* and his heirs till *B* return from Rome, and, on the happening of that event, to the use of *X* and his heirs, the use to *X* and his heirs is a shifting use, because it takes effect in defeasance of *A*'s estate. On the other hand, if an estate be limited to the use of *A* and his heirs to take effect five years hence, or to the use of *X* for ten years, and then to the use of *A* and his heirs, in both these cases the use to *A* and his heirs is a springing use, because it does not defeat an estate previously limited by the same instrument.

The recognition of these new varieties of legal interest in the land raised many difficult problems. During the sixteenth century we can discern two schools of thought. Some lawyers thought that they could be created at the will and pleasure of the settlor or testator, and that they were exempt from all the rules applicable to the limitation of legal estates. Others, impressed by the view that uses were often created for fraudulent purposes, and that they could be used to create perpetuities, thought that they ought to be subjected to all the common law rules of limitation. The result arrived at in the sixteenth century was in the nature of a compromise. The judges admitted that these future interests in land could be limited in ways unknown to the common law, e.g. by way of use a fee could be limited after a fee. But, in order to prevent the risk of the creation of a perpetuity, they laid it down that, if a future limitation could be construed as a contingent remainder, it must be so construed, so that it was liable to be destroyed in the same way as a contingent remainder was liable to be destroyed. And this rule they held to be a rule of law, so that, unlike a rule of construction, it was independent of the intention of the parties.[1] This became a permanent rule of English law. Further, in the sixteenth century they held that these interests could be destroyed by those having vested estates in ways similar to those in which contingent remainders could be destroyed; and that, as a term of years was a chattel, future interests in it could not be limited.

These two last-mentioned rules were overruled early in the seventeenth century. The court of Chancery was prepared to give relief to persons whose interests were affected by these rules. The result was that the judges of the courts of common law found themselves obliged to revise their ideas. In 1620 it was held in the case of *Pells* v. *Brown* [2] that executory devises of freeholds were not destructible; and in 1609 and 1612 it was held in *Manning's* [3] and *Lampet's* [4] *Cases* that indestructible future interests

[1] See *White* v. *Summers*, [1908] 2 Ch. at p. 263.
[2] Cro. Jac. 590. [3] 8 Co. Rep. 94b. [4] 10 Co. Rep. 46b.

in terms of years could be created by an executory devise.

Thus the future interests, both in freeholds and terms of years, which had come into existence as legal estates through the operation of the statutes of Uses and Wills, became interests which differed from legal contingent remainders in two chief respects. In the first place, they were free from the rigid rules which fettered the limitation of legal contingent remainders; and, in the second place, they were indestructible. We shall see that these results played no small part in making it clear that a new and general rule against perpetuities was needed to guard against the opportunities which the recognition of these future interests afforded to landowners of creating these perpetuities.[1]

Equitable Interests.[2]

After the passing of the statute of Uses the court of Chancery still had jurisdiction over uses not executed by the statute—uses of chattels real and personal, uses of copyholds, and uses where the feoffees had active duties to perform. On this basis the Chancellors began to build up a new system of equitable estates. The great impetus to their construction came when, in the latter half of the seventeenth century, they began to enforce the use upon a use as a trust.[3] Starting from the basis of the principles of the modern common law, they gradually created a new set of equitable estates by way of trust, which, as Lord Mansfield said,[4] answered 'the exigencies of

[1] Below, pp. 219–20, 224. [2] Holdsworth, H. E. L. vii. 134–5, 144–9. [3] Above, p. 161.

[4] *Burgess* v. *Wheate* (1759), 1 W. Bl. at p. 160.

families and all purposes without producing one inconvenience, fraud, or private mischief which the statute of Uses meant to avoid'. The fact that equity was able to jettison a large amount of the medieval law which it had naturally followed in building up the law as to the uses now turned into legal estates by the statute, was the decisive cause of its success in building up this new branch of the law. Partly by following its own conception of what was just and reasonable, partly by following the principles of the modern common law, it was able to mould these new equitable estates in such a way that they satisfied modern needs. I have already said something of this process in connexion with the development of the law as to ownership and possession; [1] and the developments which were taking place in that branch of the law were paralleled by the developments which were simultaneously taking place in the law as to these future equitable estates in the land.

In moulding these new equitable estates equity retained some of the principles which it had applied to uses before the passing of the statute of Uses. Thus it allowed that a person who took the legal estate from the trustee for value and without notice of the trust got a good title both at law and in equity; and that a person who got the land by a title paramount to that of the trustee got a title free from the trust. The great difference between the medieval and the modern equitable rules turns upon this: according to the medieval rules what was bound by the trust was the conscience and the estate of the feoffees to uses. According to the modern rules the land itself is

[1] Above, pp. 183–4.

bound by the trust—'the trust in this court', said Lord Mansfield, 'is the same as the land.'[1] It is this difference in the point of view of modern equity which explains the difference between the medieval use and the modern trust, and therefore the difference between the medieval and the modern conception of equitable estates in the land.

First, the modern law diverges from the medieval in the fact that a trust may exist though there is no trustee. No use could be declared without a feoffee to hold to the use; but, as the modern trust is regarded as attaching to the property, equity will supply the place of a trustee. Thus, where property was devised to the separate use of a married woman, and no trustees were appointed, it was held that the husband, who took the property at law, was trustee for his wife. Secondly, equity did not consider itself bound by the rules which disabled certain persons from holding to the use of others. Both the king and a corporation could be trustees. Thirdly, unlike the *cestui-que* use, whose interest was affected by all the legal incidents which befell the estate of his feoffee, the *cestui-que* trust is 'protected against his judgements and other incumbrances, and against his bankruptcy'.[2] How far the *cestui-que* trust was protected against the escheat or forfeiture of the legal estate, if a sole trustee committed felony or treason, was, for a long time, a doubtful question; and there were similar doubts in the case of an escheat owing to the failure of the heirs of a sole trustee. But, in the nineteenth century, the Legislature accepted the view of those who held that

[1] *Burgess* v. *Wheate* (1759), 1 W. Bl. at p. 162.

[2] Sanders, Uses, i. 391.

the estate of the *cestui-que* trust was not affected by these events ;[1] and this view is based ultimately on the idea that the trust binds the land itself, and not the trustee's interest in it.

As I have already pointed out, it is these equitable future interests in land which, under the Property Acts, are the sole survivors of the many future interests recognized by the old law.

The development of these various executory interests, legal and equitable, added immensely to the powers of landowners over their property. Either by settlements *inter vivos* or by will they could make elaborate laws for its future devolution. We shall now see that these powers were added to by the simultaneous development of several different kinds of powers of appointment. We shall see that some of these powers of appointment, because they gave enlarged facilities for disposition to limited owners under these settlements, helped to counteract the worst consequence of this system of settlement—the continued occupation of the land by persons with very limited rights of disposition and user. They contributed an element of elasticity to the rigid laws of those settlements by which the majority of the great estates in England had come to be fettered ; and we shall see that, in some cases, the rights conferred by them gave their owners what in substance amounted to a new variety of future interest in the land.

[1] Above, p. 38, and n. 2.

§ 3. Powers of Appointment[1]

A power, in its widest sense, is an authority or mandate given by one man to another to do some act on his behalf. The bestowal of such an authority or mandate to act on behalf of another, and the bestowal of a proprietary right on another, are obviously distinct operations, which fall under two quite distinct juridical categories. A power gives to the person on whom it is bestowed an authority or mandate to do some act, either for his own, or for some one else's benefit. On the other hand, the gift of a proprietary right bestows no authority to do anything—it simply gives the recipient the rights of an owner. The distinction is clear enough if we look at such powers as e.g. a power of attorney, which merely bestow an authority or mandate to do some specified act or acts on behalf of another. But if the authority or mandate bestowed is an authority or mandate to create new, or to revoke or suspend existing interests in property, either in favour of the recipient of the authority, or in favour of other persons, it is clear that these two very distinct things—power and property—will begin to approach one another. A person to whom a power has been given to confer a proprietary interest on himself is in effect given something like a right of property; and, if he has been given a power to confer a proprietary right upon a third person, he is in effect enabled to create a proprietary right in favour of that person, for the ultimate benefit, either of the donee of the right, or of himself, or of both. It is these powers to confer proprietary rights with which we

[1] Holdsworth, H. E. L. vii. 149–93.

are here concerned. From the sixteenth century onwards many different varieties have been developed. Without ceasing to possess many of the juridical qualities of authorities or mandates, they have all developed, some to a greater and some to a less degree, proprietary characteristics. But, because they are authorities or mandates, and have never ceased to possess many of their juridical qualities, they have added materially to the disposing capacity of landowners, and indeed of the owners of all sorts of property of a permanent kind. For this reason they have been the means of increasing the flexibility and adaptability of the land law ; and, consequently, they have added to it a new and important chapter.

Powers were used by the conveyancers mainly for two purposes. First, they were used to correct the two chief defects of a strict settlement of property. The defect that the whole property was made to devolve on the eldest son, leaving the widow and younger children unprovided for, could be obviated by giving to the father or mother powers to charge the property with sums of money for the widow's jointure, and for portions for the younger children. The defect that the common law powers of a life tenant under such a settlement were not sufficient to enable him to deal with the property to the best advantage was obviated by giving to the life tenant powers to lease and to do other things which were needed to enable the property to be used profitably. Secondly, they were employed in connexion with the law of mortgage as developed by the court of Chancery, partly to give extended powers to the mortgagee, and partly to enable the mortgagor or the mortgagee to grant leases, in order that the existence of the mortgage might not hinder the development of the mortgaged property. In fact, these powers, as thus developed by the common law and by equity, and applied by the conveyancers, have been found to be so necessary an adjunct to the land law that, in the last century, they were greatly extended by the Legislature when it wished, in the public interest, both to increase the powers of the owners of settled land and to simplify conveyances.[1]

I propose to deal very briefly with first the origins and modes of operation of powers; and, secondly, with their classification.

Origins and Modes of Operation.

From this point of view powers can be divided into four main classes.

(1) Common Law Powers. In those few localities in which a custom to devise land was recognized in the Middle Ages a testator could by his will give his executors a power to sell his land without giving them an estate in the land. The executors took no estate in the land—only a bare power; and so, without entering upon the land, they could bargain and sell to a purchaser, who thereupon acquired a right to enter.[2] These powers acquired a greatly increased importance as the result of the statute of Wills—as Coke said, 'that which in Littleton's time a man might do by custom in some particular places, he may now do generally.'[3] But, as before, the power was

[1] Below, pp. 210–12, 261, 263.
[2] Holdsworth, H. E. L. vii. 153–5.
[3] Co. Litt. 112 b.

still regarded simply as an authority or mandate to a particular person.

But the rise of uses, and the fact that settlors or testators could empower their feoffees to convey, or could empower any third person to direct their feoffees to convey, were giving an extended significance to this capacity to create powers, even before the passing of the statutes of Uses and Wills. The statute of Uses converted many of the estates, created in pursuance of these powers, into legal estates. It followed that the common law was introduced to a very much larger range of powers, all of which operated to confer the legal estate in a way very different from that in which the common law testamentary power had operated. We shall see that it is in connexion with these powers that the distinction between power and property begins to be blurred; for we shall see that, in some cases, the gift of certain varieties of these powers did confer upon the donee, in a greater or a less degree, something in the nature of a proprietary right.

(2) Powers taking effect by means of the statute of Uses. We have seen that, before the passing of the statute of Uses, the *cestui-que* use could reserve to himself, or give to another, a power to revoke the old and declare new uses.[1] As and when these uses were declared, the feoffees became trustees for the new *cestui-que* uses. Thus settlors and testators could reserve to themselves, or give to others, powers to revoke the uses already declared, and limit new uses, for the purposes of making jointures, leases, exchanges, or sales. Powers of this sort could be given after the statute;

[1] Above, pp. 163–4.

and, as a result of their exercise, and of the statute, the new uses, to which the feoffees became seised, were turned into legal estates. After the passing of the statute of Wills, testators as well as settlors could, if they liked, avail themselves of the machinery of the statute of Uses, and create by their wills powers which operated as a declaration of a use on the seisin of a person clothed with the legal estate, by the will or otherwise.

It is clear that powers of this kind are very different from a common law power given to executors or others to sell property. It is clear that persons to whom these powers were given had, sometimes to a greater, sometimes to a lesser degree, rights which were closely akin to property. This fact began to be recognized by the common law judges of the sixteenth and early seventeenth centuries. Hence they began to differentiate between powers which were merely authorities to act on behalf of another, and powers which gave to the donee something in the nature of a proprietary right.

With this leading classification of powers, and with other classifications which grew up between these proprietary powers, I shall deal when I come to consider the classification of powers.

(3) Equitable powers. The exercise of the two first of these classes of powers gave rise to legal estates. The exercise of this third class of powers gave rise to equitable interests. There were two main reasons for the growth of these equitable powers.

First, just as equity found it necessary to create new forms of equitable interests in land, through the medium of trustees, which differed in many respects from the shifting and springing uses, and executory devises, recognized by the common law;[1] just as, by the same means, it gave effect to the desires of settlors and testators to make settlements of money, stocks and shares, and other forms of permanent chattels personal, which were developing in the latter half of the seventeenth century; so, as a necessary accompaniment to these developments, it recognized powers over the equitable interests thus developed. These powers were modelled on the powers which operated by means of the statute of Uses; but, necessarily, they could only confer an equitable estate on the appointee; and, equally necessarily, they were wholly under the control of the court of Chancery. That court, by its control, not only shaped the development of these equitable powers, but also added to the common law rules regulating powers, which operated under the statutes of Uses and Wills, a large superstructure of equitable rules.

Secondly, other equitable powers, originating in the treatment by equity of the legal rights of a mortgagee, came to be recognized in the course of the eighteenth century. We shall see that a mortgagee, though the owner of the legal estate, and though that estate was absolute at law, held his estate subject to the mortgagor's equity of redemption.[2] Hence he was unable to sell free from that equity of redemption unless the mortgagor joined in the sale. To obviate the need for the concurrence of the mortgagor, it became customary, towards the end of the eighteenth century, to give to the mortgagee an express

[1] Above, pp. 200–3. [2] Below, pp. 256–7.

power of sale in the mortgage deed. Such a power obviously operates in a manner different from other equitable powers. The mortgagee had at law the legal estate, and could therefore convey it, if he had not been prevented by the fact that, in equity, his legal estate was subject to the mortgagor's equity of redemption. This power operated to release this equitable bar upon his legal rights, and thus enabled him to give a title good both at law and in equity. Similarly the express power of leasing, which was sometimes given to the mortgagee, was equally necessary, and operated in exactly the same way.

It is clear that these equitable powers resembled many of the powers operating under the statute of Uses, in that they gave to their donees rights or interests in the property over which they existed. In most cases they were something very much more than mere authorities to act on behalf of another. Hence they increased the force of the tendency, which had been operating since the passing of the statute of Uses, to give a proprietary aspect to all these powers of appointment.

(4) The modern statutory powers. We have seen that as early as 1540 [1] the Legislature had interfered to give some protection to lessees to whom leases had been granted by certain limited owners. The result was that a limited owner could, under the conditions set out in the Act, grant leases for terms which might last longer than his own interest. But, till the nineteenth century, this statute stood alone, because the various kinds of powers, which have just

[1] Above, p. 168.

been described, were considered to be adequate to meet the needs both of the general public and of the landowners. This was the opinion of the Real Property Commissioners in 1829; but when they were drawing up their report the industrial revolution was making it plain that the existing classes of powers were no longer adequate. In the first place, too much power was left to individual landowners, who might deliberately omit to give powers to the tenant for life under a settlement. The result was that, unless the tenant was prepared to face the expense of a private Act of Parliament, he might be wholly unable to develop his property. In the second place, even if a landowner wished to insert all the powers necessary to enable the tenant for life to manage and develop his estate, he might, in the age of rapid change which came in the nineteenth century, omit to insert the right powers. He could not be expected to foresee that the growth of a neighbouring town might, fifty years hence, make part of his estate valuable building land. Nor could he foresee that the discovery of minerals might convert an agricultural estate into an industrial centre.

Legislation of the nineteenth century, which culminated in the Settled Land Acts, and some of the clauses of the Conveyancing Acts, went far to meet these defects. In a manner characteristic of English law reforms, these Acts adopted and largely extended the scheme of powers worked out by the conveyancers of the seventeenth and eighteenth centuries. From this point of view these Acts may be compared to other codifying Acts of the nineteenth century. But, from another point of view, they are much more than this; for they have adapted this scheme of powers to modern conditions; and they have enlarged it, by taking into consideration, not only the needs of those taking interests under settlements, but also the needs of the actual tenants of the land and of the public at large.[1]

The Property Acts have left only two out of these four classes of powers—equitable and statutory powers.[2]

Classifications of Powers.

The distinction between powers which are merely authorities or mandates, and powers which give the donee something in the nature of a proprietary interest in the property over which they have been created, is at the root of the principal classifications of powers. From this point of view the three main lines of division between powers are (1) the division between powers simply collateral and powers which are not simply collateral; (2) the division between general and special powers; and (3) the division between ordinary powers and powers in the nature of a trust.

(1) The division between powers simply collateral and powers which are not simply collateral. The form which this division has taken in modern law has been clearly and authoritatively stated by Jessel, M.R.,[3] as follows:

> 'The first power, a power simply collateral, I understand to be a power given to a person who has no interest what-

[1] See *Bruce* v. *Marquess of Ailesbury*, [1892] A.C. at pp. 364–5 *per* Lord Macnaghten, cited below, pp. 314–15; below, pp. 315, 327–8.

[2] Cheshire, Real Property (3rd ed.), 502–3.

[3] *Re D'Angibau* (1880), 15 C. D. at pp. 232–3.

ever in the property over which the power is given. The second power, a power in gross, is a power given to a person who has an interest in the property over which the power extends, but such an interest as cannot be affected by the exercise of the power. The most familiar instance is that of a tenant for life with a power of appointment after his death. Then the third kind of power is a power exercisable by a person who has an interest in the property, which interest is capable of being affected, diminished, or disposed of to some extent by the exercise of the power. That power is commonly called a power appendant or appurtenant.'

These distinctions were only gradually arrived at in the course of the sixteenth and seventeenth centuries. The first distinction to emerge was the distinction between powers simply collateral and other powers. Then, as between these other powers, the distinction between powers in gross and powers appendant or appurtenant gradually grew up.

(2) The division between general and special powers. As early as the sixteenth century it was becoming apparent that the gift of a power which conferred upon the donee authority to appoint to any one he pleased, including himself, was difficult to distinguish from a proprietary right. In the course of the eighteenth century the interests of creditors [1] and the application of the modern rule against perpetuities [2] emphasized this fact. A person entitled to a general power of this kind has in effect property which his creditors can take; and, as its existence does not affect the alienability of the property, the period allowed by the modern rule against perpetuities is reckoned from the date of its exercise. On the other hand, a special power to appoint, e.g. among the chil-

[1] Below, p. 217. [2] Below, pp. 223 seqq.

dren of *X*, is much more in the nature of a mandate. The property is not the property of the appointor, so that it cannot be taken by his creditors ; and, as the alienability of the property is effected by the creation of such a power, the period allowed by the modern rule against perpetuities is reckoned from the date of its creation.

The large use made of these powers by settlors and testators soon made it clear that some of these special powers—powers, for instance, given to a husband to appoint amongst the children of the marriage—approach the confine of trusts. The need to distinguish between power and trust, and to regulate powers which had about them something of the character of trusts, has led to the third and latest division between powers.

(3) The division between ordinary powers and powers in the nature of a trust. In principle the distinction between powers and trusts is clear. 'Powers are never imperative: they leave the act to be done at the will of the party to whom they are given. Trusts are always imperative, and are obligatory upon the conscience of the party intrusted.'[1] The distinction is of course obvious in the case of general powers. But, in the case of special powers, it is a good deal less obvious ; and, in the case of powers simply collateral, the large control exercised by the court of Chancery, and the new conception that the trust bound the property rather than the person trusted,[2] tended to make the difference between powers and trusts very fine. And so, just as the growth of powers of appointment,

[1] *Attorney-General* v. *Lady Downing* (1767), Wilm. at p. 23 *per* Wilmot, C. J.

[2] Above, pp. 201–2.

and their development by the courts of common law after the passing of the statute of Uses, tended to give to these powers some of the characteristics of legal estates in the land; so the regard paid by equity to the interest of the persons for whose benefit powers of a fiduciary character were created, tended to give powers of this kind some of the characteristics of trusts.

In the eighteenth century the equitable rules upon this question gradually became more precise. These rules were applied by the court to special powers of appointment, in cases where it thought that the creator of the power had intended to put upon the donee of the power a duty to execute it. This development of the rules of equity was natural, and, indeed, inevitable; for, in the course of the seventeenth and eighteenth centuries, equity had assumed jurisdiction to relieve in certain cases against defective execution of powers; and to interfere in cases where there had been a fraudulent exercise of a power. This jurisdiction was based upon the principle that equity ought to give effect, if possible, to the intentions of the creators of powers; and that it ought to protect the interests of the persons intended to be benefited by their exercise; more especially when those persons were children or relatives for whom the creator of the power had a moral duty to provide. But, in the eighteenth and early nineteenth centuries, the idea that certain powers could be regarded as being in the nature of trusts was unduly extended. This extension resulted in the growth of the unfortunate distinction between exclusive and non-exclusive powers —it was held that if there was a power to appoint amongst a class, no member of the class could be excluded unless a power to exclude were specially given; and in the accompanying doctrine of illusory appointments—it was held that the appointment of a merely nominal sum to one of the class was invalid. These doctrines were got rid of by two statutes of the nineteenth century,[1] which restored to appointors the free discretion which had been taken away from them by the undue extension of the trust concept.

This legislation emphasized the discretionary aspect of powers. But, subject to this exception, the legislation of the nineteenth century has tended to emphasize their proprietary aspect. Three illustrations will make this clear. First, the tendency to allow the free alienation of all rights led to the permission to release all powers, even powers simply collateral, other than powers in the nature of trusts.[2] Secondly, the inconvenience of allowing the creators of powers to require for the execution of powers the observance of what formalities they pleased led to the enactment of statutes which provide that, whatever formalities may be required, a power to be exercised by will is well exercised by a will in the form required by the Wills Act 1837; [3] and that a power to be executed by deed is well executed by a deed attested by two or more witnesses.[4] These statutes thus assimilate the formalities required for the execution of powers to the formalities required for the disposition

[1] 11 George IV and 1 William IV, c. 46, § 1; 37, 38 Victoria, c. 37.

[2] 44, 45 Victoria, c. 41, § 52; Halsbury, Laws of England, xxiii. 64.

[3] 7 William IV, and 1 Victoria, c. 26, §§ 9 and 10.

[4] 22, 23 Victoria, c. 35, § 12.

of property. Thirdly, powers which the donee might have exercised for his own benefit are liable to be taken in execution under the Judgements Act 1838,[1] and vest in and can be exercised by the trustee in the bankruptcy of the donee.[2]

The growth of these different varieties of powers, and their development by the courts and the Legislature, show us that the law has, by a judicious mixture of the mandatory and the proprietary ideas inherent in powers of appointment, created a new and original species of interest in the land. We have seen that without them the system of strictly settling property would have been unworkable;[3] and though they have had important effects on other parts of the land law, notably on the law of mortgage,[4] it is this effect which constitutes their main contribution to its development.

§ 4. The Rules against Perpetuities [5]

We have seen that from a very early period the common law had shown a strong bias in favour of freedom of alienation;[6] and the manner in which the courts aided the frustration of the statute De Donis Conditionalibus, by giving efficacy to the common recovery, shows that this bias was maintained all through the medieval period.[7] During the Middle Ages the principle of freedom of alienation was, in fact, adequately safeguarded. But towards the

[1] 1, 2 Victoria, c. 110, § 11.
[2] 4, 5 George V, c. 59, § 38 (2) (*b*).
[3] Above, p. 205. [4] Above, pp. 205–6: below, pp. 261, 263.
[5] Holdsworth, H. E. L. vii. 193–238.
[6] Above, p. 108. [7] Above, pp. 57–8.

middle of the sixteenth century it was becoming apparent that the medieval rules were no longer sufficient. By means of the new future interests in land, which were then becoming recognized, it had become possible so to settle property that it must, for an indefinite period, continue to be enjoyed by a series of limited owners, no one of whom had complete freedom of alienation.

During the latter half of the sixteenth century landowners began to realize the fact that they could thus settle their property, and they began to make these settlements. Just as in the Middle Ages alienation into mortmain showed that landowners would, unless restrained, use their power to alienate freely so as to destroy that power,[1] so now the settlements attempted by them showed that they wished to do much the same thing, by so tying up their land that no future owner should have complete power of alienation. These settlements show that they hoped to be able to restore again those unbarrable entails which, though sanctioned by the Legislature in the thirteenth, had been finally frustrated by the courts in the fifteenth century. Thus the struggle of the courts to maintain the principle of freedom of alienation entered upon a new phase. The courts found it necessary to lay down rules to prevent settlements which created what was in effect an unbarrable entail, or, as the lawyers of the sixteenth century and later called it, ' a perpetuity.' This struggle against these attempts of the landowners resulted, in the sixteenth and seventeenth centuries, in the gradual evolution of many different rules, all designed to ensure that

[1] Above, pp. 109–10.

land should not be vested in limited owners for an indefinite period.

These rules were devised to meet the various devices employed by the landowners to create a perpetuity. They were concerned mainly with devices to make an estate tail unbarrable, or to evade the liability to destruction characteristic of contingent remainders, or of the other interests which were treated as contingent remainders.[1] But they suffered from the defects of being both too limited in their scope, and inadequate in their contents. They were too limited in their scope because they did not apply to limitations which, not being able to take effect as contingent remainders, were held to be not destructible like these remainders; and they were only applicable to property in land.[2] They were inadequate in their contents because they were, for the most part, merely negative. They condemned certain sorts of limitations, or rendered them liable to destruction in certain ways; but they gave no information to landowners as to what limitations were valid. They laid down no positive rule for their guidance. What was wanted was a rule which was both positive and negative—a rule which would tell owners of property both what settlements they might and what they might not make.

The rule required was first clearly laid down by the decision of Lord Nottingham in 1681 in *The Duke of Norfolk's Case*, which was upheld by the House of

[1] Above, pp. 194–5, 199.

[2] Till the growth of stocks and shares in the seventeenth century, land was the one form of permanent property. Other kinds of chattels personal are of a wasting character, so that settlements of them are not very usual.

Lords in 1685.[1] It was both positive and negative. According to that rule, as finally settled, any interest which must vest within a life or lives in being and twenty-one years after is valid; any interest which may vest at a period more remote is invalid. Thus the rule tells the owners of property both what they may do, and what they may not do; and it is a general rule applicable to all kinds of property. The general principle laid down in 1685, that it is the time at which a future interest must vest that must be regarded in considering whether any given limitation infringes the rule against perpetuities, was elaborated by the courts during the following centuries. But it did not abrogate the older rules except in so far as they were directly contradictory to it.[2]

This sketch of the evolution of the law indicates the main lines of division. They are as follows: the Older Rules; the Modern Rule; the Relation between these Rules.

The Older Rules.

We have seen that, with a view to prevent the creation of a perpetuity, the common law rules as to the limitation of contingent remainders, and as to their capacity to be destroyed, had been applied to some of the future estates which took effect by the operation of the statutes of Uses and Wills.[3] The older rules, therefore, centre round these rules as to contingent remainders. From this point of view these rules can be divided into two classes. First the rules which made contingent remainders destructible;

[1] 3 Ch. Cas. 1; 1 Pollex. 223; 2 Ch. Rep. 229; Swanst. 454; below, pp. 224–5. [2] Below, pp. 228–9. [3] Above, pp. 199–200.

and secondly the rules which were designed to prevent a contingent remainder from vesting at too remote a date. (i) The rules which made contingent remainders destructible[1] obviously tended to prevent a perpetuity. But we have seen that this liability to destruction was, in a large measure, obviated by the device of trustees to preserve contingent remainders.[2] Thus it happened that the second of these classes of rules had a more permanent effect in preventing the creation of perpetuities. (ii) The following three rules prevented a contingent remainder from vesting at too remote a date:

(*a*) The rule that a remainder will fail if it is not ready to vest when the precedent estate determines. This was an effectual safeguard against the creation of a perpetuity for the following reasons: A contingent remainder must be limited to take effect either after a life estate or an estate tail. If it is limited to take effect after a life estate it must vest, if at all, within the compass of a life in being. If it is limited to take effect after an estate tail it may be destroyed at any time by the process of barring the estate tail, so that its existence does not render the property inalienable. It is true that, in certain cases, the Contingent Remainders Act (1877)[3] saves from destruction contingent remainders which are not ready to vest when the precedent estate determines; but only those contingent remainders are saved which comply with the modern rule against perpetuities.[4]

(*b*) The rule that all provisos designed to prevent a tenant in tail from barring his estate tail were void.

[1] Above, pp. 194–5.
[2] Above, pp. 195–6.
[3] 40, 41 Victoria, c. 33.
[4] Above, pp. 196–7.

Many such devices were employed during the latter part of the sixteenth century. But in *Corbet's Case*,[1] *Mildmay's Case*,[2] and finally in *Mary Portington's Case* [3] they were held to be void. Henceforth it was accepted as a fundamental principle that any set of limitations designed to create a perpetuity by means of an unbarrable entail was void.[4]

(*c*) The rule which prevented the creation of a perpetual freehold, that is, an indefinite series of life estates, by way of contingent remainder. By the end of the sixteenth century it was well understood that contingent remainders could not be limited to a series of unborn persons, one after another, in such a way that a perpetual freehold was created. The rule on this subject was, for the first time, clearly laid down in Coke's argument in *Perrot's Case* in 1595.[5] He had no difficulty in showing that the creation of a perpetual freehold was in effect a perpetuity; and he laid down the rule, which has since prevailed, as to the conditions under which such a grant should be held to be valid. An estate might be limited to *A* for life, remainder to his unborn son for life; but all further limitations after the second life estate were void.[6]

[1] (1599–1600), 1 Co. Rep. 83 b.

[2] (1606), 6 Co. Rep. 40 a.

[3] (1614), 10 Co. Rep. 35 b.

[4] See Holdsworth, H. E. L. vii. 207–9.

[5] Moore, 368.

[6] At one time this rule was treated as a deduction from a supposed principle that there could not be a possibility on a possibility, or, as it was sometimes called, a double possibility. This supposed principle was applied in two ways: (1) It was applied as a reason for the view that remainders limited on too remote a contingency were invalid; but at the end of the seventeenth and in the eighteenth century the courts held that the remoteness of a contingency did not affect its validity, see Holdsworth, H. E. L. vii. 92–8; above, p. 190. (2) It was taken as a large premise which justified the

In one respect only was this rule modified. It was laid down in *Humbertson* v. *Humbertson* in 1716[1] that if an attempt was made to create a perpetual freehold by will, the court would do what it could to effectuate the testator's intention by giving to persons in being life estates and to their unborn children estates tail. This is known as the 'cypres' doctrine. It was long doubtful whether a contingent remainder could be limited after a contingent remainder, provided that the rule preventing the creation of a perpetual freehold was not infringed. It was settled in two modern cases that the second contingent remainder was valid, provided that it must vest within the period allowed by the modern rule against perpetuities.[2]

The Modern Rule.

The modern rule is thus stated by Williams[3]:

> 'The rule against perpetuities requires every future estate limited to arise by way of shifting use or executory devise to be such as must necessarily arise (if at all) within the compass of existing lives and twenty-one years after, with the possible addition of the period of gestation, in the case of some person entitled being a posthumous child. But if no lives are fixed on, then the term of twenty-one years only is allowed. And every executory estate which might

rule that a perpetual freehold could not be created by limiting a series of contingent remainders, see Holdsworth, H. E. L. vii. 212–14; but in 1910 the court of Appeal declared the non-existence of this application of the supposed principle: in their view it was a not very intelligent reason for the rule which prevented the creation of a perpetual freehold, *Re Nash*, [1910] 1 Ch. at pp. 9–10; cf. *Whitby* v. *Mitchell* (1889), 42 C. D. at pp. 501–2 *per* Kay J.

[1] 1 P. Wms. 332; cp. *Monypenny* v. *Dering* (1847), 16 M. and W. 418.

[2] *Re Frost* (1889), 43 C. D. 246: *Re Ashforth*, [1905] 1 Ch. 535.

[3] Real Property (22nd ed.), 413–14.

in any event transgress the limits so fixed will from its commencement be absolutely void.'

It is clear that this is a rule which is very different in its character from the older rules which we have just discussed.

The need for this rule arose from the fact that *Manning's Case* and *Lampet's Case* settled that executory devises of terms were not only valid but indestructible ; [1] and that the case of *Pells* v. *Brown* settled that executory interests in freeholds (other than those which took effect by way of contingent remainder) were also indestructible.[2]

But, till the decision in *The Duke of Norfolk's Case*,[3] there was much uncertainty as to the form which the rule should take. The judges did not as yet see that the crucial test as to whether or not a limitation was valid ought to depend upon the question whether it might vest at too remote a date. They were inclined rather to look at the nature of the precedent estate, and to rule that, if it was a greater estate than an estate for life, all the subsequent limitations were bad. In the case of *Child* v. *Baylie*,[4] in 1618, Bridgman unsuccessfully argued that the remoteness of the date at which the executory limitation might vest was the important matter. He continued to hold this view ; and, in fact, he drew the conveyance in *The Duke of Norfolk's Case*,[5] the validity of which depended upon its correctness.[6]

The following were the material facts of that case :

[1] Above, pp. 199–200. [2] Above, p. 199.
[3] Above, pp. 219–20 ; below, pp. 224–5. [4] Cro. Jac. 459.
[5] 3 Ch. Cas. 1 ; 2 Ch. Rep. 229 ; Pollex. 223 ; 2 Swanst. 454.
[6] Holdsworth, H. E. L. vii. 221–2.

the Earl of Arundel conveyed land to trustees for a term of 200 years on trust for Henry Howard, his second son, and the heirs male of his body; but if Thomas Howard, his eldest son, died without issue male in Henry Howard's lifetime, or if the earldom should descend upon Henry Howard, the land was to be held on trust for Charles Howard, his third son. In 1675 Henry Howard got the term assigned to himself, and suffered a recovery to the use of himself and his heirs. In 1677 Thomas Howard died without issue. The question therefore arose whether the executory trust in favour of Charles Howard was barred by this recovery. Since the assignment of the term to Henry Howard was made with notice of the trust, the assignment and the recovery could be disregarded, if the executory trust in favour of Charles was valid. Obviously its validity depended on the question whether or not it was too remote. In 1682 Lord Nottingham, contrary to the opinion of Pemberton and North, C.JJ., and Montague, C.B., whom he had called in to advise him, held that the trust was not too remote, because it must take effect, if at all, within the compass of an existing life. He therefore made a decree in favour of Charles Howard. In 1683, on a bill of review, his successor lord keeper North reversed this decision; but in 1685 Lord Nottingham's decree was restored by the House of Lords.

This case thus laid down the root principle of the modern rule against perpetuities—the validity of an executory interest depends upon the remoteness of the date at which it is limited to vest. It also laid down the principle, which was assumed in the earlier cases on executory interests, that, in considering the validity of a limitation, possible and not actual events must be considered. It was assumed in these earlier cases because the same principle was applicable to those older rules which prevented the creation of an unbarrable entail or a perpetual freehold. Limitations designed to effect this result were bad *ab initio*, quite regardless of actual events, which in fact caused a subsequent limitation to vest within a life in being. On the other hand, this principle was not applicable to the older rule, which required a legal contingent remainder to vest at or before the termination of the precedent estate of freehold; for the question whether this rule has been complied with can only be answered by reference to the actual event. We shall see that it is this difference, arising from the nature of this last-named rule, which, before the Property Acts, underlay the leading difference between the treatment of legal contingent remainders and the treatment of other future interests in property.

The Duke of Norfolk's Case did not settle the utmost limit of time at which a future interest could be made to vest. That was the work of the eighteenth and early nineteenth centuries.[1] The rule was finally settled in the form stated above [2] by the decision of the House of Lords in 1832 in the case of *Cadell* v. *Palmer*; [3] and it is only very slightly modified by the Property Act.[4]

Before the Property Acts the rule, as thus settled, was modified in only two respects by the Legislature. (i) The posthumous avarice of Peter Thellusson

[1] See Holdsworth, H. E. L. vii. 226–7. [2] Above, p. 223.

[3] 1 Cl. and Fin. 272. [4] Law of Property Act, 1925, § 163.

made it clear that trusts to accumulate property ought to be restrained within narrower limits than trusts to permit the property to be enjoyed by a series of limited owners.[1] The validity of Thellusson's will was upheld; [2] but the Legislature in 1800 passed an Act to restrain these trusts.[3] This Act and a later Act of 1892 [4] are reproduced with amendments in the Law of Property Act.[5] (ii) The Conveyancing Act of 1882 [6] provided that if a person was entitled in fee, for life, or for a term of years, and there was an executory limitation over on failure of his issue, that limitation became void so soon as any of the issue attained twenty-one. This rule is also reproduced in the Law of Property Act.[7]

The Relation between these Rules.

The relation between these rules gave rise to two different sets of questions. First, what was the relation of the modern rule to certain common law limitations which were older than it? Secondly, what was the relation of the modern rule to the older rules applicable to contingent remainders?

(1) It was long doubtful whether the modern rule was applicable to common law rights of entry for breach of condition. It was settled that it was applicable in 1899; [8] and this is now enacted by the

[1] Holdsworth, H. E. L. vii. 228–31.

[2] *Thellusson* v. *Woodford* (1797), 4 Ves. 227; S.C. on appeal, 11 Ves. 112.

[3] 39, 40 George III, c. 98.

[4] 55, 56 Victoria, c. 58.

[5] Law of Property Act, 1925, §§ 164–6.

[6] 45, 46 Victoria, c. 39, § 10.

[7] Law of Property Act, 1925, § 134.

[8] *Re the Trustees of Hollis' Hospital*, [1899] 2 Ch. 540.

Law of Property Act 1925.[1] On the other hand, it is now enacted, in accordance with the better opinion, that it does not apply to a right of re-entry for the non-payment of a rent charge.[2] Such a right is part of the estate of the owner of the rent charge. It is therefore a vested estate to which the rule is not applicable.[3]

(2) The relation of the modern rule to the older rules applicable to contingent remainders was a much more difficult question. There was no doubt that the modern rule applied to equitable contingent remainders.[4] But, first, how far did it apply to legal contingent remainders; and, secondly, were equitable contingent remainders affected by any of the older rules? The solution ultimately worked out was as follows:

(i) The older rules applicable to the limitation of legal contingent remainders[5] in effect made the creation of a perpetuity by their means impossible. They were in fact restrained more strictly than they would be restrained by the modern rule. The only instance in which they were favoured arose from the fact that, in considering whether a contingent remainder fails by reason of abeyance of the seisin, you must look, not at possible, but at actual events. Thus, if an estate was limited to *A* for life, remainder to his unborn child at any age over twenty-one, this limitation would have been void in its inception if limited in any other way than by way of legal contingent remainder; but, if limited by way of legal contingent

[1] § 4, (3).

[2] Ibid., § 162, (1).

[3] Holdsworth, H. E. L. vii. 234.

[4] *Abbiss* v. *Burney* (1880), 17 C.D., 211.

[5] Above, pp. 221–2.

remainder, it would have taken effect if the child reached the required age at or before the expiration of the precedent estate—that is within a life in being.

(ii) It was settled that the rule as to the invalidity of an unbarrable entail;[1] and the rule that, after an estate to an unborn person for life, a contingent remainder in favour of that unborn person's children was invalid;[2] applied both to equitable and to legal contingent remainders.

The results upon the law were not happy. There was, first, one rule—the rule requiring that a contingent remainder must vest at or before the expiration of the precedent estate—applicable only to such legal contingent remainders as infringed the modern rule.[3] Secondly, there were two other rules—the rules against the creation of an unbarrable estate tail and a perpetual freehold—which were applied to any set of future interests in land which had the obvious result of infringing them; and from the latter of these two rules it followed that, after an estate for life to an unborn person, a contingent remainder (legal or equitable) to that unborn person's children was invalid. Thirdly, there was the modern rule against perpetuities, which applied generally to all future limitations of any kind of property, including equitable contingent remainders, and to legal contingent remainders limited after legal contingent remainders, but not to legal contingent remainders limited after a vested estate.

In any body of law which is developed through decided cases, there comes a time when the principles underlying the cases have been so fully worked out

[1] Above, pp. 221–2. [2] *Re Nash*, [1910] 1 Ch. 1. [3] Above, p. 221.

that a restatement of the law is desirable ; and such a restatement is doubly desirable when these principles are divergent in their character, and traceable historically to different sources ; for in such a case they give rise to a body of rules, the complexity of which, though it can be explained historically, cannot be justified. In 1832 it was obvious to the Real Property Commissioners that the time for such a restatement had come ; and they made a series of suggestions as to the form which such a restatement should take. But their suggestions bore no fruit. The Law of Property Act 1925 has, however, solved these problems. It has, in effect, restated this branch of the law of property, which is one of the most important of all its branches, because it defines the chief limitation upon that essential incident of the right of property—the right of the owner to dispose of it as he will.

We must now turn from the rules which regulate the powers of landowners to deal with their property, to the rules of law which regulate the rights and duties of the persons who actually occupy the land.

§ 5. Landlord and Tenant[1]

At the close of the medieval period the decay of villein tenure had caused a large extension of the practice of letting land to farmers for terms of varying duration ; and, during the sixteenth and seventeenth centuries, the policy of encouraging the farmer and the agricultural industry made for the continuance and extension of this practice. 'For the most part', said Coke in *Walker's Case*,[2] 'every man is lessor or

[1] Holdsworth, H. E. L. vii. 238–96.

[2] (1587), 3 Co. Rep. at f. 23 a.

a lessee.' In this period, therefore, we see the formation of one of the peculiar features in the English land system—the fact that 'the great bulk of the land is not cultivated by the owner, but by tenant occupiers.' [1] This, it has been said, 'is a feature in the English land system not less singular in Europe than the law and custom of primogeniture.' [2] Nor are these two singular features wholly unconnected. The practice of strictly settling land, which grew up during this period, aimed at and succeeded in effecting the same results as were effected by the law of primogeniture. It tended to promote the accumulation of estates, and ensured their descent as one whole to a single proprietor. But, except in the case of those parts of these estates which were occupied by copyholders,[3] the only way in which these proprietors could exploit their properties was by letting them on lease to tenant farmers. Thus it happened that, during this period, these two factors—the agrarian policy of the state, and the law and custom of primogeniture as artificially extended by the system of strict settlement—united to make the relation of landlord and tenant a very common relation in the country at large. At the same time the growing commercial prosperity of the country made for the growth of urban districts, and the extension of this relationship to urban properties. Naturally, therefore, the law of landlord and tenant began to develop during this period, and its main principles began to be settled upon their modern basis.

[1] Brodrick, English Land and English Landlords, 198, citing Caird, Landed Interest, 46, 47.

[2] Ibid.

[3] Above, pp. 42–5.

I shall trace the history of some of the more salient features of this large chapter of our modern law under the following heads: The Varieties of Tenancies, their Incidents, and Creation; The Obligations of the Lessor; The Obligations of the Lessee; Covenants Running with the Land and the Reversion.

The Varieties of Tenancies, their Incidents, and Creation.[1]

I have already described the main varieties of tenancies—tenancies for life or lives, tenancies for terms of years, tenancies at will, from year to year, and at sufferance.[2]

Technically tenancies for life or lives and tenancies for terms of years fell into the two widely separate categories of freehold and chattel interests. The tenant for life or lives had certain advantages which explain the prevalence of this form of tenancy. We have seen that, during the greater part of the medieval period, it was the freeholder alone who could get specific restitution; and later, when this had ceased to be a distinguishing feature of a freehold interest,[3] it still continued to possess other advantages over a chattel interest. It conferred the Parliamentary franchise; and the interest of a tenant who held under a lease for lives was not liable on his death for his simple contract debts.

On the other hand, the lease for years had other advantages which eventually tended to make it more popular than the lease for life or lives. For instance, its duration was definite; and this advantage, obvious even in the case of agricultural leases, was even

[1] Holdsworth, H. E. L. vii. 239–50.

[2] Above, pp. 60–5, 71–3. [3] Above, p. 72.

more obvious in building and mining leases. It was a chattel interest; and this meant that its devolution upon an intestacy was governed by the more rational rules applicable to personal property. A lease for years could, while a lease for life could not, be limited *in futuro*;[1] and it can still be so granted, provided that it takes effect not more than twenty-one years from the date of the instrument creating it.[2] It is not surprising, therefore, that during the seventeenth and eighteenth centuries these leases for terms of years tended to replace leases for life or lives. It would seem that, down to the period of the Napoleonic wars, farmers generally held their land upon leases for fixed terms—often for twenty-one years; and the period of twenty-one years allowed by the statute of 1540,[3] and generally permitted by powers inserted in strict settlements, was the period allowed by the Settled Land Acts, till the Act of 1925. Agriculture was the most important form of industry down to the period of the industrial revolution; so that it is not surprising that the forms of other leases, such as building and mining leases, were not settled till the nineteenth century. In 1805 Lord Eldon regarded the insertion in a marriage settlement of a power to grant a building lease for 99 years as unusual.[4] But it is not improbable that some such period was then becoming the normal period; and it is clear from the provisions of the earlier Settled Land Acts that, towards the end of the nineteenth century, 99 years had become the usual period for a building lease, and 60 years for a

[1] Above, pp. 112, 191.

[2] Law of Property Act, 1925, § 149 (3).

[3] Above, p. 168.

[4] *Attorney-General* v. *Owen* (1805), 10 Ves. at p. 560.

mining lease. In this, as in other respect, these Acts codified the existing conveyancing practice.[1]

But though technically there were great differences, and substantially there were some differences, between leases for life or lives and leases for terms of years, they were fundamentally similar. Perhaps the best illustration of this fundamental similarity is the manner in which some of the principles applicable to the tenure of, and estates in, freehold interests in land were applied to the relation of lessor and lessee for a term of years. Thus, in the first place, fealty was due from lessor to lessee. In the second place, the lessor, by reason of the tenure which existed, could distrain. In the third place, the different effects of an assignment and an under-lease by a lessee for years may be compared to the different effects of a conveyance in fee simple and a conveyance for a smaller estate by the owner of the fee. In the case of an assignment the assignee steps into the place of the assignor, and becomes liable to pay the rent and to perform covenants in the lease which run with the land. It may thus be compared to an alienation in fee simple, as the result of which the alienee holds, not of the alienor, but of the alienor's lord. On the other hand, in the case of an under-lease a new estate is created which is held by the under-lessee of the under-lessor; and, because it is a new and a different estate, the under-lessee is not liable upon any of the covenants in the head lease. It may thus be compared to the creation by a tenant

[1] The Settled Land Act 1925 § 41 allows, in the case of building leases, terms of 999 years; in the case of mining leases, terms of 100 years; in the case of forestry leases, terms of 999 years; in the case of any other lease, terms of 50 years.

in fee simple of a life estate, as the result of which the life tenant held of the tenant in fee simple. Since the Property Acts, in fact, it is only in the relation of landlord and tenant that the doctrine and consequences of tenure have any real significance.[1]

A lease for life or lives could be created in any of the ways in which a freehold interest could be created —by feoffment, fine, recovery, or by a conveyance operating under the statute of Uses. A term of years could be created by the owner of the freehold by means of a conveyance operating under the statute of Uses, or otherwise by words or writing. The statute of Frauds required leases for lives and for years to be in writing signed by the parties, except leases for a term not exceeding three years at a rent of at least two-thirds of the value of the property demised;[2] and the Real Property Act 1845 required a deed in all cases in which the statute of Frauds had required writing.[3] The provisions of these two statutes are reproduced by the Law of Property Act 1925.[4]

None of these leases, except leases which took effect by the operation of the statute of Uses, could take effect without a physical transfer of possession. Just as a feoffment was inoperative to confer an estate without livery of seisin, so a lessee, before entry, got no estate, but only an *interesse termini*. This *interesse termini* gave him a certain interest in the property, but no complete estate, e.g. he could not take a release of his lessor's interest till he had entered.[5] The Law of Property Act 1925 has abolished the necessity

[1] Above, p. 38.
[2] 29 Charles II, c. 3, §§ 1 and 2.
[3] 8, 9 Victoria, c. 106, § 3.
[4] §§ 52 (1) (2) *d*, 54.
[5] Holdsworth, H. E. L. vii. 247.

for entry to perfect a lease, and with it the doctrine of the *interesse termini*.[1]

The Obligations of the Lessor.[2]

As early as the fifteenth century it was recognized that when land was let for a term of years the relation of landlord and tenant gave rise to an implied covenant for quiet enjoyment and title. But this implied covenant was not satisfactory either to lessor or lessee. It was not satisfactory to the lessee, because it ended with the expiry of the lessor's estate. It was not satisfactory to the lessor, because it extended, not only to his own acts, but to the acts of those who claimed by title paramount. It therefore became customary for lessors and lessees to make express covenants; and it was held that these covenants 'qualified the generality of the covenant in law and restrained it by the mutual consent of both parties'.[3] These express covenants were more satisfactory to the lessee, in that their obligation did not end with the expiry of the lessor's estate. They were more satisfactory to the lessor, in that they were generally so worded that they extended only to the acts of the lessor and those claiming under him, and not to the acts of those who claimed by title paramount. In fact, by the beginning of the seventeenth century, on a lease, just as on a sale of the fee simple,[4] express covenants were usually entered into, that the lessor had the right to demise, for quiet enjoyment, for further assurance, and against incumbrances; to

[1] § 149 (1) (2).
[2] Holdsworth, H. E. L. vii. 250–61.
[3] *Nokes's Case* (1599), 4 Co. Rep. at f. 80 b.
[4] Below, p. 247.

which was later added, on the assignment of a lease, the covenant that the lease is subsisting, and that the lessor's covenants have been performed.

The only other obligation of the lessor of which it is necessary to say anything is the obligation resulting from a covenant, sometimes inserted in leases, to renew the lease. These covenants were held to be valid in the latter part of the sixteenth century;[1] and in 1715 it was held by the House of Lords that a covenant of this kind, though it was for perpetual renewal, was not void as infringing the rule against perpetuities.[2] As Gray has pointed out, if the covenant for renewal is absolute, the decision is correct. It does not infringe the rule, because the covenant to renew 'is part of the lessee's present interest. The right which the present possessor of land has to continue or drop his possession is not a right subject to a condition precedent.'[3] It creates, as Jessel, M.R., said, 'an equitable estate from the time of its execution.'[4] But, as Mr. Cyprian Williams has pointed out,[5] this reasoning does not apply to a case where the covenant to renew is not absolute. It does not apply, for instance, to a case where the lessee's right is limited to arise, only on giving notice within a particular time, and paying a specified fine. The allowance of the validity of such a covenant for perpetual renewal is, as Jessel, M.R., said,[6] an exception from the rule against perpetuities, no

[1] *Chapman* v. *Dalton* (1565), Plowden, 286.

[2] *Bridges* v. *Hitchcock*, 5 Bro. P.C. 6.

[3] Gray, Perpetuities, 194.

[4] *Moore* v. *Clench* (1875), 1 C.D. at p. 452.

[5] 42 Solicitors' Journal, 630; and Gray agrees, Perpetuities, 195.

[6] *L.S.W.R.* v. *Gomm* (1882), 20 C.D. at p. 579.

doubt permitted because it was established when the rule against perpetuities was as yet young,[1] and before any one had realized that such covenants, in effect, created an equitable interest to which the rule should be applied.[2] That being so, it is not surprising to find that the courts will not construe a covenant for renewal as a covenant for perpetual renewal unless such an intention clearly appears;[3] and that it has been decided, in accordance with the views expressed by Mr. Cyprian Williams,[4] that an option of purchase given to a lessee for years, to be exercised at a period which may infringe the rule against perpetuities, is invalid.[5]

The Obligations of the Lessee.[6]

The most important of the lessee's obligations are (1) his duty to pay rent; (2) his liabilities in respect of waste; (3) his liabilities on conditions or covenants against assignment or underletting; (4) his liabilities in respect of fixtures.

(1) Rent. We have seen that two very different ideas have contributed to the formation of the rules relating to rent—the medieval idea that rent is a thing issuing out of the land, and similar in many of its incidents to an estate in the land; and the modern idea that the obligation to pay rent is a personal obligation founded on contract.[7] In our modern rules of law on this subject we can see traces of both those very different ideas.

[1] Above, p. 224. [2] See 42 Solicitors' Journal, 630.

[3] *Baynham* v. *Guy's Hospital* (1796), 3 Ves. at p. 298.

[4] 42 Solicitors' Journal, 628–30, 650.

[5] *Woodall* v. *Clifton*, [1905] 2 Ch. at pp. 259–66 *per* Warrington, J.

[6] Holdsworth, H. E. L. vii. 261–86. [7] Above, pp. 98–9.

(i) *The medieval idea.* (*a*) The fact that rent was recoverable by the real actions emphasized its similarity to corporeal estates in the land ; and, though the real actions are things of the past, the right of distraint for non-payment of rent still illustrates its close connexion with the land and the chattels thereon. (*b*) As rent was regarded as a species of property, it was never looked upon as a mere chose in action. Therefore it was always assignable. A rent reserved belonged to the landlord as part of his reversion, and could be assigned with that reversion. (*c*) The nature of the remedies provided for the non-payment of rent gave rise to the rule that it cannot be reserved out of an incorporeal thing. Though itself an incorporeal thing, it must be solidly attached to visible land, because otherwise it would be difficult to exercise the remedy of distraint.[1] It is true that a contract can be made to pay for the use of an incorporeal thing ; but such a payment is not a true rent. This rule, subject to a modification introduced by the Law of Property Act 1925,[2] is still a rule of English Law.[3] (*d*) Since rent was regarded as issuing out of the land, it followed, first, that it was not due till the end of the time fixed for payment, till, that is, the lessee had taken the profits of the land ; and, secondly, that if the lease ended before the time fixed for payment, there could be no apportionment, so that the rent ceased to be due. The strictness of the latter principle was, it is true, modified ; but it still worked considerable injustice till it was swept

[1] *British Mutoscope and Biograph Co.* v. *Homer*, [1901] 1 Ch. at p. 675.

[2] § 122 (1).

[3] Cheshire, Real Property (3rd ed.), 319.

away by the Apportionment Act 1870,[1] which provided that rents and other periodical payments should accrue from day to day, and should be apportionable in respect of time accordingly.

(ii) *The contractual idea.* Even when Coke was writing, it was clear that the relation of lessor and lessee involved the elements both of contract and conveyance.[2] Between lessor and lessee there was both privity of contract and privity of estate; and an action for debt for rent reserved on a lease for years lay at common law.[3] Hence if a lessee assigns his estate, though privity of estate has ceased, privity of contract remains, and he continues to be liable for the rent. In 1709 personal actions were allowed to be brought for rent reserved on grants of estates of freehold or inheritance.[4] This tended to emphasize the contractual aspect of rent; and, as we have seen, the rule that rent could not be reserved out of an incorporeal thing could be evaded by making a contract to pay for its use.[5]

The conception of rent as a sum due by virtue of a contract tended to liberalize the old rules. But in one respect it tended to make them more rigid. If a man had contracted to pay rent he was bound by his contract, whatever happened to the land or the premises.[6] The only mitigations allowed to the lessee's liability were in the cases where the lessor had himself evicted the lessee from the whole or a part of the premises, or where the lessee had been evicted from the whole of the

[1] 33, 34, Victoria, c. 35.

[2] 'In every lease for years there is a contract between lessor and lessee,' *Walker's Case* (1587), 4 Co. Rep. at f. 22 b.

[3] Litt. § 58. [4] 8 Anne, c. 14, § 4. [5] Above, p. 239.

[6] *Paradine* v. *Jane* (1647), Aleyn at p. 27.

premises by some one claiming by a title paramount to that of the lessor. In these cases the rent was suspended during the continuance of the eviction. Since these mitigations of the lessee's liability were obviously fair, they have become part of our modern law.

(2) Waste. The medieval rules as to waste were during this period developed both by common law and equity.

The common law courts developed the law as to permissive waste and meliorative waste. Both Coke [1] and Blackstone [2] laid it down that tenants for life and years were liable for permissive waste, i. e. waste occasioned by acts of omission. But cases decided in the early years of the nineteenth century leave it doubtful whether tenants for years are liable for permissive waste; [3] and it has been decided that tenants for life are not liable.[4] The common law held strictly to the view that any act which altered the character of the property was waste—even though the effect of the act was to raise its value. This is meliorative waste.[5] This strict rule of the common law was adhered to as late as 1671.[6] But before that date some judges were inclined to adopt the more reasonable rule that an act which did not diminish the value of the property, and did not prejudice the inheritance, could not be waste. This was held to be the right view by Denman, C.J., in 1833.[7]

1 Second Instit. 145.

2 Comm. ii. 283.

3 *Herne* v. *Bembow* (1813), 4 Taunt. 764; *Jones* v. *Hill* (1817), 7 Taunt. 392 negative the liability; but there are a series of cases to the contrary, see *Davies* v. *Davies* (1888), 38 C.D. 499.

4 *Re Cartwright* (1889), 41 C.D. 532.

5 Co. Litt. 53 a.

6 *Cole* v. *Green*, 3 Lev. 309.

7 *Doe d. Grubb* v. *Burlington*, 5 B. and Ad. 507.

On the basis of the common law doctrines as to waste, the court of Chancery erected a considerable superstructure of equitable rules. These rules concerned chiefly tenants holding limited interests under settlements; but some of them affected all tenants. They affected the legal rules in three main directions. First, equity followed the law and applied the legal rules applicable to legal estates to equitable estates. Secondly, equity laid down rules as to the power of the tenant to deal with the property which sometimes enlarged, and sometimes restricted, his legal powers. It enlarged his powers in that it allowed a tenant for life under a settlement to cut ripe timber, the proceeds being held on trust, as to the income for the tenant for life, and as to the capital to the first tenant for life without impeachment of waste.[1] It restricted his powers in that, from an early date, it restrained a tenant unimpeachable for waste from making an inequitable use of his powers;[2] and, as the result of this interference, it created and developed the conception of equitable waste. Thirdly, since the old common law action for waste was very defective, equity gave the better remedy of an injunction; and this fact induced the common law courts to supersede the old action for waste by an action on the case.[3] The action on the case superseded the old action for waste for reasons somewhat similar to those which caused the action of ejectment to supersede the real actions. The old action was

[1] *Waldo* v. *Waldo* (1846), 12 Sim. 107.

[2] *Vane* v. *Lord Barnard* (1716), 2 Vern. 738.

[3] See *Woodhouse* v. *Walker* (1880), 5 Q.B.D. at pp. 406–7; Holdsworth, H. E. L. vii. 280–81.

abolished in 1833 with the real actions,[1] so that, at the present day, the remedy for waste is an action for damages, supplemented, where necessary, by the equitable remedy of injunction.

(3) Conditions or covenants against assignment or underletting. We have seen that the common law has always endeavoured to maintain freedom of alienation;[2] and that, with this object in view, it has declared to be void any attempts to prevent a tenant in fee simple from alienating his fee, or a tenant in tail from barring his entail.[3] But the imposition of a restraint upon the power of a tenant for life or years to assign or underlet was a different matter. As the rules against waste proved, these tenants had not complete freedom of disposition; and it is quite clear that the relation of landlord and tenant, and the exigencies of estate management, make the power to impose some sort of restraint desirable. The legality of these restraints was recognized by Coke in *Mildmay's Case.*[4] Coke also laid it down that, though such a condition was lawful, yet a grant made in breach of it was valid.[5] This view has prevailed;[6] and it has also been settled that the operation of such a condition is restricted to assignments made by the lessee himself, so that it does not apply when the property passes by operation of law, for instance on death or bankruptcy.[7]

(4) Fixtures. Anything annexed to the soil be-

[1] 3, 4 William IV, c. 27, § 36.

[2] Above, p. 108.

[3] Above, pp. 106, 221–2.

[4] (1606) 6 Co. Rep. at f. 43 a.

[5] Co. Litt. 223 b.

[6] *Williams* v. *Earle* (1868), L.R. 3, Q. B. at p. 750.

[7] Holdsworth, H. E. L. vii. 282, n. 4.

comes the property of the owner of the soil—*quicquid plantatur solo, solo cedit.* Therefore at the termination of his lease the tenant must give up all articles originally fixed to the property, or which have become fixed to it during the term.[1] In the sixteenth century there are signs that the courts were beginning to realize that too rigid an adherence to this principle might be bad for trade. In 1704 effect was given to this view by the decision in *Poole's Case.*[2]

In that case, Holt, C.J., held that a soap-boiler 'might well remove the vats he set up in relation to trade, and that he might do it by the common law (and not by virtue of any special custom) in favour of trade and to encourage industry; but after the term they become a gift in law to him in reversion, and are not removable'. But he held that this exception operated only in the case of trade fixtures —'there was a difference between what the soap-boiler did to carry on his trade, and what he did to complete the house, as hearths and chimney-pieces which were not removable'.

Poole's Case became the starting-point of the modern rule which gives to a tenant the right to remove 'trade fixtures', and things accessory to them, provided, as later cases have decided, that their removal does not involve serious damage to, or the destruction of, the premises demised.[3] But, in respect to other fixtures, *Poole's Case* followed the

[1] *Herlakenden's Case* (1589), 4 Co. Rep. at ff. 63 b, 64 a; *Liford's Case* (1615), 11 Co. Rep. at f. 50 b.

[2] I Salk. 368.

[3] *Lawton* v. *Lawton* (1743), 3 Atk. at p. 14; 2 Smith, Leading Cases (10th ed.) 204.

strict rule of the earlier cases. In this respect the more recent cases have adopted a more liberal attitude. If the chattel is so fixed to the land or building that it can be removed without causing appreciable damage,[1] the test, as to whether it is or is not a fixture, has come to depend on the question whether it is fixed to land or buildings for more convenient use as a chattel, or whether it is fixed to the land or building for the more convenient use of the land or building. If it is affixed for the purpose of more convenient use as a chattel, it is not a fixture and is removable by the tenant. If it is affixed for the more convenient use of the land as land or the building as a building, it is a fixture and cannot be removed.[2]

In respect of one most important industry—the agricultural industry—the exception in favour of trade fixtures was not applied. That it was not applied is mainly due to the unfortunate decision of Lord Ellenborough in *Elwes* v. *Maw.*[3] In that case he explained away certain earlier decisions and dicta, in which the opinion had been expressed that the agricultural industry should be regarded as a trade, and that agricultural tenants should be allowed to remove chattels fixed to the land for the purpose of their trade.[4] He refused to regard agriculture as a trade, followed the general law, and ruled that, as the buildings in that case had been fixed to the land for its more convenient use as land, they could not

1 *Wake* v. *Hall* (1883), 8 A.C. at pp. 204–5 *per* Lord Blackburn.

2 Ibid.; cp. *Holland* v. *Hodgson* (1872), L.R. 7 C.P. at pp. 334–5 *per* Blackburn, J.; *Hobson* v. *Gorringe*, [1897] 1 Ch. at pp. 189–91.

3 (1802), 3 East 38.

4 At pp. 55–7; cp. 2 Smith, Leading Cases (10th ed.), 205–6.

be removed. This decision put agricultural tenants in a less advantageous position than tenants who carried on any other trade; and, in consequence, it has been necessary for the Legislature to intervene and give them that right to remove trade fixtures, which had long ago been allowed by the courts to other traders.[1]

Covenants running with the Land and with the Reversion.[2]

In dealing with this subject I shall first say something of covenants relating to the land as between vendors and purchasers of estates in fee simple, since the law on this matter has had some influence upon the evolution of the law as to similar covenants as between landlord and tenant. I shall then deal with these covenants as between landlord and tenant. Finally, I shall say something of the additions made by equity to these legal rules.

(1) Covenants relating to the land as between vendors and purchasers of estates in fee simple. As a general rule a covenant binds only the parties to it or their representatives. But, in the Middle Ages, the law recognized certain covenants which had a wider operation. They were regarded as being, in a sense, annexed to an estate in the land. In this respect they have some analogy to easements. But they differ from easements in that they can be enforced only by the person who has the same estate as the original covenantee; while an easement binds the

[1] 14, 15 Victoria, c. 25, § 3; 46, 47 Victoria, c. 61, § 34, 8 Edward VII, c. 28, § 21; 13, 14 George V c. 9.

[2] Holdsworth, H. E. L. (3rd ed.), iii. 157–66, vii. 287–92.

land itself, so that not only can those who have the same estate as the original covenantee take advantage of it, but also his tenants, and his lord who took the land by escheat. At law covenants do not run with the land. They run with a particular estate in the land to which they have been annexed; and this is true both of these covenants as between vendor and purchaser, and of the covenants which run with the land or the reversion as between landlord and tenant. The conception of covenants running with the land (as distinct from a particular estate in the land) is, as we shall see, a later conception due to equity.[1]

These covenants originated in the old obligations, express or implied, of a vendor to warrant the title of the purchaser. But, in the course of the sixteenth and seventeenth centuries, these warranties gave place to the modern covenants for title—covenants for seisin,[2] for the right to convey, for quiet enjoyment, for freedom from incumbrances, and for further assurance. Two questions then arose. First, how far would either the benefit or the burden of these and other covenants relating to the land run with it? Secondly, how far would they run with the reversion?

(i) As early as 1369 it was, in effect, settled by *Pakenham's Case*[3] that *the benefit* of covenants relating to land, made with a purchaser of the land, would run with his estate in the land.

[1] Below, p. 253.

[2] The vendor covenanted that he was seised of the very estate that he purported to convey; this covenant fell into disuse, see Holdsworth, H. E. L. (3rd ed.) iii. 163, n. 4; the others survived, and are now implied on a conveyance by a vendor 'as beneficial owner', see Cheshire, Real Property (3rd ed.), 677–8.

[3] Y.B. 42 Ed. III, Hil. pl. 14; cp. Holmes, Common Law, 395–8.

Pakenham sued a prior for breach of the prior's covenant made with Pakenham's great-grandfather that the prior and convent should celebrate divine service weekly in his chapel. The plaintiff claimed, not as heir, but as assignee; and it was held that he was entitled to recover—'he is tenant of the land, and it is a thing which is annexed to the chapel, which is in the manor, and so annexed to the manor'. Similarly it was held in 1582 that, where *A* had enfeoffed *B* in return for certain services, and granted that if the feoffee, his heirs, or assigns were distrained for greater services, he (the feoffee), his heirs, or assigns could levy a distress in *A*'s manor, the assign of *B* could take advantage of the covenant.[1]

It is clear from *Pakenham's Case* that the covenantor need not necessarily be connected with the land. In that case the prior was a stranger. But, as early as 1401, it was recognized that the assign must, to enable him to sue, have the land to which the covenant was annexed.[2] An assign cannot, like an heir, rely on the privity of contract: he can only rely on privity of estate. Hence we get the modern rule that the benefit of covenants made with the purchaser of land will, if they relate to the land, run with that purchaser's estate in the land, that is, they can be enforced by successive tenants of that estate.[3] In modern law covenants for title have superseded the medieval warranties express or implied. They are at the present day by far the commonest class of

[1] Moore, 179.

[2] Y.B. 2 Hen. IV Mich. pl. 25 (p. 6); *Spencer's Case* (1583), 5 Co. Rep. at f. 18 a.

[3] 1 Smith, Leading Cases (10th ed.), 72.

covenants, the benefit of which runs with the estate in the land.

Whether or not *the burden* of a covenant made by a purchaser of the land would run with his estate in it was long an unsettled question. But the better opinion was that it would not. This was the view of Holt, C.J.;[1] and it was decided to be good law in the case of *Austerberry* v. *Corporation of Oldham*.[2] 'I am not', said Lindley, L.J.,[3] 'prepared to say that any covenant which imposes a burden upon land does run with the land, unless the covenant does, upon the true construction of the deed containing the covenant, amount to either a grant of an easement, or a rent charge, or some estate or interest in the land.'

(ii) The second question, how far these covenants ran with the reversion, is more simple. In the case of a grant in fee simple there is no reversion with which the covenant can run.[4] On the other hand there can be a reversion after the grant of an estate less than an estate in fee simple. In the case of these estates, therefore, the question arises whether and under what conditions covenants could run with the reversion. But in such cases the tenant holds of the reversioner, so that the law applicable to these covenants depends upon the rules as to the conditions under which covenants will run with the estate in the land or the reversion as between landlord and tenant. To the consideration of this question we must now turn.

[1] *Brewster* v. *Kitchell* (1697), 12 Mod. 166.

[2] (1885) 29 C.D. 750.

[3] At p. 781.

[4] Above, pp. 66–7.

(2) Covenants relating to the land as between landlord and tenant. Before the sixteenth century the law on this topic was very uncertain.[1] The foundations of the modern law were laid by a statute of 1540,[2] and by the rules in *Spencer's Case*,[3] which was decided in 1583.

The occasion for the passing of the statute of 1540 was the large transfer of reversionary interests which followed on the dissolution of the monasteries, and on the gift of these reversions by the king to various favoured persons. It enacted that the grantees of these and other reversions were to have the same rights against the lessees and their assigns for the non-payment of rent and non-performance of the covenants in the lease as the original lessors had; and, conversely, that lessees and their assigns should have the same rights against the assignees of the reversion and their assigns as they had against the original lessors.

It is clear that this statute made a wholly new departure in this part of the law of landlord and tenant. In the first place, it gave to assignees of the reversion a right to enforce, and put these assignees under a duty to fulfil, covenants in leases. In the second place, it gave to assignees of the land the right to enforce, and put them under a duty to fulfil these covenants. But the provisions of the Act were very wide. It contained no sort of definition as to the kind of covenants which were to run with the land or the reversion. This and other matters were left for the courts to elucidate in the light of the scanty authority which then existed. In the light of the

[1] Holdsworth, H. E. L. vii. 287–8.

[2] 32 Henry VIII, c. 34.

[3] 5 Co. Rep. 15a.

guidance given by the Act and of the existing principles of the law, and in the light of the new situation created by the Act, they performed their task of interpretation with considerable skill.

(i) The first need was to ascertain the kind of covenants to which the statute applied. This was finally met by the decision in *Spencer's Case* in 1583,[1] which was based partly on the older rules applicable to the case of vendor and purchaser of an estate in fee simple, and partly on the obvious needs of landlords and tenants. If the covenant touched or concerned the estate in the land demised or something actually on it, not only the benefit, but also the burden of it, ran with that estate. Probably the rule that the burden ran with the estate in the land as well as the benefit was due to considerations of convenience, and was perhaps new law.[2] Such lessees could not create permanent charges on the land in the same manner as owners in fee simple. Moreover, there were not the same dangers that by such covenants the land would be rendered inalienable. If, however, the covenant related to something to be newly done on the land demised, there was nothing in being to which the covenant could be annexed.[3] After some hesitation it was laid down

[1] 5 Co. Rep. 15a.

[2] 'If the law should not be such, great prejudice might accrue to him; and reason requires that they who shall take benefit of such covenant when the lessor makes it with the lessee, should, on the other side, be bound by the like covenant when the lessee makes it with the lessor'; it was therefore said that 'the covenant is appurtenant and goeth with the land,' at f. 17b.

[3] 'It cannot be appurtenant or annexed to a thing which hath no being,' at f. 16a.

that the benefit and burden of such covenants would only run with the estate in the land if assigns were named; and, though this rule has been criticized,[1] it was law till its alteration by the Law of Property Act 1925.[2] It is obvious that neither principle touches covenants merely collateral, i. e. those which have no reference to the land demised. Such covenants, therefore, can never run with the estate in the land.[3] The same principles as were applied to covenants running with the estate in the land were applied to covenants running with the reversion.[4] A long line of cases has decided what sort of covenants do, and what do not, come within the various categories of covenants defined in *Spencer's Case.*[5]

(ii) Secondly, in accordance with the principle generally applied by the common law,[6] these covenants ran, not with the land or the reversion, but with the actual estate in the land, and with the actual reversion to which they were originally annexed. An assignee of part of the land, or of a particular estate in the whole reversion, e. g. a grantee of the reversion for life or years, gets an estate with which the covenants will run, by virtue of the Act of 1540, and in accordance with the rules in *Spencer's Case*; and the assignee of the reversion of part of the land can take the benefit of the covenants. On the other hand, an under-lessee is not an assignee of the land, since he takes a new and a different estate, so that, except by virtue of express stipulation, he is neither

[1] 1 Smith, Leading Cases (10th ed.), 66–9.

[2] § 79 (1).

[3] *Spencer's Case*, 5 Co. Rep. at f. 16b.

[4] Ibid. at f. 18a.

[5] 1 Smith, Leading Cases (10th ed.), 65–6.

[6] Above, p. 247. Below, pp. 253, 286–7.

bound by, nor can he enforce the covenants in his lessor's lease. Conversely, if the reversion on a lease was destroyed, e. g. by merger, there was nothing with which the covenants could run, so that the lessee could rely only on the personal liability of the original lessor. The law as to under-lessees is still the same; but the consequences of the rule that the covenants could only run with the reversion to which the covenants were originally annexed were found to be so inconvenient, that the rule was first modified and finally swept away.[1]

(iii) We have seen that, though these covenants were annexed to the land, the original lessee remained liable after an assignment.[2] Though privity of estate had disappeared, privity of contract remained. On the other hand, the liability of an assignee, since it depends wholly on privity of estate, ceases when he makes an assignment.

(3) The rules of equity. We have seen that one of the leading differences between the medieval use and the modern trust consisted in the fact that, while the medieval use bound the conscience of the feoffees to uses and the estate which they took, the modern trust binds the land itself.[3] Just in the same way, the rules of equity as to covenants running with the land differ from the rules of the common law in that the benefit and burden of the covenant is attached, not to the estate of the covenantor and covenantee, but to the land itself. Starting from this principle, equity developed a set of rules which not only disregarded the common law distinctions between covenants entered into as between vendor and purchaser

[1] 4 George II, c. 28, § 6; 8, 9 Victoria, c. 106, § 9; 44, 45 Victoria, c. 41, §§ 10, 11. [2] Above, p. 248. [3] Above, pp. 201–2.

of an estate in fee simple, and covenants entered into as between landlord and tenant, but also the distinction between assignees and under-lessees.

The starting-point of this development was the case of *Tulk* v. *Moxhay*, which was decided in 1848.[1] That case, and the cases following it,[2] have laid it down that if a covenant, which is negative in substance, is entered into by the owner of Blackacre with the owner of Whiteacre, and the covenant is for the benefit of Whiteacre, then any person, who gets any interest in Whiteacre, can sue any person who gets any interest in Blackacre with actual or constructive [3] notice of the covenant. It is only a person who gets a legal estate in Blackacre for value and without notice of the covenant who is not bound. It should be noted, first, that the covenant must be negative in substance—e. g. a covenant to use the premises only for certain defined purposes; [4] secondly, that it must be for the benefit of land still belonging to the covenantee—if the covenantee sells all his land he cannot sue an assign of the covenantor; [5] thirdly, that the covenantee must have intended to attach the benefit of the covenant to the land retained by him; [6] and, fourthly, that an assign of the covenantee must show that the benefit of the covenant has been assigned to him.[7]

[1] 2 Ph. 774. [2] See Cheshire, Real Property (3rd ed.), 229–38.

[3] For the meaning of this term see above, p. 148, n. 1.

[4] *Haywood* v. *Brunswick Building Society* (1881) 8 Q.B.D. 403.

[5] *Formby* v. *Barker*, [1903] 2 Ch. 539. Cp. *London County Council* v. *Allen* [1914] 3 K.B. 642.

[6] *Renals* v. *Cowlishaw* (1879), 11 C.D. 866.

[7] *Rogers* v. *Hosegood*, [1900] 2 Ch. 388; *Reid* v. *Bickerstaffe*, [1909] 2 Ch. 305.

In the nineteenth and twentieth centuries further developments in the law have been made in cases where an owner has, in pursuance of a building scheme, laid out his land in plots, and taken identical covenants from each purchaser of a plot in order to preserve the amenity of the property. In such a case, although each purchaser has only covenanted with the vendor of the plots, and not with the other purchasers, they can sue one another for any breach of the covenants, or they can sue the vendor if he releases any one purchaser from the obligations of the covenant.[1]

The Property Acts have made some emendations in these rules legal and equitable; but the main principles of the law on this matter remain unchanged.[2]

§ 6. Mortgages

The modern law of mortgage is partly the product of the large superstructure of principles and rules which equity has erected on a very meagre common law basis,[3] and partly the result of the manner in which the conveyancers have adapted the rules of law and equity to the needs of their clients. The rules of equity are concerned with the establishment and elucidation of the new conception of a mortgage which equity originated. The work of the conveyancers is mainly concerned with the elaboration of the rights of mortgagors and mortgagees, and the remedies of the mortgagee.

[1] The best summary of the law on this topic is contained in the judgement of Parker J. in *Elliston* v. *Reacher*, [1908] 2 Ch. 374.

[2] See the Law of Property Act 1925, §§ 78, 79, 84; Land Charges Act 1925, §§ 10 (1), D (ii), 13 (2).

[3] Above, p. 70–1.

The Rules of Equity.

We have seen that, in the latter half of the fifteenth century, a common form of mortgage was a conveyance to the mortgagee of the fee simple, or other the whole estate of the mortgagor, with a condition that, if the debt was paid by a fixed date, the mortgagor could re-enter.[1] This condition was superseded in this period by a proviso for reconveyance.[2] The strictness with which this proviso was construed by the courts of common law made a recourse to equity very necessary; and equity was ready to interpose, either on the ground that payment had been prevented by the sharp practice of the mortgagee, or on the ground that the strict construction of the proviso might amount, in cases where payment had been delayed by accident, to the enforcement of a penalty, or possibly on the ground that it might be tantamount to the enforcement of an usurious contract.[3] But, towards the end of the sixteenth and at the beginning of the seventeenth century, there was a further development. The Chancellor began to take the view that a mortgage was, after all, only a security for a debt; and that therefore the title to equitable relief did not depend upon the reason why the mortgagor had failed to redeem at the day, or upon the nature of the contract. It was enough that it was a mortgage transaction, intended to secure to the mortgagee a fixed sum and interest thereon, and,

[1] Above, p. 71. [2] Turner, Equity of Redemption, xlv.

[3] Lord Parker, in his judgement in *Kreglinger* v. *New Patagonia Meat Co.*, [1914] A.C. at pp. 54–5, gives some support to this view; he there said that the statutes against usury had something to do with the equitable rule as to clogs on the equity of redemption, as to this see Holdsworth, H. E. L. vi. 664, n. 6.

subject thereto, to leave the mortgagor substantially the owner of the property. Moreover the fact that the mortgagee had sold the property to a purchaser without notice could not affect the mortgagor's rights—he was the owner, and, as the mortgagee merely held the property as a security for the debt, he could only convey it subject to the mortgagor's rights. In 1639–40, in the case of *Bacon* v. *Bacon*, it was said that 'the Court will relieve a mortgage to the tenth generation, though the purchaser had no notice'.[1] It followed that the mortgagor, though he had lost his legal right to redeem, had an equity of redemption, which was an equitable interest in the property. It is from this principle that the rules governing modern law of mortgage have been deduced.

(1) Mortgagors in early days were, and at the present day often are, needy persons. To maintain their equitable ownership, they must be prevented from making bargains which might destroy that ownership. This was the origin of the rule that any stipulations which tend to clog or fetter an equity of redemption are invalid.[2] Mortgagors, it was soon seen, must be prevented from assenting to stipulations which would either prevent the exercise of their power to redeem, or which would prevent them, on redeeming, from getting back the property in the same unfettered condition as it was in when it was mortgaged. For instance, if a publican mortgaged his public house to a brewer, and it was stipulated that the publican must buy all his beer from the brewer, this was a valid stipulation so long as the

[1] Tothill, 133; for an explanation of this rule see L.Q.R., xlvii, 428–9.

[2] *Howard* v. *Harris* (1683), 1 Vern. 190.

mortgage lasted. But if it was provided in the mortgage deed that, after the mortgage had been paid off, he must still go on buying beer from the brewer, this stipulation was invalid as a clog on the equity of redemption. He had mortgaged a free public house, and, on redemption, he would get back something less valuable—a tied public house.[1]

This rule originated at a time when mortgages were usually made by needy landowners, upon whom pressure could easily be put to contract themselves out of their equities of redemption. But, in modern times, its stringency was often felt to be inconvenient. A person or a company might be quite solvent, and yet need a temporary loan—why should not the parties to such a transaction make what stipulations they pleased ? This difficulty has been got over by drawing a distinction between bargains which are invalid as a clog on the equity of redemption, and collateral bargains which are not. It was laid down in *Kreglinger* v. *The New Patagonia Meat Co.*[2] that a collateral bargain is valid, provided that it is not a clog on the equity of redemption, i. e. provided that it does not either prevent the mortgagor from redeeming, or prevent him, on redemption, from getting the property restored to him in the same condition as it was in before the mortgage ; and provided that it is in other respects just and equitable.[3]

[1] *Noakes* v. *Rice*, [1902] A.C. 24.

[2] [1914] A.C. 25.

[3] Ibid. at p. 61. The stricter view that all collateral advantages were invalid as clogs on the equity of redemption prevailed in *Bradley* v. *Carritt*, [1903] A.C. 253 ; the modern view prevailed in *De Beers Consolidated Mines* v. *British South Africa Co.* [1912] A.C. 52, and in *Kreglinger* v. *New Patagonia Meat Co.*; the stricter

(2) A mortgagee, because he is the legal owner of the property, had a right to take possession. But, since equity regarded him, not as the owner, but only the holder of a security for his loan, it held him very strictly to account for any advantages, in excess of his interest on his loan, which he got by taking possession.[1]

(3) If the mortgagee died, the money (for which the land was only a security) was payable, not to his heir, but to his executor; and, conversely, till the enactment of the Real Estate Charges Acts [2] (commonly known as Locke King's Acts), if the mortgagor died, the mortgage debt was payable primarily, not by his heir out of the land, but by his executor out of his personal property.

(4) On the other hand it was recognized that it would not be fair to the mortgagee to prevent him from dealing with the property as his own if he could not get payment. At about the same period, therefore, as the equity of redemption was recognized we get the foreclosure decree, which cuts short this equity unless the mortgagor pays by a fixed date.

At the end of the seventeenth century this new conception of a mortgage, which gave the mortgagor an equitable estate in the mortgaged property, was already beginning to raise further problems. In the

view was better adapted to an age in which most mortgages were made by needy landowners: the modern view to an age in which they are often made by solvent business men, see *Samuel* v. *Jarrah Timber Corporation*, [1904] A.C. at pp. 326–7 *per* Lord Macnaghten.

[1] See *White* v. *City of London Brewery Co.* (1889), 42 C.D. 237.

[2] 17, 18 Victoria, c. 113; 30, 31 Victoria, c. 69; 40, 41 Victoria c. 34.

first place, because the mortgagor had an estate or interest in the property, he had something which he could sell or mortgage; and so it became possible for the mortgagor to mortgage his property more than once. What were the rights of the successive incumbrancers ? There was no doubt that the mortgagee who had the legal estate had the priority ; and that, normally, as between the mortgagees of the equity of redemption, the maxim *prior est tempore potior est jure* applied. But what if a later equitable incumbrancer got in the legal estate ? Could he hold it till his whole claim was satisfied ? It was settled that he could, if at the time when he made his advance he had no notice of an intervening mortgage—'when the equities are equal the law prevails'; and thus the foundation of the doctrine of tacking was laid.[1] In the second place, though equity had given large privileges to the mortgagor, it did not forget its maxim that he who comes to equity must do equity. It would not allow a mortgagor, who had mortgaged two properties to a mortgagee, to redeem one, and leave the mortgagee with an insufficient security for the other debt.[2] This principle seems soon to have hardened into the fixed rule that the mortgagee in such a case could hold both the properties as security for his whole debt.[3] In other words, we have reached the doctrine of consolidation. But as yet these two doctrines of tacking and consolidation are only

[1] *Marsh* v. *Lee* (1670), 1 Ch. Cas. 162.

[2] *Purefoy* v. *Purefoy* (1681), 1 Vern. 29.

[3] *Shuttleworth* v. *Laycock* (1684), 1 Vern. 245. For these doctrines as finally developed see Cheshire, Real Property (3rd ed.), 604–8, 615–17; the Conveyancing Act 1881 abolished consolidation unless the right was expressly reserved in the mortgage deeds or one of them; this is reproduced in the Law of Property Act 1925, § 93.

in their initial stages. They have not as yet been elaborated into a series of fixed and detailed rules, which sometimes seem to lose sight of the equities on which they were originally based.

The Practice of the Conveyancers.

The practice of the conveyancers was directed to the manipulation of the rules of law and equity in such a way that the property should be put to the best use, and that the mortgagee should be given adequate remedies.

It soon became apparent that, if land was mortgaged, neither mortgagor not mortgagee could grant leases for a fixed term of years. The mortgagor could not grant such a lease because he had conveyed the legal estate to the mortgagee. The mortgagee could not grant such a lease because his lessee might be ousted if the mortgagor exercised his equity of redemption.[1] To obviate this inconvenience express powers of leasing were inserted in the mortgage deed, exercisable by whichever of the two parties to the mortgage was in possession of the mortgaged property. We have seen that the mortgagee's power took effect as an equitable power.[2] On the other hand the mortgagor's power took effect as a power, operating under the statute of Uses, to declare that the mortgagee held his legal estate to the use of the lessee for the term desired. It was so usual to insert these powers that it was provided by the Conveyancing Act 1881 that they should be implied in all mortgages made by deed.[3]

[1] Above, p. 257. [2] Above, pp. 209–10.

[3] § 18 ; a similar power is given by the Law of Property Act, 1925, § 99 (1)–(3).

The remedies of the mortgagee depended at law upon the mortgage deed. The mortgagee deed consisted of two distinct parts. First a conveyance of the property by the mortgagor to the mortgagee, subject to a proviso that the mortgagee should reconvey the property, if the money were repaid at a fixed date—usually six months from the date of the mortgage; and, secondly, a personal covenant by the mortgagor to pay the sum advanced and interest. At law the mortgagee could enter upon the property at any time because it was his; and he could also sue upon the covenant. Equity modified the mortgagee's legal rights in three ways. First, as we have seen, it gave the mortgagor an equity of redemption in addition to his legal right to redeem. This right could be exercised at any time during the existence of the mortgage. But it could be put an end to if the mortgagee applied to the court to declare that the mortgagor be foreclosed from his equity of redemption. On such an application the court makes an order for foreclosure *nisi*, i. e. an order that the mortgagor be foreclosed unless within a fixed date (usually six months) he pays the principal and interest. In default of payment the order is made absolute at the date fixed, and the mortgagee gets his legal estate discharged from the mortgagor's equity of redemption. Secondly, if, after getting such a decree, the mortgagee sues on the personal covenant, the foreclosure may be 're-opened', i. e. the court will give back to the mortgagor his equity of redemption, so that, if he pays what is due, he can get back the property. Thirdly, we have seen that, though the mortgagee can enter upon the property at any time, equity held him so strictly to account that it was very rarely a profitable course to pursue.

In order to improve the rights of the mortgagee the conveyancers employed two devices. In the first place, they inserted in the mortgage deed a clause which gave the mortgagee a power to sell in certain events—e. g. if the principal money had been demanded and not paid within three months, or if interest was in arrear for two months. In the second place, they inserted in the mortgage deed a power to appoint a receiver—a power generally exercisable in the same events as those upon which the power of sale was exercisable. The receiver was appointed by the mortgagee but went into possession *as agent of the mortgagor*. He received the rents and profits, paid the interest due to the mortgagee, and handed over the balance to the mortgagor. Thus the mortgagee got the advantages of going into possession without the disadvantages. These were such usual powers that it was provided by the Conveyancing Act 1881 that they should be implied in all mortgages made by deed.[1]

The Law of Property Act 1925 has made very extensive changes in the law of mortgage. It was not consistent with the scheme of the Act to allow the mortgagee to continue to have the legal estate, and the mortgagor only an equitable estate. On the other hand, to give mortgagor the legal estate and the mortgagee only an equitable estate, would be to leave the mortgagee very insufficiently protected.[2] To meet this difficulty the old form of mortgage has been abolished, and a return has been made to an

[1] See now the Law of Property Act 1925, §§ 101–7, 109.

[2] See Cheshire, Real Property (3rd ed.), 569–70.

older form which was often used in the seventeenth century. The mortgagor demises the land to the mortgagee for a long term of years, subject to a proviso that the term shall cease when the mortgagor repays the loan.[1] Thus both mortgagor and mortgagee have legal estates.[2] If the mortgagor wishes to make a second mortgage, he leases the land to the second mortgagee for the original term plus one day, subject to the term of the first mortgagee. Thus both the first and the second mortgagees have legal interests. The result is that the doctrine of tacking is abolished, subject only to a very special exception if an advance is made to secure not only the sum lent, but also further advances, and the other conditions specified in the Act are satisfied.[3] Great changes have also been made by the Law of Property and the Land Charges Acts 1925 in the rules as to the priority of successive mortgages. But, in spite of all these changes, a great deal of the old law survives. Neither the doctrine of consolidation, nor the rules as to the invalidity of clogs upon the equity of redemption are affected; and the rights and remedies of mortgagor and mortgagee remain substantially as they were under the old law. It is therefore necessary to know something of the way in which the old law was evolved if we would understand the meaning of these rights and remedies.

[1] Bridgman's book of Precedents in Conveyancing, which was published at the end of the seventeenth century, Blackstone's Commentaries, ii. 158, and the form prescribed by a statute of 1777 (17 Geo. III, c. 53), show that this form of mortgage was usual in the seventeenth and eighteenth centuries; see Holdsworth, H. E. L. vii. 375 n. 11; below, p. 323, n. 4.

[2] Cheshire, Real Property (3rd ed.), 570; see ibid. 577–81 for other forms of mortgage, legal, statutory, and equitable. [3] Ibid. 625–8.

§ 7. Incorporeal Things

I have dealt in the first chapter with the principal types of incorporeal things which are important in the land law. We have seen that during the Middle Ages the law as to one very important class of these incorporeal things—the class of easements—was not fully developed.[1] The law on this topic was developed during the seventeenth, eighteenth, and the first half of the nineteenth centuries, and mainly in the last part of this long period. At this point, therefore, I shall say something of the history of the law of easements.[2]

Both the term 'easement' and the thing itself were known to the medieval common law. At the latter part of the sixteenth century it was described in Kitchin's book on courts, and defined in the later editions of the 'Termes de la Ley'.[3] That definition is as follows: 'An easement is a privilege that one neighbour hath of another by writing or prescription without profit, as a way or a sink through his land or such like.' From the point of view of modern law this definition is obviously defective in that it does not say that the 'writing' must be under seal, and does not say anything about the existence of a dominant tenement. But these defects in the definition are instructive, because they indicate that the law as to easements was as yet rudimentary.

It was still rudimentary when Blackstone wrote.[4] In fact, right down to the beginning of the nineteenth

[1] Above, p. 102.

[2] Holdsworth, H. E. L. vii. 321–42.

[3] For this book see ibid. v. 401.

[4] Comm. ii. 35–6.

century, there was but little authority on many parts of this subject. Gale, writing in 1839, said,[1] 'the difficulties which arise from the abstruseness and refinements incident to the subject have been increased by the comparatively small number of decided cases affording matter for defining and systematizing this branch of the law. Upon some points indeed there is no authority at all in English law.'

The industrial revolution, which caused the growth of large towns and manufacturing industries, naturally brought into prominence such easements as ways, water-courses, light, and support; and so Gale's book became the starting-point of the modern law, which rests largely upon comparatively recent decisions.

But, though the law of easements is comparatively modern, some of its rules have ancient roots. There is a basis of Roman rules introduced into English law by Bracton, and acclimatized by Coke; and there are a number of rules originating in the remedies for the infringement of an easement—the assize of nuisance, and its successor the action on the case. The law, as thus developed, sufficed for the needs of the country in the eighteenth century. But, as it was no longer sufficient for the new economic needs of the nineteenth century, an expansion and an elaboration of this branch of the law became necessary. It was expanded and elaborated partly on the basis of the old rules, which had been evolved by the working of the assize of nuisance, and its successor the action on the case; partly by the help of Bracton's Roman rules; and partly, as Gale's book shows,

[1] Easements, Preface to the first ed.

by the help of the Roman rules taken from the Digest, which he frequently and continuously uses to illustrate and to supplement the existing rules of law.

These, then, are the conditions under which the modern law has grown up. I shall deal (1) with the differentiation of easements from other rights analogous thereto; and (2) with the evolution of the main principles of the modern law.

(1) The differentiation of easements from other rights analogous thereto.

In modern law it is well established that an easement is a right of property appurtenant to a dominant tenement. Since it cannot exist in gross, it is distinct from a customary right in the nature of an easement; since it is a right of property, it is distinct from a personal licence to use; and, since it gives to the owner of the dominant tenement rights additional to those which the law gives him as owner, it is distinct from a natural right incident to ownership. It was only gradually that easements came to be thus clearly differentiated from these analogous rights.

(i) It was the better opinion in the sixteenth century that there could not be an easement in gross.[1] But it was not definitely settled that this was the law till 1868.[2] The reason why this principle

[1] Holdsworth, H. E. L. vii. 324.

[2] 'There can be no easement properly so-called unless there be both a servient and a dominant tenement. . . . There can be no such thing according to our law, or according to the civil law, as an easement in gross,' *Rangeley* v. *Midland Railway Co.*, L.R. 3 Ch. App. at pp. 310–11 *per* Lord Cairns.

remained so long doubtful was due to a failure to distinguish between easements proper and customary rights in the nature of easements. The wording of one of the resolutions in *Gateward's Case* [1] helped to perpetuate this confusion. It runs as follows: 'A custom that every inhabitant of such a town shall have a way over such land either to the church or market, &c., that is good, for it is but an easement and no profit.' This suggested that these customary rights were essentially similar to true easements, and naturally suggested that an easement could, like these customary rights, exist in gross. Thus Blackstone, when dealing with rights of way, thinks that a way may be either granted to an individual or attached to a dominant tenement; [2] and dicta can be cited which support this view.[3] Two lines of thought contributed to get rid of this confusion between easements properly so called, which must be appurtenant to a dominant tenement, and customary rights in the nature of easements. First, it had been settled in 1850 that the extent of an easement was limited by the needs of the tenement to which it was attached.[4] But if an easement in gross was allowed to be created no such limitation of its extent was possible. It would therefore in effect be a new incident attached to the enjoyment of property, which could not be limited, as a customary right is limited, by reasonableness,[5] or as an

[1] (1607) 6 Co. Rep. at f. 60 b.

[2] Comm. ii. 35–6.

[3] See *Dovaston* v. *Payne* (1795), 2 Hen. Bl. 527; *Mounsey* v. *Ismay* (1865), 3 H. and C. at p. 498.

[4] *Ackroyd* v. *Smith*, 10 C.B. at pp. 187–8; below, p. 272.

[5] See *Gateward's Case* (1607), 6 Co. Rep. at f. 60 b.

easement is limited, by the needs of the dominant tenement. This, in effect, was the *ratio decidendi* in *Hill* v. *Tupper*,[1] in which it was held that a grant by a canal company of the sole right of letting pleasure boats for hire on the canal did not create a right of property in the grantee. Secondly, Bracton had held the view that rights of this kind were always praedial. Gale had called renewed attention to the rules of Roman law on which Bracton's text is based; and had distinguished from true easements appurtenant to a dominant tenement, both customary rights and mere personal licences to use.[2] Both these lines of thought contributed to the clear statement of the distinction which was made by Lord Cairns in 1868.[3]

(ii) By the end of the fifteenth century an easement was distinguished from a licence by the fact that a licence is, and an easement is not, revocable.[4] But what was the position of a licence coupled with a grant? This question was dealt with by Vaughan, C.J., in his famous judgement in *Thomas* v. *Sorrel*.[5]

> 'A dispensation or licence properly passeth no interest, nor alters or transfers property in any thing, but only makes an action lawful, which without it had been unlawful. As a licence to go beyond the seas, to hunt in a man's park, to come into his house, are only actions which, without licence, had been unlawful. But a licence to hunt in a man's park, and carry away the deer killed to his own use; to cut down a tree in a man's ground, and to carry it away the next day after to his own use, are licences as to the acts of hunting and cutting down the tree; but as to the carrying away of the deer killed, and tree cut down, they are grants.'

1 (1863) 2 H. and C. at pp. 127, 128.

2 Easements (7th ed.), 9.

3 Above, p. 267, n. 2.

4 Y.B., 20 ed. IV, Trin. pl. 2.

5 (1674) Vaughan at p. 351.

These cases, and others which followed them, were elaborately reviewed in the judgements of the court in *Wood* v. *Leadbitter* in 1845;[1] and the conclusion was reached that all licences were revocable, but that, if they were coupled with a grant, they were irrevocable. But it is obvious, first, that when the court talked of a grant, they meant the grant of some ascertainable property which is capable of being granted;[2] and, secondly, the court itself decided in that case that such a grant must have been validly made, so that if (as in that case) the grant was of an incorporeal right over land, which could not be granted without a deed, and no deed was executed, the licence was revocable.

There can be no doubt that the judgement in this case is a masterly historical analysis of the evolution of the law as to the nature of a licence. But in one point the application of the common law rule was modified by equity. Equity would, in certain cases, give effect to a grant made for value though not under seal.[3] This is, of course, a perfectly intelligible modification, and is similar in character to the manner in which equity modified the law, by enforcing verbal contracts to purchase interests in land, in cases in which there had been part performance. Unfortunately a desire to do substantial justice led the court of Appeal, in the case of *Hurst* v. *Picture Theatres Ltd.*, to disregard the rule that a grant must be the grant of some ascertainable property, and, in

[1] 13 M. and W. 838.

[2] See *Warr* v. *London County Council*, [1904] 1 K.B. at pp. 721–3 *per* Romer, L.J.

[3] *Duke of Devonshire* v. *Eglin* (1851), 14 Beav. 530; *Frogley* v. *Earl of Lovelace* (1859), John. 333.

consequence, both to make a wholly new extension of the equitable modification of the legal rule, and to cast unfortunate and undeserved doubts upon the principles laid down in *Wood* v. *Leadbitter.*[1]

(iii) For a considerable period the distinction between natural rights, which belong to every owner of property as such, and easements, was by no means clearly grasped. The chief reason for this confusion was the fact that the form of action—in the Middle Ages the assize of nuisance and later the action on the case for a nuisance—was used to remedy the infringement of both natural rights and easements. One of the rules laid down for the competence of these remedies was the rule that, to succeed in his action, a plaintiff must show that the nuisance complained of had been caused while he was in possession of the freehold. This seems to have been the origin of the rule laid down by Blackstone, that a person who acquires property adjoining another property where a nuisance is already established has no cause of action. 'If', he said,[2] 'my neighbour makes a tan-yard so as to annoy and render less salubrious the air of my house and gardens, the law will furnish me with a remedy; but if he is first in possession of the air, and I fix my habitation near him, the nuisance is of my own seeking, and must continue.' But this really amounts to saying that a man could acquire an easement to disturb another's natural rights by mere usage, however short, provided that the plaintiff was not in a position to complain when the nuisance was set up. Obviously this introduced a

[1] [1915] 1 K.B. 1; and see an article on this case by Sir J. Miles, L. Q. R. xxxi. 217.

[2] Comm. ii. 402–3.

confusion between the limits of natural rights and easements which was not got rid of till this doctrine was swept away by decisions of the nineteenth century.[1]

(2) The evolution of the principles of the modern law.

(i) Because an easement is appurtenant to land, the extent of the rights conferred by it is limited in the same way as other incorporeal rights appurtenant or appendant are limited. Thus a right of way appurtenant to a house can only be used for purposes connected with the house. The older authorities had laid it down that if a way was appurtenant to a house, it could only be used by the owner for the time being of the house. It followed, therefore, that it could only be used to go to and from that house, and not for the purpose of going to and from a more distant point. Partly for this reason, partly by making use of the analogy of profits *à prendre*, and partly because any other construction would facilitate what the law now refuses to allow—the creation of a novel mode of enjoying property—it was held in *Ackroyd* v. *Smith* in 1850 [2] that the extent of the rights conferred by an easement must be limited to purposes connected with the dominant tenement.

(ii) It was a rule of Roman law, perhaps recognized by Bracton,[3] that the causes of easements must be permanent. That means that the rights attached to the dominant tenement and exercised over the ser-

[1] *Elliotson* v. *Feetham* (1835), 2 Bing. N.C. 134; *St. Helen's Smelting Co.* v. *Tipping* (1865), 11 H. L. C. 642.

[2] 10 C.B. at pp. 187–8; above, p. 268.

[3] At f. 233 a.

vient tenement must be of a permanent character.[1] Cases of the nineteenth century, chiefly connected with rights to water, have, in effect, applied this rule. They have laid it down that the exercise of rights of a purely temporary character cannot create an easement which will entitle the owner of a neighbouring property, who is benefited by their exercise, to insist on their continuance. In *Arkwright* v. *Gell* [2] this principle was applied to a claim to a continuance of a flow of water through an artificial watercourse constructed for a temporary purpose.

(iii) Until the decision of the case of *Keppel* v. *Bailey* in 1833 [3] the question of the number and variety of easements which a landowner might create does not appear to have been considered. In that case Lord Brougham laid it down that 'incidents of a novel kind cannot be devised, and attached to property, at the fancy and caprice of the owner'; [4] because, if that were permitted, owners could impress on the holding of land 'a peculiar character which would follow the land into all hands however remote'.[5] It is clear that the reason for this rule is to be found in the fact that an easement was appurtenant to land,[6] and that it was coming to be recognized that it gave rise to a permanent right. It should also be remembered that it was just about the same time that the modern rule against perpetuities was finally fixed;[7]

[1] Gale, Easements (7th ed.), 15–17.

[2] (1839), 5 M. and W. 203.

[3] 3 My. and K. 517.

[4] Ibid. at p. 535.

[5] Ibid. at p. 536.

[6] 'Every close, every messuage might be held in a separate fashion; and it would hardly be possible to know what rights the acquisition of any parcel conferred, or what obligations it imposed,' ibid.

[7] Above, p. 226.

and it is clear that a power to fix permanently a peculiar character on the holding of land at the caprice of the owner might be detrimental to the freedom of alienation.[1] To some extent the freedom thus denied to landowners has been restored by the growth of the equitable doctrines as to restrictive covenants.[2] Moreover it should be observed that Lord Brougham only denies that new easements may be created 'at the fancy and caprice of the owner'. Lord St. Leonards said that 'the category of easements must alter and expand with the changes that take place in the circumstances of mankind'.[3] And this would seem to be the better opinion.[4]

(iv) The common law follows the Roman law in making the duty of the servient owner a merely passive duty, and placing upon the dominant owner the duty of doing all that is necessary to make his right effectual.[5]

(v) It was settled in the sixteenth century that easements, like other incorporeal things, if created expressly, must be created by deed.[6] It was also settled that they could be created by implication. But for some time there was some doubt as to the principle upon which a grant would be implied. According to one view a grant of a continuous and apparent easement would be implied in favour of either vendor or purchaser on a severance of two tenements. Such easements were treated as being analogous to natural

[1] This point was made in the argument, 2 My. and K. at p. 525.

[2] Above, pp. 253–5. [3] *Dyce* v. *Hay* (1852), 1 Macq. 305.

[4] See *Attorney-General of Southern Nigeria* v. *John Holt and Co.*, [1915] A.C. at p. 617, where Lord St. Leonards' dictum is cited with approval; and cp. Cheshire, Real Property (3rd ed.), 256–8.

[5] *Pomfret* v. *Ricroft* (1669), 1 Wms. Saunders at p. 322.

[6] Co. Litt. 9 a.

rights. It followed from this theory that, on a severance of two tenements, a continuous and apparent easement might arise, either by implied grant, or by implied reservation. But though this view was held by Gale, it is now established, in accordance with the views of Kelynge, J.,[1] and Holt, C.J., that the creation of such easements is based on the principle that a man shall not derogate from his grant. 'If', said Holt, C.J.,[2] 'the builder of the house sells the house with the lights and appurtenances, he cannot build upon the remainder of the ground so near as to stop the lights of the house. . . . But if he had sold the vacant piece of ground and kept the house, without reserving the benefit of the lights, the vendee might build against his house.' This case is the starting-point of the modern law.[3] With the acquisition of easements by prescription I shall deal in the following section.

(vi) That an easement was extinguished by unity of seisin, because no man can have a servitude over his own property, was stated by Bracton,[4] and accepted by Littleton [5] and Coke. But it was pointed out by Coke that this extinguishment would only occur if the two properties were held for equally 'high and perdurable' estates.[6] Otherwise the unity of possession will only cause a suspension. On severance, a new easement may arise by implication; but, as Brooke pointed out, it is not the old, but a new easement.[7] Any permanent alteration of the dominant tenement, which makes the continuance of the easement

1 *Palmer* v. *Fletcher* (1663), 1 Lev. 122.

2 *Tenant* v. *Goldwin* (1705), 2 Ld. Raym. at p. 1093.

3 See *Wheeldon* v. *Burrows* (1879), 12 C.D. at p. 51.

4 At f. 220 b.

5 § 561.

6 Co. Litt. 313 a, 313 b.

7 Ab. *Extinguishment*, pl. 15.

impossible, or permanently alters the burden on the servient tenement, destroys the easement.[1] The question how far mere non-user will destroy an easement was long a very uncertain question. Coke seems to have thought that it was only non-user for as long a period as would suffice to establish a prescriptive right which would have any effect;[2] but the modern authorities seem to show that in all cases the question depends upon whether, from the non-user, the existence of an intention to abandon can be deduced.[3]

§ 8. The Statutes of Limitation and Prescription

The manner in which lapse of time affects title to interests in land differs according as the interest is corporeal or incorporeal. In the case of corporeal interests the effect of lapse of time is not to give a positive title, but to bar the action and (under modern statutes) to extinguish the title of the former owner. On the other hand, in the case of certain incorporeal rights over land, lapse of time gives a positive title. For corporeal interests the law provides a Real Property Limitation Act: for certain incorporeal rights it provides a positive prescription—analogous to the *usucapio* of Roman Law.

The Real Property Limitation Acts.

We have seen that periods of limitation were provided for certain of the real actions, and for the action of ejectment, by statutes of Henry VIII's and James

[1] *Luttrel's Case* (1601), 4 Co. Rep. at ff. 87 b, 88 a.
[2] Co. Litt. 114 b.
[3] *Crossley* v. *Lightowler* (1867), 2 Ch. App. at p. 482.

I's reigns.[1] These statutes affected, not the title to the property, but the right of action to recover it. They were superseded by an Act of 1833,[2] which was amended by an Act of 1874.[3] These two Acts differ from the older Acts in that they not only bar the action of the former owner, but also extinguish his title. If an owner makes no claim for a period of twelve years after his right to the land accrued, his action is barred and his title is extinguished. But if the person in possession of the land has made a written acknowledgement of his title, then time runs from the date of the acknowledgement. There are provisions for extensions of the time if the owner is under the disabilities of infancy, coverture, or lunacy when the right to the land accrued; and also for persons entitled in remainder or reversion. The Acts apply to the interests of a mortgagor or mortgagee in possession, so that possession by either for twelve years without acknowledging the title of the other will bar the other's action and extinguish his title; [4] and in this case the disabilities of infancy, coverture, and lunacy will not prevent the operation of the statute.[5] The statute applies to rents and tithes in the hands of laymen; and a special period of limitation is provided for advowsons. This statute is not affected by the Property Act.[6]

[1] Above, pp. 167–8. [2] 3, 4 William IV, c. 27.

[3] 37, 38 Victoria, c. 57.

[4] Note that when the right of action to recover the property, and the title, are extinguished, the right to sue on the covenant in the mortgage deed is also barred, *Sutton* v. *Sutton* (1882), 22 C.D. 511. [5] Williams, Real Property (22nd ed.), 576.

[6] For details of the modern law see Cheshire, Real Property (3rd ed.), 793–804.

The question now arises, why does English law only bar the action and extinguish the title of the former owner ? Why does it stop short of conferring a positive title on the possessor ? The answer is to be found in the English theory of possession and ownership. We have seen that the person seised or possessed is regarded by the law as the owner, and that he has the rights of an owner as against all the world except as against a person who can show a better right.[1] It follows that all the law need do when it wishes to secure the rights of a person who is seised, against a person who has a better right to seisin, is to bar that better right. A system of *usucapio* which, by lapse of time, turns *possessio* into *dominium* is unnecessary, and, having regard to the English theory of seisin and possession, unintelligible. If a person is seised, and if the title of the person with the better right to seisin is barred, he has the best and the only title which the law can give. It is not the fact, as has sometimes been said, that the Real Property Limitation Acts operate as a 'statutory conveyance'. Lord Cozens Hardy, M.R., in *In re Atkinson and Horsell's Contract*,[2] has shown that to talk of a statutory conveyance in this connexion is erroneous, and has clearly laid down the true principle.

> 'My present view', he said, 'is that the phrase "statutory conveyance" and so on, is a loose metaphorical term, and that the true view is this, that whenever you find a person in possession of property, that possession is prima facie evidence of ownership in fee, and that prima facie evidence becomes absolute when once you have extinguished the right of every other person to challenge it. That is the effect of S. 34 of the Real Property Limitation Act,

[1] Above, pp. 125–8, 180–1.

[2] [1912] 2 Ch. at p. 9.

and that explains how the person who has been in possession for more than the statutory period does get an absolute legal estate in the fee, and there is no one who can challenge the presumption which his possession of the property gives.'

Prescription.[1]

Certain kinds of incorporeal rights can be claimed by prescription. If, in the case of a right in gross, a man can show that he and his ancestors, or, if, in the case of a right appendant or appurtenant, he can show that he and all those whose estate he has, have enjoyed these rights from before the time of legal memory, he gets a positive title to these rights. It was settled (not without some conflict of opinion) [2] that the time of legal memory was the year 1189—a date fixed by analogy to the rule made in 1275 as to the period of limitation for a writ of right.

The principle underlying the rule that user from before the time of legal memory confers a title has varied in different periods of our legal history. I must say something, first, of the earlier theory, and, secondly, of the modern theory, because both have left their traces upon our modern law.

(i) In the twelfth and thirteenth centuries the law regarded the power of a landowner to create interests in his land from a peculiar point of view. The man who limited an estate was regarded as making, by the form of his gift, a special law for that estate, differing from the ordinary law which would have governed it if it had not been thus limited. A man who charged his land with rent, or who gave to a

[1] Holdsworth, H. E. L. (3rd ed.) iii. 166–71, vii. 343–52.

[2] Ibid. iii. 161, n. 5, vii. 343–5.

stranger a right of common, or who gave a neighbour a right of way, subjected his land to a special law in favour of the grantee. Such grantee, if his right was questioned, must show that he was entitled; and this he could only do in three ways. He might either produce the deed, the 'specialty', by which this special law was made; or he could prescribe, i.e. show that he had enjoyed the right from time immemorial; or he could show that in the district, in which the land was situated, there was a special custom which entitled all persons in his position to the right claimed. In all these three cases the claimant succeeded because he was able to set up a special law applicable to his case. The deed was conclusive. The user for so long a period was equally conclusive, because no evidence from before the time of legal memory could be of any avail to show that the user was wrongful. Custom, if proved, set up a special local law for the district which, if reasonable, might supersede the common law. Both custom and prescription set up a special law. The difference was that one was local, the other personal.

This idea was the cause of a rule which limited the number of things which could be acquired by prescription. It was only things which needed an express limitation to create them—things 'against common right'—which could be so acquired. Certain forms of services were recognized as the ordinary accompaniments of free tenure. Therefore they did not require to be created by an express limitation. Similarly certain incorporeal rights, such as common appendant,[1] were attached to the holding of property by the law.

[1] Above, pp. 94–5.

These things were ' of common right ', or, as we should say, they were natural rights incident to ownership. Therefore they need not and cannot be prescribed for. On the other hand, common appurtenant or easements being ' against common right ' could be prescribed for.

(ii) Before the end of the medieval period the theory upon which prescription was allowed to operate had changed. As the things against common right which could be prescribed for were normally created by a deed of grant, it came to be thought that prescription was based, not so much on a personal law in favour of the person seised, as on the fact that such immemorial user was conclusive evidence of a grant made before the time of legal memory. This was a theory very different from the older theory; and it entailed different consequences. Both theories, it is true, prevented tenants for limited interests from prescribing in their own names ; for on either theory prescription is use from before the time of legal memory; and, as Blackstone puts it,[1] ' it is absurd that they should pretend to prescribe, whose estates commenced within the memory of man.' On the other hand, the newer theory proved fatal to the claims of unincorporate communities to prescribe for profits *à prendre*. Such communities may indeed avail themselves of a customary right in the nature of an easement, but they cannot prescribe because they cannot take a grant ; and, as profits *à prendre* cannot be claimed by custom, they cannot claim rights of this kind.

It was settled also that the rules, which Bracton had copied from Roman law, as to the nature of the

[1] Comm. ii. 265.

user required to found a prescriptive right were part of English law. In English as in Roman law, that user must be *nec vi, nec clam, nec precario*—it must be, that is, open and as of right.

These rules show us that by the end of the medieval period the main characteristics of prescription at common law had been reached. Prescription is a mode of acquiring certain incorporeal rights over land by a user, which must be open and as of right, from before the time of legal memory. Such user has this effect because it supplies the place of a lost grant; and since it operates in this way, no prescriptive title can be acquired unless a grant of the thing is legally possible.

The doctrine which required for a prescriptive title user from before 1189 was productive of great hardship, which grew greater with lapse of time. The courts tried to mitigate the hardship by holding that proof of enjoyment as far back as living witnesses could speak raised a presumption of enjoyment from before 1189. But this was only a presumption which was capable of being rebutted. As the Real Property Commissioners pointed out in 1829,[1]

> 'a right claimed by prescription is always disproved by showing that it did not or could not exist at any one point of time since the commencement of legal memory, or, although it originated before the commencement of legal memory, that at some subsequent period the servient tenement . . . and the dominant tenement . . . once belonged to the same individual, whereby the prescriptive right was extinguished.'

To obviate these inconveniences recourse was had to a new device, which was suggested by, if it did not

[1] First Report, 51.

originate in, the rule that every prescriptive title is founded on a presumed grant made before the time of legal memory.[1] The essence of this new device is the rule that, in order to support a title by long possession to some incorporeal thing, a deed granting that thing will be presumed after a certain lapse of time. The time after which such a deed of grant would be presumed was fixed at twenty years, by analogy to the period after which the action of ejectment was barred.

We can see signs of this doctrine as early as 1607. But, owing to the strictness of the common law rule of pleading that all deeds relied on must be produced, it did not make much way till this rule of pleading was modified in 1789.[2]

Down to the end of the eighteenth century this presumption of a grant after twenty years enjoyment was merely a rebuttable presumption of law. During the nineteenth century the strength of this presumption had been increasing; and some lawyers considered that the presumption had become irrebuttable. But, as the case of *Angus* v. *Dalton* [3] showed, the opinions of the lawyers were much divided on this point.

Thus the action of the courts in developing a law of prescription had produced a body of rules which were neither certain nor convenient. A litigant who relied on prescription at common law might succeed if he could show thirty or forty years user. On the other hand, a litigant who could show eighty or a hundred years user might fail, if e.g. unity of seisin were proved to have existed some two centuries ago.

[1] Above, p. 281. [2] *Read* v. *Brookman*, 3 T.R. 151.
[3] (1881), 6 A.C. 740.

A litigant who relied on the presumption of a lost grant would probably succeed if he could prove twenty years user as of right. But was evidence admissible to prove that no such grant was ever made ? And if a jury did not believe that such a grant had ever been made, could they find against him ? On these matters no certain conclusion had been reached.

In 1832 the Legislature attempted to apply a remedy ; [1] but its attempts have resulted in making the law still more confused than it was before. It did not (except in the case of the right to light) abolish the existing modes of acquiring a title by prescription. It simply added one more to the existing modes. The effect of the Act shortly stated is as follows : If an easement has been enjoyed openly and as of right without interruption for twenty years, it cannot be defeated by the fact that at some period, later than 1189, it did not exist ; but it may be defeated by any other method permissible at common law. If an easement has been enjoyed openly and as of right without interruption for forty years, the right is indefeasible unless it has been enjoyed by virtue of a written consent or agreement. In the case of a profit the rules are the same, but the periods are thirty and sixty years respectively. In the case of the right to light enjoyment for twenty years gives a title, unless the right was enjoyed by virtue of a written agreement.

The two chief defects of this Act are as follows :

(i) It provides that the periods fixed for acquiring a prescriptive title are to be the periods ' next before action brought '. It follows that an enjoyment for a period longer than that fixed by the Act will not con-

[1] 2, 3 William IV, c. 71.

fer a title, unless at the end of it there is a litigation as to the existence of the right. Moreover, the Act provides that no act shall be deemed to be an interruption of the enjoyment unless it has been acquiesced in for one year. The result is that if there has been an enjoyment for a longer period than that fixed by the Act, and if at the end of that longer period, and before litigation begins, there is an interruption acquiesced in for more than a year, no claim can be made under the Act. Obviously it would have been much more sensible to provide that the period was to run from the beginning of the enjoyment—just as under the Real Property Limitation Act time runs against the owner from the date when his right to enter or to bring an action accrued.[1]

(ii) The second defect of the Act is its bad drafting. In the first place, it is left quite uncertain what easements and profits come within the scope of the Act. Until the decision in the case of *Angus* v. *Dalton*,[2] it was more than doubtful whether the easement of support came within it. It is not even now certain whether rights in gross are within its scope. In the second place, its reference in § 8 to 'any such way or other *convenient* water-course' has puzzled generations of judges and text-writers. In the third place, the interpretation of its provisions with regard to the easement of light, which are quite different from its provisions with regard to other easements, long remained doubtful.

[1] As to the reason why the framers of the Act adopted this course see Holdsworth, H. E. L. vii. 351–2; in effect they confused the mode in which prescription operates with the mode in which a statute of limitation operates.

[2] (1881), 6 A.C. 740.

It is, I think, true to say that no branch of English law is in a more unsatisfactory state than the law of prescription. It is odd that the branch of the land law which most requires to be restated should have been left wholly untouched by the Property Acts.

Note on the two cases of Tichborne *v.* Weir (1892), 67 L.T. 735, and In re Nisbet and Potts' Contract, [1905] 1 Ch. 391.

These two cases, which, at first sight, may appear to be difficult to reconcile, illustrate very clearly (1) the difference between the common law conception that a covenant runs with the *estate in the land to which it is annexed*, and the equitable conception that a covenant runs *with the land itself*; and (2) the mode of the operation of the Real Property Limitation Act, and the fact that it depends on the common law theory of seisin and possession.

The facts in the case of *Tichborne* v. *Weir* were as follows: the plaintiff's predecessor in title was seised of a house in fee simple. In 1802 she leased it to Baxter for eighty-nine years. The lease contained a covenant to repair. Baxter made an equitable mortgage of the premises to Giraud, and Giraud entered on the premises in 1836. In 1836 Baxter disappeared, and Giraud remained in occupation of the premises till 1876. During that period he paid the rent reserved in Baxter's lease to the lessor. In 1876 Giraud assigned the lease to the defendant. The defendant entered and paid the rent till the term ended in 1891. He then delivered up possession to the plaintiff. The plaintiff sought to make him liable on the covenant to repair. *Held* that he was not liable. The Real Property Limitation Act had barred the action and extinguished the right of Baxter ; but it had not vested Baxter's lease in him. As he had not taken Baxter's estate, he was not bound by the covenant to repair, which ran with that estate (see the judgement of Kay, L.J., at p. 737). To the argument that he was estopped by the payment of rent from denying that he had taken Baxter's estate, it was said that such payment estopped him from disputing the title of the plaintiff, but it did not estop him from denying that he was bound by the terms of the lease. It estopped him from denying that he was a lessee : it did not estop him from denying that he was the holder of Baxter's lease.

The facts in *In re Nisbet and Potts' Contract* were as follows : Thomas Headde acquired a title to property under the Real Property Limitation Act. Headde in 1890 conveyed the land to the predecessors in title of Nisbet. In 1903 Nisbet agreed to sell the land to Potts. Potts discovered that, before Headde had acquired his title, the land had been subject to restrictive covenants. The question was : Did these covenants bind Headde ? If they did, Potts was bound and a good title had not been shown : if they did not, Potts was not bound and a good title had been shown. *Held* that Headde was bound by the covenants. In equity restrictive covenants bind the land. Any one who gets the land is bound by them, no matter what estate in the land he takes, unless he can prove that he is a purchaser for value without notice. Potts was a purchaser for value. But he could not prove that he had no constructive notice, for the following reason : if Real Property Limitation Act had conferred a new estate on Headde at the end of twelve years, there would have been much force in the contention that Potts had no notice. In that case the new estate, because it was new, would have been free from all preceding restrictions, and there would have been nothing of which Potts could have had notice. But the Act does not operate in this way. It bars the action and extinguishes the title of the former owner. It does not give a new estate to the new owner. The person in possession has all along been regarded by the law as owner, except as against the person who can prove a better right. Now that the better right is barred his title is absolute. But this theory of possession involves this further consequence. As the man in possession has all along been assumed to be the owner, he must have got his ownership regularly. If this had been the case, he would have had actual or constructive notice of the covenants. He is therefore bound by them and so is his successor in title (see Maitland, Equity, 170).

§ 9. CONVEYANCING [1]

We have seen that in the Middle Ages the forms of conveyance at the disposal of the freeholder fell into two main classes—those which took effect by the act of the parties, and those which depended for their efficacy upon the machinery of the court.[2] Under the first head fell feoffments with livery of seisin, releases, surrenders, confirmations, exchanges, partitions, and, for incorporeal things, deeds of grant; and under the second head fell fines and recoveries. We have seen, too, that the most essential part of a conveyance of corporeal hereditaments was the livery of seisin.[3] Un-

[1] Holdsworth, H.E.L. vii. 353–87. [2] pp. 111 seqq. [3] pp. 112–13.

less the feoffee was already in possession, an actual livery of seisin was required; and even in the case of some of these incorporeal things which lay in grant, something equivalent—such as attornment or actual user of the right granted—was required.[1] A lease for a term of years created only an *interesse termini* till the lessee had entered.[2] But it was coming to be recognized that the right to incorporeal things passed by mere deed of grant; [3] and we have seen that in the case of all conveyances, the need to indicate the intent with which seisin had been delivered, and to define the rights and duties of the various parties to different dispositions of property, had made a deed, and often a very elaborate deed, a necessary accompaniment to a livery of seisin.[4] The forms of these deeds, whether deeds poll or indentures, and their contents, had already attained fixity in the medieval period; and, though, in this period, their contents were necessarily modified by changes in the law, they are the basis upon which the modern system of conveyancing has been built up.

Just as medieval rules retained their importance in other branches of the land law because they were the basis upon which the modern law was founded, so in the law of conveyancing—all the medieval modes of conveyance continued to be available to landowners all through this period. But, just as in other branches of the land law, medieval rules and doctrines tended to become modified, and sometimes to be superseded by the new rules which had grown up during this period, so in the law of conveyancing these medieval

[1] Above, pp. 129–30. [2] Above, p. 120.
[3] Above, p. 130. [4] Above, pp. 113–14.

modes of conveyance tended, for ordinary purposes, to be superseded by the new modes of conveyance, which the rise of uses and the passing of the statute of Uses had rendered possible. And what was in substance a new mode of conveying land sprang up in consequence of the power to devise conferred by Henry VIII's statute of Wills.

These new modes of conveyance affected the law of conveyance in three main directions:—In the first place, they made it possible to create or transfer an estate in the land without an actual livery of seisin. For this reason the deed or other document which evidences the transfer became in most cases, and, after the passing of the statute of Frauds,[1] in all cases, an essential and necessary element in a conveyance. In this way a great impetus was given to the tendency, which was proceeding all through the medieval period, to make the deed which evidenced the intent with which livery of seisin was delivered of more importance than the actual livery of seisin. In the second place, the greatly increased powers of disposition which the statutes of Uses and Wills conferred upon landowners necessarily added to the complication of the instruments by which these powers of disposition were exercised. In the third place, in their work of thus adapting the law of conveyancing to the modern land law, the lawyers were allowed a very free hand. Till the reforms of the nineteenth century, the only two statutes of general importance which directly affected this branch of the law were the statute of Enrolments [2] and the statute of Frauds. Thus the

[1] 29 Charles II, c. 3, §§ 1–3.

[2] 27 Henry VIII, c. 16 ; above, p. 159.

whole system of modern conveyancing was the joint work of the courts and the conveyancers. Hence, when the main principles of the modern law had been settled by the courts in the sixteenth, seventeenth, and eighteenth centuries, the practice of these conveyancers, who settled the common forms which carried out in practice the principles of the law, tended to be treated by the courts as such cogent evidence of the law, that it can be regarded almost as a secondary source of the law.

In this section I shall say something, first, of the new forms of conveyance which depend on the statute of Uses ; secondly, of the devise ; and, thirdly, of the influence of the practice of the conveyancers upon the law.

The New Forms of Conveyance.

We have already seen that the direct result of the statute of Uses and the statute of Enrolments was to make a bargain and sale of a freehold interest in lands, if enrolled within six months, operative to convey the legal estate in that interest.[1] In the course of the sixteenth century a covenant to stand seised for good consideration[2] came to have the same effect. But we shall see that these two new conveyances suffered from several defects, which prevented them from wholly superseding the older modes of conveyance ;[3] and that, at the beginning of the seventeenth century, they were being superseded by the conveyance by way of bargain and sale for a term, followed by a com-

[1] Above, p. 159.

[2] For the meaning of this term see below, p. 292.

[3] Below, p. 293.

mon law release.[1] This conveyance, being free from many of the defects of the bargain and sale of a freehold interest enrolled, and of the covenant to stand seised, became the most general mode of conveyance for the creation and transfer of all kinds of interests in real property; and it continued to hold this position till it was superseded by the new conveyances introduced by the legislation of the nineteenth century. I shall therefore consider, in the first place, the bargain and sale enrolled and the covenant to stand seised; and, in the second place, the bargain and sale for a term coupled with a release.

(1) The bargain and sale enrolled and the covenant to stand seised. The essence of the conveyance by bargain and sale was the pecuniary consideration; for a bargain and sale means an agreement to sell accompanied by actual payment. The consideration might be of purely nominal value; and it need not move from the person or persons to whom the property was to be conveyed. Under the statute of Enrolments bargains and sales of freehold interests must be enrolled within six months. The enrolment related back to the bargain and sale.

The essence of the covenant to stand seised was 'good' as distinct from 'valuable' consideration; and good consideration was blood relationship or marriage. It followed that it was only to those who could be brought within the consideration by virtue of blood relationship or marriage that such a conveyance could be made; so that if, for instance, *X*, in consideration that *B* married his daughter, cove-

[1] Below, pp. 293–5.

nanted to stand seised to the use of *B* and his daughter, remainder to *C*, the remainder to *C* was void, 'for that he is a stranger to the consideration.'[1]

Both the bargain and sale enrolled and the covenant to stand seised suffered from several defects. The publicity of the bargain and sale, which was secured by the enrolment, rendered it distasteful to the landowners; but this was perhaps the least of its defects. By reason of the fact that the bargainee was a *cestui-que* use, no use could be limited on his estate;[2] so that neither a springing use nor a power to lease, which would be executed by the statute of Uses, could be limited on a bargain and sale in fee. The covenant to stand seised avoided the defect of publicity; but it suffered from even more fatal defects than the bargain and sale. We have seen that by it a conveyance could only be made to those who came within the consideration of blood relationship or marriage. Hence no power to lease could be reserved on such a conveyance; and, what was worse, no limitations to trustees to preserve contingent remainders could be made. For these reasons, therefore, these conveyances, in the course of the seventeenth century, gradually gave place to a form of conveyance which avoided these defects—the bargain and sale for a term coupled with a release.

(2) The bargain and sale for a term coupled with a release. We have seen that at common law a lease for a term, followed by a release, was a recognized mode of conveyance; but that this conveyance could not take effect until the lessee had entered under the

[1] 2 Rolle, Ab. 784, pl. 5; cp. Sanders, Uses, ii. 99.

[2] Above, p. 160; Sanders, Uses, ii. 62.

lease.[1] The effect of the statute of Uses was to dispense with the necessity for entry under the lease; for the bargain and sale created the situation of a vendor seised to the use of the purchaser for a term, and the statute converted the use into actual possession without any need for an entry by the purchaser. This being the case, it is clear that such a purchaser could take a release from the lessor, and so acquire the freehold without entry. Thus a bargain and sale for a term which, by virtue of the statute of Uses, conveyed the actual possession without entry, coupled with a release which operated at common law, could pass the freehold, without livery of seisin and without the need for enrolment. It was the established tradition of the seventeenth century that this device was invented by Sir Francis Moore (1558–1621)—a member of St. John's College, Oxford, and a distinguished lawyer and member of Parliament, best known from the authorship of the reports which bear his name, and his Reading on Charitable Uses. The efficacy of this mode of conveyance was recognized by the courts in 1621 in the case of *Lutwich* v. *Mitton*, [2] and in 1629 in the case of *Iseham* v. *Morrice*.[3] Its validity was assumed by Bridgman; and it is clear that, during the latter part of the seventeenth century, it was rapidly becoming the ordinary form of conveyance. The only important instance in which it could not be used was in the case of a conveyance by a corporation. Since a corporation could not be seised to a use, it could not take advantage of these new methods of conveyance, and was obliged, till 1845, to convey by the old method of feoffment and livery of seisin.

[1] Above, p. 115. [2] Cro. Jac. 604. [3] Cro. Car. at p. 110.

We have seen that this mode of conveyance avoided the disadvantage of publicity which was inherent in the bargain and sale enrolled. It also avoided the other disadvantages both of the bargain and sale enrolled, and of the covenant to stand seised. The release operated at common law. It was a conveyance which took effect by way of 'transmutation of possession'.[1] Therefore uses could be limited on the seisin so conveyed, and powers of appointment could be given, which could take effect out of the releasee's seisin, and so convey the legal estate to the appointee. It is not surprising, therefore, that it became the ordinary mode of conveyance till 1841, when a release was made sufficient.[2] In 1845 the modern deed of grant was substituted.[3]

The Devise.

(1) The nature of a devise. In consequence of the prohibition of a will of lands at the end of the thirteenth century,[4] landowners lost the power to devise directly. This power only survived in a few towns in which a custom to devise was recognized. We have seen that they regained this power, indirectly, by means of feoffments to uses.[5] Thus the will of land was a direction to the feoffees to uses as to the disposition of the *cestui-que* use's property after his death. It differed neither formally nor materially from any other directions which a *cestui-que* use might give to his feoffees. It was therefore an instrument which had quite as many of the characteristics of a conveyance as of a

[1] That is, the possession is transferred by the common law, and not by the operation of the statute of Uses.

[2] 4, 5 Victoria, c. 21, repealed by 37, 38 Victoria, c. 96.

[3] 8, 9 Victoria, c. 106. [4] Above, pp. 103–4. [5] Above, p. 149.

will; and, when wills of land were permitted by Henry VIII's statute of Wills, both lawyers and land-owners considered that the will of lands made by virtue of the Act, was a transaction of a kind essentially similar to a will of lands made through the machinery of the use. Like it, it did not take effect till death; and, like it, it was essentially a conveyance of the whole or part of the estate belonging to the testator when it was made. 'As all real property lawyers know', said Jessel, M.R., in *Sugden* v. *Lord St. Leonards*,[1] 'in ancient times it was customary for great landed proprieters to make, not only separate wills of real and personal estate, but several wills of real estate. I have seen as many as three ancient wills of different portions of the real estate of the testator, devoting an estate to different purposes. . . . If the testator intended to found two families, he was often desirous that this will should accompany the muniments of title to his estate, and, therefore, he made separate wills.' It followed that, as under the older law, the only land which could pass by such a will was land of which the testator was seised both at the time of the making of his will and of his death.

The consequences of this rule were followed out with the ruthless logic which was characteristic of the lawyers of the sixteenth, seventeenth, and eighteenth centuries. Because a will was a conveyance of the land which the testator then had, and of that land only, it was necessary for him 'to republish his will or to make a new one as often as he acquired other property'.[2] If he disposed of his property, and re-

[1] (1876), 1 P.D. at p. 237.

[2] Real Property Commission, Fourth Report, 24.

acquired it before his death, or if he mortgaged his estate, and, on payment of the debt, it was reconveyed to him, the same result followed. These doctrines were swept away by the Wills Act 1837,[1] which in effect enacts that all wills, whether of realty or personalty, shall be 'ambulatory' i.e. shall take effect as if executed immediately before the testator's death.

(2) The forms required for the making and revocation of wills. Henry VIII's statute of Wills required a will of land to be in writing ; but it was not required to be written by the testator or to be signed by him. In 1666 a will was upheld which was written on loose sheets of paper, dictated by the testator to an attorney, though the testator had said that, as he intended to write them over again, he would not sign or publish them, but that in the meantime they should be his will.[2] This case is said to have caused the enactment of the clause of the statute of Frauds which required all devises of lands and tenements to be in writing, and signed by the testator, or by some one else in his presence and by his direction, and to be attested in the presence of the testator by three or four credible witnesses.[3]

No forms were prescribed for the revocation of wills before the statute of Frauds. That such wills were revocable had been admitted from the earliest times. It was also well settled that acts of total or partial destruction raised a presumption of an intention to revoke or alter a will ; and that a revocation might be implied from a later disposition of his property by a testator, or from certain alterations in his personal cir-

[1] 1 Victoria, c. 26, § 24. [2] *Stephens* v. *Gerard*, 2 Keble, 128.
[3] 29 Charles II, c. 3, § 5.

cumstances, e. g. by marriage in the case of a woman, or by marriage and the birth of a child in the case of a man.[1] The statute of Frauds required that an express revocation must be effected by some other will or codicil in writing, or by some other writing of the testator signed in the presence of three or four witnesses.[2]

These rules applied only to wills of freehold. Wills of copyhold were governed by different rules; and there were different rules for personalty, and for particular kinds of property, e. g. money in the public funds. The Real Property Commissioners in 1833 found that there were ' ten different laws regulating the execution of wills under different circumstances '.[3] This monstrous state of the law was remedied by the Wills Act of 1837, which was based largely on the recommendations of the Commissioners. Taking a very broad view of the effect of that Act, it may be said that, in respect to the nature of a will, the model of a will of personal estate has been followed; and that, in respect to the forms required for the making and revocation of a will, the model of a will of freeholds has suggested some of the provisions of the modern law.[4]

In fact that Act was the first considerable step taken by the Legislature to realize one of the chief aims of the Property Acts—the assimilation of the law of real and personal property.

[1] Under the Wills Act 1837, § 18, marriage, whether of a man or a woman, generally revokes a will; but the Property Act 1925, § 177 (1), provides that a will expressed to be made in contemplation of marriage is not revoked by the marriage contemplated.

[2] 29 Charles II, c. 3, § 6.

[3] Fourth Report, 12–13.

[4] For the provisions of the Act as to the making and revocation of Wills see Cheshire, Real Property (3rd ed.), 751–3, 767–70.

The Practice of Conveyancers and the Law.

In the Middle Ages a class of professional conveyancers had not arisen.[1] During the sixteenth and seventeenth centuries the growth of the complexity of the law caused the beginnings of the growth of such a class. In the course of the eighteenth century the continued increase in the complexity of conveyances, and in the rules of law and equity, and the fact that other branches of the common law, notably commercial law, were coming to be quite as important as the land law, had, at the end of that century, made the conveyancers a class very much apart from other legal practitioners. Mr. Tyrrell stated that Serjeant Hill (1716–1808) was the last lawyer of eminence who both practised as a conveyancer and attended to the business of the courts.[2] It is clear from Mr. Tyrrell's evidence that, at the beginning of the nineteenth century, an intimate knowledge of the law of real property was almost confined to a comparatively small number of eminent conveyancers; and that the majority of lawyers—barristers as well as judges—depended for their information upon the opinions and writings of these conveyancers.

Under these circumstances, it is not surprising to find that, from the beginning of the eighteenth century onwards, the practice and opinions of these conveyancers have been appealed to as the best evidence of the existing state of the law upon many questions connected with the land law. That practice and these opinions are not law; and if they are founded on

[1] Above, p. 111.

[2] Real Property Commission, First Report App. 564.

an erroneous view of the law they will be disregarded. But, subject to these qualifications, they are regarded by the courts as cogent evidence of the law. In fact the practice of conveyancers is the foundation of many sections of the Conveyancing and Settled Land Acts—these Acts have codified it, and have thus given it the dignity of statute law, just as other Acts on other topics have codified our case law.

§ 10. General Conclusions

In the Middle Ages the land law, because it was the most important branch of English law, was the most highly developed and the most technical part of the common law.[1] The rise and growth of the use had shown that, even in the fourteenth and fifteenth centuries, its rules and doctrines were too narrow ;[2] and large developments of, and additions to, its rules and doctrines were obviously needed to bring them into conformity with the new political social and economic ideas and wants of the modern English state. The adaptation of this highly developed and technical body of law to the changed world which was opening in the sixteenth century was a difficult task. But the common lawyers rose to the occasion ; and, on the foundation of the medieval land law, erected, with the help of the Legislature, the elaborate superstructure of the modern law. In later centuries, these rules of the modern law became the foundation of new equitable developments ; just as, in an earlier period, the rules of the medieval common law had been the foundation on which the medieval Chancellors had constructed the law as to uses.

[1] Above, pp. 136–8. [2] Above, pp. 145–51.

Till the end of the eighteenth century, this system met the needs of different classes of landowners. No doubt some of its rules were clumsy, some were uncertain, and some were inequitable. But on the whole they were just and flexible rules. The sixteenth century was not marked in England, as it was marked in Germany, by a peasant revolt ; and the settlement in England of the position of the copyholder removed a set of grievances which, in France, were among the causes of the first French Revolution.[1] Moreover, the rules of the modern land law impeded neither the economic developments of the sixteenth and seventeenth centuries, nor the progress of the industrial revolution of the latter part of the eighteenth and the beginning of the nineteenth centuries. Its rules were approved, as we shall see in the next chapter, by the Real Property Commissioners in 1829. We shall see also that their approval had no small influence in shaping the course of the reforms made in the land law in the nineteenth century.

[1] Maine, Early Law and Custom, 299 seqq.

CHAPTER IV

THE ERA OF REFORM (1833–1925)

THE era of reform begins in the second quarter of the nineteenth century. After the passing of the Reform Act of 1832 a series of statutes was passed to carry into effect the recommendations of the Real Property Commissioners who, between 1829 and 1833, had issued four Reports on the law of real property. A new period of reform begins in the second half of the nineteenth century; and, early in the twentieth century, we can see the beginnings of the movement which has led to the recasting of the law by the Property Acts; I shall therefore divide the history of the law during this era of reform into these three periods.

§ 1. THE SECOND QUARTER OF THE NINETEENTH CENTURY

'The Blackstonian era', says Dicey,[1] 'was a period of natural strength and of most reasonable national satisfaction; and he adds that 'in the ordinary course of things the law of England would have been amended before the end of the eighteenth, or soon after the beginning of the nineteenth century.'[2] But the French Revolution and the Napoleonic wars delayed changes which the rapidly changing social and economic condition of the country rendered absolutely necessary. It was this delay which made necessary

[1] Law and Opinion in England (1st ed.), 79, n. 1.
[2] Ibid. 123.

the sweeping changes in English law which followed the passing of the Reform Act of 1832.

The Commissioners on the Law of Real Property issued their first report in 1829, their second report in 1830, their third report in 1832, and their fourth report in 1833. The legislation of the first half of the nineteenth century, which followed upon those reports, destroyed many anomalies; and, in the fields of conveyancing and procedure, it substituted a simpler mechanism for the complex expedients imposed upon the law by its historical development. 'Old abuses fell like leaves in autumn. Fines were not saved by their antiquity, nor recoveries by their absurdity, nor real actions by their costliness. . . . Our sense of historical continuity was not keen enough to save 'the casual ejector', or the 'common vouchee'. A decent oblivion was provided for John Doe and Richard Roe. The law of inheritance itself did not altogether escape the touch of the innovator.'[1] We have seen that the law, both as to prescription and as to the limitation of actions for the recovery of land, was reformed.[2] But, in spite of all the labour and research which are embodied in these four reports and their appendices, the legislation which they produced only resulted in a preliminary clearing of the ground. It did little directly in the direction of assimilating the law of real and personal property. The reason for this is to be found in the circumstances of the time, which prevented a just appreciation of the causes which kept these two bodies of law so far apart.

When the Real Property Commission was appointed,

[1] Maitland, Collected Papers, i. 198–99.

[2] Above, pp. 277, 284–5.

and when the Commissioners made their reports, the influence of the great landowners, both in Parliament and in the local government, was very extensive. To a very large extent England had been governed by the great landowners during the eighteenth century. Their political achievement, measured by a comparison between the position and prosperity of the country at the beginning and the end of that century, was one which no merely democratic community has ever yet been able to show; and we have seen that, till the end of the eighteenth century, the land law met the needs of different classes of landowners.[1] It is true that, at the beginning of the nineteenth century, England was becoming a manufacturing country. But the social and political influence of the landed gentry continued to be felt. Joshua Williams in 1862 could state as a notorious fact that 'every man who accumulates a fortune immediately lays it out in the purchase of land, with a view to found a family and to perpetuate his name.'[2] Bagehot, writing in 1866, could say that in the House of Commons 'the landed gentry far surpass any other class', and that 'men who study the structure of Parliament, not in abstract books, but in the concrete London world, wonder, not that the landed interest is very powerful, but that it is not despotic.'[3]

It is not surprising, therefore, that the Real Property Commissioners, when they issued their first report in 1829, were influenced by these political and social conditions. They recommended, as we have seen, reforms in many branches of the law, but they

[1] Above, p. 301. [2] Juridical Society's Papers, ii. 599.
[3] English Constitution, 163, 164.

gave unstinted praise to its substantive principles. They said: [1]

'We have the satisfaction to report that the Law of Real Property seems to us to require very few essential alterations; and that those which we shall feel it our duty to suggest are chiefly modal. When the object of transactions respecting land is accomplished, and the estates and interests in it which are recognized are actually created and secured, the Law of England, except in a few comparatively unimportant particulars, appears to come almost as near to perfection as can be expected in any human institution. The owner of the soil is, we think, vested with exactly the dominion and power of disposition over it required for the public good, and landed property in England is admirably made to answer all the purposes to which it is applicable. Settlements bestow upon the present possessor of an estate the benefits of ownership, and secure the property to his posterity. The existing rule respecting perpetuities has happily hit the medium between the strict entails which prevail in the northern part of the Island . . . and the total prohibition of substitutions, and the excessive restriction of the power of devising, established in some countries on the Continent of Europe. In England families are preserved, and purchasers always find a supply of land in the market. A testamentary power is given, which stimulates industry and encourages accumulation; and while capricious limitations are restrained, property is allowed to be moulded according to the circumstances and wants of every family. Where no disposition is made by will, the whole landed estate descends to the son or other heir male. This, which is called the Law of Primogeniture, appears far better adapted to the constitution and habits of this kingdom than the opposite Law of Equal Partibility, which, in a few generations, would break down the aristocracy of the country, and, by the endless subdivision of the soil, must ultimately be unfavourable

[1] First Report, pp. 6–7.

to agriculture, and injurious to the best interests of the State.'

We have seen that the legislation recommended by the Commissioners swept away archaisms, and made much needed reforms in the substantive law. But the reform which the Commissioners thought most essential was not so much these reforms in the substantive law, as a reform in the law as to conveyancing. In their second report they emphasized the insecurity of titles, and the expense of the then existing system of conveyancing; and they made a careful analysis of the causes of these evils. The cure which they advocated was the establishment of a general register of conveyances. This project had been frequently discussed from the sixteenth century onwards, and repeated attempts had been made to establish a system of registration. Of these projects and attempts I shall at this point say a few words, since, I think, that they had some influence upon the Commissioners' views on this matter.

A comprehensive scheme for the registration of conveyances had formed part of Henry VIII's proposals for the reform of the land law.[1] But though his proposal to deal with the problem of the use had taken legislative form in the statute of Uses, his proposal to establish a register of conveyances never took shape. All that was passed was the statute of Enrolments,[2] which was, as Bacon said,[3] simply in the nature of a proviso to the statute of Uses. A scheme for the registration of conveyances was one of the proposals

[1] Holdsworth, H. E. L. iv. 457–9; above, p. 153.
[2] 27 Hen. VIII, c. 16.
[3] Reading, Works (ed. Spedding), vii. 432.

put forward at the time of the Commonwealth ; but, unlike other proposals then made for the reform of the law, it was not lost sight of at the Restoration. Hale, so Roger North tells us,[1] 'had turned that matter in his thoughts, and composed a treatise not so much against the thing (for he wishes it could be) as against the manner of establishing it ; of which he is not satisfied, but fears more holes may be made than mended by it.' It is probable that a tract advocating the enrolling and registering of all conveyances of land, which is printed in the Somers 'Tracts',[2] contains Hale's proposals. Francis North favoured a more extensive proposal—a register of titles[3] ; and in the eighteenth century Blackstone lamented the secrecy of conveyance which conveyances to uses had rendered possible, and considered that the project of a general register for deeds, wills, and other acts affecting real property, was worthy of consideration.[4]

A very good account of the attempts made in the seventeenth and eighteenth centuries to establish some sort of a general register is given by Mr. Tyrrell in a communication which he made to the Real Property Commission in 1829.[5] After noticing the proposals in the time of the Commonwealth for the establishment of a general register, he says :

> 'Bills for the same purpose were brought in . . . during the reign of Charles II in 1663, 1664, 1670, and 1677 ; in the reign of James II in 1685 ; in the reign of William III in 1693, 1694, 1697, 1698, and 1699 ; in the reign of George II in 1734 and 1758 ; and the last of such bills was in-

[1] Lives of the Norths, i. 142.

[2] Vol. xi. 81–90.

[3] Lives of the Norths, i. 141–2.

[4] Comm. ii. 342–3.

[5] First Report, Appendix at p. 525.

troduced by Mr. Serjeant Onslow in 1816, but it was not read a second time. With the exception of the Act for regulating the Bedford Level, the first local Act (for the West Riding of Yorkshire) was passed in 1703, and it was followed in 1706 by the Act for the East Riding, and in 1707 by the Act for Middlesex. The reasons for passing these Acts, which are stated in the preambles, are equally applicable to the whole kingdom. . . . At the same time that the bills were passed for establishing local registers in Yorkshire and Middlesex, similar bills were brought in for the counties of Berkshire and Huntingdonshire. Bills of the same nature were also proposed for Derbyshire in 1732, twice for Surrey in 1709 and 1728, and twice for Northumberland, of which the last was in 1784. However, the only other bill which has passed was that for the North Riding of Yorkshire in 8 Geo. II. It appears that most of these bills were introduced in the House of Commons upon petitions by the Magistrates and the Grand Jury of the county stating "that lands were secretly conveyed by ill-disposed persons, and that several who had purchased lands or lent money thereon, had been undone by prior or secret conveyances or incumbrances." '

Thus, although local registers were established for Yorkshire and Middlesex, all attempts to establish a general register failed. The cause was partly, as Roger North rightly says, the hostility of the legal profession, and partly and consequently the fact that, for the most part, these Bills represented rather crude attempts to legislate upon a very complicated subject. But no doubt the main cause of their failure was the great complication which the statutes of Uses and Wills and the doctrines of equity had introduced into the land law.

I think that the fact that the question of registration had been thus discussed at intervals during the seventeenth and eighteenth centuries helped the

Commissioners to arrive at the conclusion that this was the best solution of the problem. What they did not see, and what a body of men impressed with the fundamental excellence of the land law could not be expected to see, was the impossibility of combating these evils simply by a mechanical device of this kind. It was impossible to make titles secure, and to get cheap conveyancing, so long as the law permitted a large series of estates, present and future, legal and equitable; so long as it continued to have two sets of rules for succession on intestacy, and two sets of representation on death; so long as conveyances were needlessly lengthy; so long as the system of strict settlement admitted of the creation of all sorts of charges upon land; so long as estates in common were admitted; and so long as the system of mortgaging land remained unreformed.

This erroneous view taken by the Commissioners—first, that little change was needed in the substantive rules of the land law; and secondly, that most of its defects could be cured by establishing a registry of titles or conveyances—has had a large effect on the subsequent history of the movement for the reform of the land law. It has led reformers to concentrate on schemes of registration rather than on direct changes in the substantive rules of the land law; and, consequently, it has blinded them to the fact that changes in these substantive rules are a condition precedent to the establishment of a successful system of registration. It was only gradually that this fact became evident during the second half of the nineteenth century. That it then became evident was due partly to the unsuccessful attempts which were made to establish a general register either of titles or conveyances, and partly to changes in economic and political conditions, which caused a great change in men's ideas as to the fundamental excellence of the land law. Both these two sets of causes produced reforms in the land law during the last half of the nineteenth century, which were the conditions precedent for the final reform made by the Property Acts.

§ 2. The Second Half of the Nineteenth Century

In the latter half of the nineteenth century economic and political ideas were changing. The advantages resulting from the existing system of settlements, and from the law of primogeniture, which were extolled by the Commissioners in 1829, were receding into the background, and the disadvantages resulting from the existing system of conveyancing were coming into the foreground. The Commissioners on the Registration of Title reported in 1857 that 'There is a general insecurity of title and apprehension of risk, even when, to all external appearance, there is an absence of any ground for suspicion.' [1] 'What are the evils of which the public complain?' said Joshua Williams in 1862.[2] 'Chiefly I apprehend these—delay, expense, and uncertainty as to the amount of delay and expense. Insecurity, when a purchase has once been made, is not an evil that appears to be generally felt; but, with regard to mortgages, complaints are sometimes heard of the insecurity of a second mortgage and the difficulty of mortgaging a second time.'

[1] Parliamentary Papers, 1857, Sess. 2, vol. xxi, 258–9.

[2] Juridical Society's Papers, ii. 589.

In these circumstances it was only natural that attention should be turned to the remedy which the Commissioners had put forward in 1830—the remedy of a general register either of titles or of conveyances.

The difference between these two rival schemes of registration was clearly explained by the Commissioners, who reported in 1878–9. They said : [1]

> 'That registration of titles is in the abstract to be preferred to registration of assurances may at once be conceded, for the former aims at presenting the intending purchaser or mortgagee with the net result of former dealings with the property, while the latter places the dealings themselves before him, and leaves him to investigate them for himself. In one case he finds, so to speak, the sum worked out for him ; in the other he has the figures given him, and has to work out the sum for himself.'

A Bill for the registration of legal titles only, and not equitable interests, was preferred by a Committee, which reported in 1853, to a Bill for the registration of conveyances ; [2] and in 1857 the Commissioners appointed to consider the registration of title took the same view, and produced a scheme to give effect to it.[3] It should be noted that the consideration of this scheme produced suggestions, many of which were indorsed by later Commissions and by distinguished real property lawyers, and some of which have been substantially enacted by the Property Acts. Thus it was suggested that no form of interest, except the fee, charges on the fee, and leases, should be put on the register,[4] and that trusts should be kept off the

[1] Parliamentary Papers, 1878–9, vol. xi, *ix*.

[2] Parliamentary Papers, 1852–3, vol. xxxvi. 399.

[3] Parliamentary Papers, 1857, Sess. 2, xxi. 245.

[4] Ibid. 277.

register.[1] But Lord Westbury's Act of 1862,[2] and Lord Cairns's Act of 1875,[3] which provided for the registration of title, were both failures. As Charles Sweet pointed out: 'Lord Westbury's experiment taught us that a system of registration of title, to be successful, must not be too rigid. Lord Cairns's experiment taught us that a voluntary system is foredoomed to failure.' [4]

It is in the Report of a Committee of the House of Commons appointed, in view of this failure, to consider the steps which should be taken to simplify the title to land, to facilitate its transfer, and to prevent frauds on purchasers and mortgagees, that we can find some suggestions which bore immediate fruit in amending Acts, and others which the Property Acts have at length adopted. We can find also other suggestions which the Property Acts have adopted in two papers contributed to the Juridical Society in 1862 by Wolstenholme [5] and by Joshua Williams.[6]

The Commissioners were agreed that, as a first step to simplify titles, it was necessary to repeal the statute of Uses—'that stronghold of conveyancing pedantry';[7] and this was also the opinion of Joshua Williams.[8] They pointed out that the great obstacles to the establishment of a system of registration of

[1] Parliamentary Papers, 1857, Sess. 2, xxi. 281–2; see also the sketch of a bill, approved by the Commissioners, App. at p. 394 seq. which, *inter alia*, reformed the system of mortgage, and reformed certain technicalities in the creation and limitation of estates.

[2] 25 and 26 Victoria, c. 53.

[3] 38 and 39 Victoria, c. 87.

[4] L. Q. R. xxviii. 6.

[5] Juridical Society's Papers, ii. 533–52.

[6] Ibid. 589–628.

[7] Parliamentary Papers, 1878–9, vol. xi, *ix*.

[8] Juridical Society's Papers, ii. 622–3.

titles were the complication of estates and interests which were legally possible.

> 'If', they said, 'an Act of Parliament could be passed . . . either prohibiting the owner of property from tying it up or charging it except in a particular manner, or giving to the possessory proprietor the right of dealing with it as if it were his own; in other words, if the law either recognized nothing but estates in fee-simple, or gave to the holder of land the same power of disposition which the holder of stock now enjoys, the registration of title would be as easy as the title would be simple.'[1]

Wolstenholme, in 1862, made a proposal, directed towards the same objects, which the Property Acts have in effect adopted.[2] He proposed that legal estates should be limited to estates in fee-simple and terms of years absolute, and that mines, easements, and rent charges should only be grantable for these two estates.[3] All other estates should be equitable. The tenant for life under a strict settlement should have the legal fee, but should not be able to dispose of it without the consent of the trustees.[4] In case of a sale the beneficial interests should attach to the purchase price, and should cease to attach to the land.[5]

The Commissioners also recommended that a real representative should be appointed for freehold interests in land, in whom estates of inheritance should vest in the first instance;[6] and to this suggestion Wolstenholme[7] and Joshua Williams[8] agreed. Joshua Wil-

[1] Parliamentary Papers, 1878–9, vol. xi, *vi*. [2] Below, p. 323.
[3] Juridical Society's Papers, ii. 544; see also Parliamentary Papers, 1878–9, vol. xi. 248.
[4] Juridical Society's Papers, ii. 547, 548. [5] Ibid. 548.
[6] Parliamentary Papers, 1878–9, vol. xi. *viii*.
[7] Juridical Society's Papers, ii. 547, 548; Parliamentary Papers, 1878–9, vol. xi, 248. [8] Juridical Society's Papers, ii. 615.

liams suggested the abolition of the pernicious system by which conveyancers were paid by the length of the conveyance, and the substitution of an *ad valorem* scale of payments ; [1] and this opinion was indorsed by the Commissioners, who also recommended that short statutory forms should be substituted for the lengthy common form clauses to be found in all conveyances.[2] Both Joshua Williams [3] and the Commissioners [4] agreed that the existing form of mortgages should be abolished. A charge on land should be substituted which should give the mortgagee the same remedies which were given by the existing form of mortgage. Joshua Williams emphasized the inconvenience of tenancies in common, and suggested that, if tenants in common exceeded a certain number, any person holding a share to a certain amount should be able to compel a sale.[5]

The wisdom of these suggestions was enforced by changes in economic and political conditions. That economic conditions were a main cause of the legislation initiated by the Settled Land Act, 1882, was explained by Lord Macnaghten in *Bruce* v. *Marquess of Ailesbury*.[6] He said : [7]

> 'A period of agricultural depression, which showed no sign of abatement, had given rise to a popular outcry against

[1] Juridical Society's Papers, ii. 594–601 ; he said, at p. 598 : 'I have before now met with some who seemed to think that their sole duty to their principals consisted, first in expanding every idea into the largest possible number of words, and secondly, in making as many deeds as possible out of every transaction.'

[2] Parliamentary Papers, 1878–9, vol. xi, *vii–viii*, *xiv*.

[3] Juridical Society's Papers, ii. 619–20.

[4] Parliamentary Papers, 1878–9, vol. xi, *xiii*, *xiv*.

[5] Juridical Society's Papers, ii. 624–5.

[6] [1892] A.C. 356.

[7] Ibid. at pp. 364–5.

settlements. The problem was how to relieve settled land from the mischief which strict settlements undoubtedly did in some cases produce, without doing away altogether with the power of bringing land into settlement. That was something very different from the task to which Parliament addressed itself in passing the Settled Estates Acts. In those Acts the Legislature did not look beyond the interests of the persons entitled under the settlement. In the Settled Land Act the paramount object of the Legislature was the well-being of settled land.'[1]

Maitland, in his paper on the 'Law of Real Property', which was written in 1879, passed by in silence the argument of the Commissioners on the Law of Real Property in 1829 for the maintenance of primogeniture—the argument that it was a mainstay of the aristocracy—and showed that it was unfair to children, and that the law of inheritance, of which it was a part, introduced endless complications into the law.

> 'The advocates of primogeniture are fond of laying stress on the fact that few landowners die intestate. Is it not a little one—This is their favourite plea. No, we reply, the abuse is not a little one. It is for the sake of the heir-at-law that we disorder the whole of our jurisprudence. In order to postpone women to men, in order to make a will which no one wants made, we render our law unknowable by any save experts. If after all our efforts we fail in attaining our worthless objects, if daughters and younger sons are not disinherited, this is but an additional argument for reform. We undergo all the evils of having two systems of property law, and have nothing to show for it. You cannot prove that a law is good by showing that all sensible men continue to evade it.'[2]

The result of the discussions of schemes for the registration of title, and of these economic and political

[1] For the effect of the Act see note at p. 327.

[2] Collected Papers, i. 193–4.

reasons for reform, was not the establishment of any general and compulsory system of registration of title, or changes in any of the fundamental principles of the law of real property. The Act of 1875,[1] which provided for the registration of title, was, as we have seen, a purely voluntary Act; and it was not till 1897 that Lord Halsbury provided a machinery for applying it compulsorily to a county or a part of a county.[2] The chief result of all these movements for reform was the passing of much legislation to effect those reforms in the law which had been shown to be obviously necessary. In 1857 the Commissioners on Registration of Title had expressed the opinion that 'the establishment of a register should only be part of a general plan for amending the law of real property',[3] and Joshua Williams agreed with this view. In 1862 he said: 'The remark that a general measure of registration should follow rather than precede beneficial alteration in the law itself is one in which I entirely agree. If the alterations be beneficial the sooner they are introduced the better.'[4] This, in fact, was the course pursued. The Partition Act, the Vendor and Purchaser Act, the Conveyancing Acts, the Settled Land Acts, and the Land Transfer Act, 1897, introduced many of those partial reforms which had been advocated during the latter part of the nineteenth century. But they were all partial and, to a large extent, unconnected reforms. They all helped on the simplification of conveyancing, but, with the exception of Part I of the Land Transfer Act, 1897,[5] they

[1] 38 and 39 Victoria c. 87.
[2] 60 and 61 Victoria, c. 65.
[3] Parliamentary Papers, 1857, Sess. 2, vol. xxi, 299.
[4] Juridical Society's Papers, ii. 607.
[5] Above, p. 76.

did little to effect any assimilation between the law of real and the law of personal property. The main essential features of the law of real property still held their ground. Dicey called attention to this fact in 1905 in his paper on 'The Paradox of the Land Law'.[1] He said:

> 'To the student of legal history the development of the English land law from 1830 to 1900 presents this paradox: incessant modifications or reforms of the law, which extend over seventy years, and have certainly not come to an end, have left unchanged, in a sense almost untouched, the fundamentals of the law with regard to land. . . . The paradox of the modern English land law may thus be summed up: the constitution of England has, whilst preserving monarchical forms, become a democracy, but the land law of England remains the land law appropriate to an aristocratic State.'

This state of things was attributed by Dicey to the history of public opinion on the subject of the reform of the land law. The landowners desired no fundamental changes, and those who wished for reform were divided; and so, though piecemeal reforms which cured obvious evils were effected, no large and thoroughgoing reform was undertaken. But I think that it was due in part to the fact that the need for fundamental changes in the substantive principles of the law had been obscured by the manner in which those who desired such changes had concentrated their energies, not on schemes for the reform of the substantive law, but on schemes for the registration of titles or conveyances; and the pursuance of this policy was, I think, not unconnected with the views held by the Real Property Commissioners in 1829.

[1] L. Q. R. xxi. 221.

But though no general register of conveyances or titles was established, legislation of the eighteenth and nineteenth centuries did establish registers of various charges upon land. An Act of 1777 [1] established a register for annuities and rent-charges for life or lives, and the Judgements Acts of 1838 [2] and 1839 [3] established registers of judgements and *lites pendentes* affecting lands. In 1887 provision was made for the registration of deeds of arrangement.[4] As has been pointed out, a register of this kind is quite distinct from a general register of titles or conveyances.[5] It is, in fact, rendered essential by the absence of a general system of registration of title. 'This springs from the fact that, in addition to such charges and encumbrances as may be revealed by an examination of the deeds, there are a whole series of liabilities, not imposed by any deeds, and therefore unmentioned in the deeds, permitted by law, of which a purchaser may be held to have notice, constructive or otherwise, and which therefore become binding on him.' [6] We shall see that the registration of these charges upon land has acquired a greatly increased importance in the new scheme of law inaugurated by the Property Acts.[7]

§ 3. The Genesis of the Property Acts

After the war many causes made it impossible to leave the land law in the condition in which it was

[1] 17 George III, c. 26.

[2] 1 and 2 Victoria, c. 110.

[3] 2 and 3 Victoria, c. 11.

[4] 50 and 51 Victoria, c. 17.

[5] J. S. Stewart Wallace, 'The Land Charges Act in Jurisprudence,' L. Q. R. xli. 179–80.

[6] Ibid. 176.

[7] Below, p. 324.

in 1914; the paradox, to use Dicey's phrase, had become too glaring, and public opinion was prepared for larger measures of reform. One cause, Sir Leslie Scott tells us,[1] was his experience as chairman of the Lands Requisition Committee, which showed up 'the expenses and delays of land transfer in England as compared with newer countries'. Another cause which made some reform necessary was the break-up of large estates. This process was assisted by the dissipation of the nation's capital, which is the necessary result of the burden of heavy death duties; for they prevent saving, by taking and spending on other purposes money which would otherwise be profitably invested; and they encourage extravagance by penalizing thrift. These causes rendered it necessary to facilitate and cheapen the transfer of land; and it was inevitable that many other rules of the land law—notably the law of primogeniture—should come under review. Sir Leslie Scott's Committee, which reported on land transfer in 1919, at length took the step of denying directly the view which had been taken by the Commissioners on the Law of Real Property in 1829. Instead of praising the law of real property and putting most of the blame for its admitted inconveniences on the system of conveyancing,[2] it gave effect to a view which had for some time been gaining ground, and said that 'the main defects in the existing

[1] For the facts contained in this and the ensuing paragraphs I have relied mainly on Sir Leslie Scott's little book, 'The New Law of Property Explained'; it contains his speech on the second reading of the Law of Property Bill, 1922, with an introduction, and it also contains notes by B. B. Benas; see also J. H. Johnson, The Bibliography of the New Property Acts, L. Q. R. xlii. 67.

[2] Above, pp. 305–6.

system of Conveyancing do not lie in the Conveyancing Acts or in the practice of Conveyancing, but in the general law of Real Property '.[1] This view was not only technically correct; it was also in accordance with the trend of public opinion. It was clear that institutions which, according to the Commissioners of 1829, were the buttresses of aristocracy, were likely to fare even worse in our post-war than they had fared in our pre-war society.

It was clear in 1919 that no extension of the system of registration of title was possible—opinions were then, and still are, too much divided ; and so it was decided to follow deliberately the course which, almost accidentally, had given rise to very many of the reforms of the nineteenth century. We have seen that the various Commissions which had reported on schemes of registration of title, and the various statutes which had been passed in consequence of their recommendations, had not succeeded in introducing any general compulsory system of registration of title, but that they had been the means of suggesting many useful reforms in the law.[2] It was now resolved to follow up this method of approach—to begin by reforming the substantive law of real

[1] Reports, &c., 1919 (Cmd. 424), vol. xxix, p. 9 ; this was the view of Charles Sweet in 1912, see L. Q. R. xxviii, 10–11, 25 ; and of the Land Transfer Commissioners (1909–11), ibid. 21, 25 n. 1—though it was beyond the scope of their commission to report on the advisability of amendments to the Law of Real Property. Sir Arthur Underhill in his pamphlet entitled 'The Line of Least Resistance' (Butterworth, 1919), p. 38, has pointed out that this was also the view of the Committee of 1878 on Land Titles and Transfer—'To legislate for the registration of titles without, as a preliminary step, simplifying the titles to be registered, is to begin at the wrong end.'

[2] Above, p. 312–17.

property and by simplifying conveyancing. Necessarily the existing Land Transfer Acts, dealing with registration of title, were amended and altered so as to bring them into line with the new law. But it was agreed that there should be no attempt to introduce any further measure of compulsory registration of title till the Acts had been in operation for ten years. At the end of this period the working of the Acts may result in a definite decision of the long controverted question as to the expediency of a general compulsory system of registration of title.

The history of the manner in which the Property Acts have assumed their present shape is shortly as follows: The story begins with a Bill of 1895, drafted by Wolstenholme and Sir Benjamin Cherry, which dealt with the subject-matter of Part I of the Act of 1922, i. e. the assimilation of the law of real and of personal property. This was followed by Draft Bills dealing with Settled Land, Conveyancing, Trustees, and Personal Representatives. In 1908 a Royal Commission was appointed to consider the working of the Land Transfer Acts, which was presided over by Lord St. Aldwyn. This was followed by Lord Haldane's Bill, introduced just before the war, the main object of which was to assimilate the law of real and personal property. The Committee set up in 1919, to advise as to the action to be taken to facilitate and cheapen the transfer of land, indorsed the views of the Royal Commission of 1908; and requested Sir Benjamin Cherry to recast, and put into one Bill, the series of Draft Bills dealing with various parts of the land law. This Bill was introduced in the House of Lords by Lord Birkenhead in 1920. After many amendments in a Joint Committee of both Houses, and consultations with the Law Society and many other bodies, the Bill finally passed both Houses in 1922—a result which was, as Sir Leslie Scott has pointed out, due in great measure to the skill, knowledge, and tact of Lord Birkenhead. Subsequently the Act of 1922 (except those parts of it which relate to enfranchisement of copyholds, extinguishment of manorial incidents, and the conversion of perpetually renewable leases into long terms) was repealed, and its contents were split up into the series of Property Acts which came into force on January 1st, 1926.[1]

The contents of these Acts to a large extent assemble, consolidate, and carry to their logical conclusion the reforms already made in the law by the legislation of the nineteenth century ; and, where they introduce new law in order to carry those reforms to their logical conclusion, they often reproduce suggestions which had already been made with this object in view. The simplification of tenure effected by getting rid of copyhold was thought desirable, but not possible, by the Real Property Commissioners in 1832,[2] but it is the logical result of the diminution of copyhold which has followed from the facilities given for its enfranchisement by the legislation of the nineteenth century. Obviously the abolition of

[1] For the series see above, p. 1, n. 1.

[2] 'Having explained the reasons why it appears to us so expedient that copyhold tenure should be changed into common socage, we are obliged to confess that, after deep deliberation, we have not been able to discover any means of speedily attaining so desirable an object. . . . We have found the difficulties great in proportion as the need for change is urgent,' Third Report, 17.

such customs as borough English and gavelkind was also the logical consequence both of the simplification of tenure and of the new scheme of intestate succession introduced by the Acts. We have seen that the reduction in the number of estates to estates in fee-simple and for a term of years absolute had been suggested by Wolstenholme as early as 1862,[1] and that the repeal of the statute of Uses had been suggested by Joshua Williams in the same year, and by the Commissioners who reported in 1878–9.[2] That a new system of intestate succession for all kinds of property was needed had been emphasized by Maitland in 1879.[3] It was, in fact, necessary, both in order to assimilate the law of real and personal property, and in order to pave the way to a simplified law as to the administration of assets. From the latter point of view, it carries to its logical conclusion the change made by Part I of the Land Transfer Act, 1897. The change in the manner of effecting a mortgage had been suggested by Joshua Williams in 1862, and by the Commissioners who reported in 1878–9.[4] The inconvenience of tenancies in common

[1] Above, p. 313. [2] Ibid.

[3] Collected Papers, i. 171 seq.; above, p. 315.

[4] Above, p. 314. Mr. Lightwood, Law Journal, xl. N. S. 46–7, has observed that in earlier days a mortgage by the demise of a term was the most usual way of effecting a mortgage. He points out that it is so stated by Davidson Conveyancing Precedents (2nd ed.), vol. ii, Pt. ii, 852 note, and that this was the form required by section 27 of the Universities and Colleges Estates Act, 1858. This view is also supported by the fact that in the second edition of Bridgman's Conveyances (1690) there are several precedents of mortgages by demise, and only one of a mortgage in fee, and by the testimony of Blackstone, Comm. ii. 158. For the reasons why this form was superseded see Davidson, loc. cit., and Mr. Lightwood's article.

had been pointed out by Joshua Williams as early as 1862.[1]

The great change made in the direction of cheapening and facilitating the transfer of land consists in the careful provisions for keeping equities off the title. To effect this object the Acts contain many new provisions; but that these provisions had been, to some extent, foreshadowed by the machinery of the Settled Land Acts and the Land Charges Acts appears from the memorandum of 1921 on Law of Property Bill: [2]

> 'Whilst preserving the present law that a purchaser for value of a legal estate in land can in good faith, without notice, obtain a good title, it reduces the number of cases in which a purchaser will be affected by notice to a minimum. This reduction is effected—(*a*) by introducing a trust for sale in certain cases; (*b*) by adopting and extending the principle of the Settled Land Acts, by which the conveyance by a person having the power of disposition overrides all the equities subsisting under the settlement—the equities attaching to the proceeds of the sale; (*c*) by requiring certain rights affecting the land to be registered in one of the registers kept under the Lands Charges (Registration and Searches) Acts, and making such rights liable to be overridden on a conveyance of the legal estate to a purchaser, unless the rights are registered, notwithstanding that the purchaser may have notice of them.'

This outline of the history of the land law shows that throughout the long history of this branch of the law, and right down to the recent legislation, three main tendencies have been apparent.

[1] Above, p. 314.

[2] Reports, &c. 1921 (Cmd. 1287), vol. xxix, at p. 4.

In the first place, the Legislature has had a larger share in shaping the land law than it has had in shaping any other branch of private law. The legislation of Edward I, the Tudor legislation as to uses and wills, the statute of tenures, and the legislation of the nineteenth century, show that, at all periods in the history of the land law, statutes have been the parents of a great many of its fundamental principles, and the starting-points of new epochs in its development.

In the second place, the tendency which Maitland discerned in the law of the thirteenth century to make what was formerly the law for the great men the law for all, is also discernible all through its history. It was the desire of the owners of great estates to make permanent settlements of their property which caused directly the development and elaboration of some of the most salient characteristics of the land law of the eighteenth century, and indirectly the development of that rule against perpetuities which set a definite limit to the fulfilment of this desire. Most of the large powers which the law, as thus developed and elaborated at the instance of the owners of great estates, conferred on these landowners, belong now to all the landowners; for the new Acts allow nearly all the results, which could formerly be accomplished by the creation of legal estates, to be accomplished by the creation of equitable interests.

In the third place, from the sixteenth century onwards, the law of real property and the law of personal property have exercised a reciprocal influence upon one another. This is very evident if we compare the law relating to chattels real with the law relating to freehold interests. The law relating to chattels real borrowed from the law relating to freehold interests some of its rules as to tenures and estates, and some of its rules relating to covenants which run with the land. On the other hand, the law relating to freehold has borrowed more from the law relating to chattels real. It has borrowed the power of devise, the form of action by which freeholds came to be protected, and the machinery by which they devolved upon the heir or devisee. Moreover, the rule against perpetuities, devised in the first instance to govern settlements of freehold interests and chattels real, was extended to all kinds of property as soon as the necessity for so extending it appeared. The Property Acts push this tendency to its logical conclusion. On the one hand, the rules regulating conveyances of land are designed to make (so far as this is possible) these conveyances as simple and cheap as conveyances of personalty—the simplicity of a conveyance of stocks and shares has been taken as an example to be followed; and one of the rules formerly only applicable to personalty—the rule in *Dearle* v. *Hall*[1]—has been applied to land.[2] On the other hand, the capacity to create an estate tail has been extended to owners of personalty.[3] For all kinds of property a new uniform system of succession on intestacy has been devised, which is much more akin to the old rules as to personalty than to the old rules as to realty.[4]

[1] (1823) 3 Russ. 1. [2] Law of Property Act, 1925, § 137 (1).

[3] Ibid. § 130 (1); above p. 76.

[4] Administration of Estates Act, 1925. Part IV; above p. 76.

Sir Leslie Scott, speaking of the Property Acts, has said: 'This vast monument of human energy has been built by the hands of many builders. More than half a century of law reformers have contributed to it.' This is a considerable understatement. If there is any truth in the history which I have endeavoured to relate, it would be more true to say that some five centuries of law makers and law reformers have contributed to it. Revolutionary as the new Acts may at first sight appear, they are historically the product of the efforts of a long series of judges, conveyancers, and legislators; and their provisions are a striking illustration of the continuity of the history of the land law. They are, as Sir Leslie Scott has said, 'not revolution but evolution'. Like the other great reforms in the past, they will, no doubt, become the foundation upon which the judges and conveyancers will build up a new fabric of property law, related to the old in somewhat the same way as the modern law of real property, constructed on the basis of the statutes of Uses and Wills, was related to the medieval land law.

Note on the Settled Land Act, 1882

(above, pp. 314–15)

To attain the paramount object of the Act it was necessary to 'strike off from the land the fetters imposed by settlements'.[1] The existence of these fetters was due to the fact that land under settlement was in the possession of a tenant for life,[2] who, because he was

[1] *In re* Mundy and Roper's Contract [1899] 1 Ch. at p. 288 *per* Chitty L.J.

[2] Above, p. 164.

only a tenant for life, had not got the powers needed for the proper management and development of the land. It is true that additional powers might be conferred upon him by the settlor;[1] but we have seen that changes in economic conditions had made this expedient inadequate. These powers were not always conferred, and, if conferred, they might not be sufficiently extensive.[2] The Settled Land Act 1882 struck off the fetters imposed by settlements by giving to the tenant for life, and other limited owners under settlements, large powers of sale, leasing, mortgaging, and otherwise dealing with the settled land; and by prohibiting any attempt to negative these powers or to fetter their exercise. At the same time it safeguarded the interests of other beneficiaries under the settlement, by shifting the trusts of the settlement from the land to the money realized by the exercise of the power of sale or other powers given to the tenant for life; and it further safeguarded these interests by providing that this money must be paid to the trustees of the settlement or into court.[3]

[1] Above, pp. 205–6. [2] Above, p. 211.

[3] *In re* Mundy and Roper's Contract [1899] 1 Ch. at pp. 288–9, *per* Chitty L.J.

Strict Settlements, 164; use of

INDEX

Q

www.ingramcontent.com/pod-product-compliance
Lightning Source LLC
LaVergne TN
LVHW091524200926
848483LV00002B/295

* 9 7 8 1 5 8 4 7 7 2 6 2 0 *